The Dark Descent

**Contributions to the Study of
Science Fiction and Fantasy**

THE
DARK
DESCENT

Essays Defining
Stephen King's Horrorscape

Edited by
TONY MAGISTRALE

Foreword by
Joseph A. Citro

Contributions to the Study of Science Fiction and Fantasy, Number 48
Marshall B. Tymn, Series Editor

Greenwood Press
New York • Westport, Connecticut • London

Library of Congress Cataloging-in-Publication Data

The Dark descent : essays defining Stephen King's horrorscape / edited
  by Tony Magistrale; foreword by Joseph A. Citro.
      p. cm. – (Contributions to the study of science fiction and
  fantasy, ISSN 0193-6875 ; no. 48)
    Includes bibliographical references and index.
    ISBN 0-313-27297-2 (alk. paper)
    1. King, Stephen, 1947- – Criticism and interpretation.
    2. Horror tales, American – History and criticism.   I. Magistrale, Tony.   II. Series.
  PS3561.I483Z629   1992
  813'.54 – dc20   91-36705

British Library Cataloguing in Publication Data is available.

Library of Congress Catalog Card Number: 91-36705
ISBN: 0-313-27297-2
ISSN: 0193-6875

First published in 1992

Greenwood Press, 88 Post Road West, Westport, CT 06881
An imprint of Greenwood Publishing Group, Inc.

Printed in the United States of America

The paper used in this book complies with the
Permanent Paper Standard issued by the National
Information Standards Organization (Z39.48-1984).

10 9 8 7 6 5 4 3 2 1

This book is dedicated to
Jennifer Magistrale, and Helen and Katherine Tederous:
In honor of St. Catherine's Court
and all points in between

Contents

FOREWORD
The King and I

JOSEPH A. CITRO

I don't know Stephen King and he doesn't know me. Still, I can tell you far more about him than he can tell you about me.

In fact, just about everyone can talk about King. They have a pet theory, a bit of privileged information, or a personalizing notion. Some offer friend-of-a-friend insights on the caliber of urban legends. I've heard *Kingisms* ranging from the benign to the bizarre:

"A friend of my dad's played baseball with him in college."

"You know, he drinks beer right on stage when he lectures."

"He's really into kids, *loves* kids."

"Actually, he hires former students to write his books."

"He's possessed. No shit. Those headaches he talked about in *Playboy?* They're a sure sign demons make him do all that writing."

Because of his books (which publishers count like McDonald's counts hamburgers), feature films, and made-for-TV movies, King has materialized in some form to each of us.

Books about King sell in staggering numbers, at unbelievable prices. One of the most recent, the limited edition of Stephen Spignesi's *The Official Stephen King Encyclopedia,* sells for $175.00 a copy! Book businesses have grown up because of him (Time Tunnel and The Overlook Connection, to name two of many). One wonders how many people this one-man industry helps to employ.

Not only has he become a colossal force in our culture, but in our economy as well.

This foreword is not an analysis of King's impact on popular culture. It is merely a subjective peek at the way King touches my life. Though I am not a publisher, bookseller, critic, or scholar, King is particularly conspicuous in my line of work. I write horror fiction.

And he's all around me, an inescapable presence, an all-encompassing force, like something from a horror novel.

It all began in 1987, when my novel, *Shadow Child,* hit the stands. I simply couldn't figure out how the book's cover art related to the story. It showed a colorful, cadaverous-looking clown holding a bouquet of bright balloons. But hey, there was no clown in my book! See, I hadn't read *It* at the time. Obviously, the publisher had. And they were targeting my book for millions of other people who had. *Shadow Child* did well, selling over 100,000 copies. I guess I have Stephen King to thank. But its publication gave me no real sense of literary independence.

King even haunted the reviews that began to appear. His presence manifested as a yardstick, the one against which the rest of us are measured. (Citro's *"Dark Twilight* illustrates what Stephen King has shown us all. . . .")[1]

In 1988 my next novel appeared with an endorsement by an internationally known author and anthologist. It proclaimed (in all caps, no less), "CITRO DOES FOR VERMONT WHAT KING DID FOR MAINE." The same quote followed me through two more books and one more publisher. No one bothered to explain exactly what I had done for – or to – Vermont, or what King did for Maine. All I know for sure is that publishers will go to any length to get King's name on my books.

At book signings people unfamiliar with my work (and that includes just about everybody) examine my book at arm's length as if it were some repugnant, alien object. They ponder, then ask, "Is it anything like Stephen King's?"

Next I'll unfailingly hear my all-time favorite line, "I don't read horror, but I *do* read Stephen King."

Once a woman told me the only books she ever reads are King's. In effect, she seemed to boast, "I grew up on him."

At a recent book signing a gaggle of what appeared to be high school girls paraded past me and my stack of *Dark Twilight*s. Like piranha they fairly tore at a floor-to-ceiling display of *Needful Things.* King sold more books at my signing than I did. Invisible himself, but an awesome competitor.

He has been just as intrusive in the Dr. Jekyll half of my career, that of a teacher. In a course I'm currently professing with the catchy title "Novel-Writing Workshop," fourteen out of sixteen students (that's 14 out of 16!) cited King as either their favorite writer or listed him among their top three. Several said they wanted to write like King. One admitted having read only three novels this year – all King's.

A student told me, "Boy, he sure has a way with words."

Another said, "His novels keep you turning pages. . . ."

Some expressed their views on paper. "It was . . . only upon reading Stephen King's *The Dark Half* about a month ago that I realized horror was what I really wanted to write."

Another on the same book: "I believe that overall the plot, characterization, climax, and denouement of the novel was (*sic*) successful."

And another: "King never gives me a reason to like his main character. The other characters are flat. . . . There's nothing to the story. . . ."

This sort of commentary, in person or on paper, is the first rung of the critical ladder, that is, personal opinion – what publishers like to call "word of mouth."

The next rung is where the book reviewers perch. (Ever ask yourself what horror writers are afraid of? The answer is right here: reviewers.) With souls of doves or vultures, these self-appointed experts offer to guide us through myriad confusions of the literary marketplace. But their usefulness – beyond simple publicity – is on a par with the flip of a coin.

All writers long to be reviewed. And I'm sure Mr. King would agree that any review is good for one's career (though a favorable review can lift the spirit). Yet very few of us give much credence to the cotton-candy concepts of these low-rent critiques. We know how it works. It's an old-boy network of foes and fans, back-slappers and back-stabbers, undignified at best, but a necessary evil in the fiction of fear.

For me the following event put reviews into a telling perspective:

Thanks to some editorial carelessness one of my books, *The Unseen*, was reviewed twice in the same magazine. One reviewer praised the characterization, but found the premise "ludicrous." The other reviewer called my premise "superlative," but said my characters needed, "fleshing out."

What's a writer to believe? Who's a consumer to believe? What good's a review?

Moving one rung up the critical ladder we find the so-called "critic." From this slightly increased altitude, their vision is often broader. They talk about "trends in the field." They flex literary and educational muscles, forcing us to explore such tedious terrain as whether "terror" or "horror" is the higher form of fear. They debate hackneyed questions: should we use a more appropriate name for the horror genre, like "dark fantasy" or *conte cruelle?* Or they assert, as pioneering *Kingologist* Doug Winter likes to remind us: horror is not a type of literature; it's an emotion.

Ho-hum.

Reviewers and critics might be well-intended or foul-spirited folks. Often they have axes to grind or reputations to make, or break. Some are opportunists (like those quick to parasite on King's popularity). Others earnestly try to make sense of a mind as it tries to make sense of our world and the cosmos in which it spins.

All make judgments which are usually in conflict. And, okay, conflict is right, good, healthy, and supremely American! But is it useful? I bet even King – who has attained an altitude to which the critical ladder cannot extend – cannot remain indifferent to such nonsense.

Although we are placed very differently in the market – he camping out atop Parnassus, me in perpetual mid-list crisis – I suspect we have at least this in common: we are dissatisfied with the "It's cool/it sucked" state of criticism. It isn't useful. It doesn't enlighten.

This book has nothing to do with the high-culture, low-culture debate. When a writer's canon embeds itself so completely in our social awareness and cultural subconscious, it has something potent to recommend it. To deny King's worth, it seems to me, is to deny the society in which we live.

The Dark Descent is not a descent at all. Here, as in his other fine books, Tony Magistrale's scholarship has lifted the focus on King's work high above reviewer rhetoric and petty critical squabbles. These essays transcend the critical ladder and meet King on his own ground. Magistrale has editorially sustained purity of literary discourse that is wonderfully free of judgment.

King is with us.

That's what this is all about.

Yes, he sure keeps us turning pages. He will for a long time to come. Here's why. . . .

NOTE

1. *Dark Twilight* by Joseph A. Citro. Reviewed by Ed Gorman in *Mystery Scene* (January, 1991).

Acknowledgments

There are several people to whom I owe a debt of gratitude beginning with Stephen King and his secretary, Shirley Sonderegger, for their encouragement and consultation throughout the writing of this book; their prompt and courteous assistance in granting us permission to use Mr. King's material is greatly appreciated. In addition, the individual contributors are sincerely thanked for making this book a reality. They labored at great lengths to create a collection distinguished by its consistent level of quality. Each chapter went through multiple drafts until the author and I felt the argument was right. Marilyn Brownstein, Senior Editor of the Humanities Division at Greenwood Press, was instrumental in encouraging this project from its inception and maintained her patience with me on several frantic occasions. Marshall Tymn, who is still recovering from an automobile accident, was responsible for guiding this book to Greenwood; may he get well soon. Much of the editorial work on this manuscript was performed during a sabbatical leave provided by the University of Vermont.

This collection, however, would probably not exist in its current form were it not for a long conversation I shared with Michael Morrison and Len Mustazza poolside one sunny March afternoon two years ago at the International Conference for the Fantastic in the Arts in Fort Lauderdale, Florida. Mike and Len helped to define both the theoretical premises for this collection as well as its place in King scholarship. If ever there was justification needed for spring-break vacations in the sun, may *The Dark Descent* long serve as exemplary testament.

Stephen King Chronology

1947   Born, Stephen Edwin King, September 21, in Portland, Maine, second son to Donald and Nellie Ruth Pillsbury King.

1949   Donald King, Stephen's father, leaves the house on a trip to the store and never returns.

1954   Begins to write short fiction modeled after the science fiction and adventure stories he reads and sees at the movies.

1962–66   Attends high school in Lisbon Falls, Maine. Plays tight end on the varsity football team. Begins writing *Getting It On* (published as *Rage*).

1966–70   Undergraduate years as an English major at the University of Maine, Orono. Writes column, "King's Garbage Truck," for the weekly school newspaper. The column reflects his changing political views: from Nixon apologist in 1968 to political activist who calls for a general student strike on April 24, 1969. As a sophomore, King enrolls in Burton Hatlen's Modern American Literature course where he is introduced to the naturalists, Steinbeck, Hemingway, and Faulkner. Completes first novel, *The Long Walk*, in 1967. Meets Tabitha Spruce who is also a UMO undergraduate. Works as a laborer in an industrial laundry.

1971–73   Marries Tabitha Spruce. Begins teaching English at Hampden Academy, Hampden, Maine. Lives in mobile home where he publishes several short stories and sells *Carrie* to Doubleday.

Begins writing *Second Coming* ('*Salem's Lot*). Completes *The Running Man*, which is rejected by Doubleday. Stephen's mother dies of cancer.

1974   *Carrie* is published. Writes first draft of *The Shining;* begins work on *The House on Value Street* (published as *The Stand*). Moves with wife and daughter to Boulder, Colorado.

1975   '*Salem's Lot* is published. Completes first draft of *The Stand*. Returns to Maine and purchases a home in Bridgton. University of Maine, Orono, establishes special depository for the Stephen King collection that has since expanded to include the bulk of the writer's manuscripts, galleys, and working drafts.

1976   Film version of *Carrie,* directed by Brian De Palma opens.

1977   *The Shining* and *Rage,* the first novel to appear under the Richard Bachman pseudonym, are published. Completes first drafts of *The Dead Zone* and *Firestarter.* Introduced to Peter Straub on a three-month trip to England.

1978   *The Stand* and *Night Shift* are published. Writer-in-Residence, University of Maine, Orono. Teaches classes in creative writing and gothic fiction. Uses the latter course to launch theories on the gothic genre, which will serve as the basis for *Danse Macabre* and several other nonfictional essays (e.g., introductions to *Night Shift* and to recent editions of Shelley's *Frankenstein* and Stevenson's *Doctor Jekyll and Mr. Hyde*).

1979   *The Dead Zone,* Bachman's *The Long Walk* are published. Completes first drafts of *Christine, Pet Sematary,* and *Danse Macabre.* Concludes teaching duties at UMO.

1980   *Firestarter,* "The Mist," and "The Monkey" are published. Completes first draft of *It.* Buys current residence, a Victorian mansion on West Broadway, in Bangor, Maine. Release of Stanley Kubrick's film adaptation of *The Shining.*

1981   *Cujo, Danse Macabre,* and the third Bachman title, *Roadwork* are published. Receives Career Alumni Award from the University of Maine.

1982   *Different Seasons,* "The Raft," and fourth Bachman book, *The Running Man* are published. Begins writing *The Talisman* with Peter Straub. Wins World Fantasy Award for "Do the Dead Sing?" ("The Reach") and Hugo Award for *Danse Macabre.* Active role as both scriptwriter and actor in film *Creepshow,* directed by George Romero.

1983   *Christine* and *Pet Sematary* are published. Completes first drafts of *The Talisman, The Tommyknockers,* and *The Eyes of the Dragon.* Film versions open of *Cujo,* directed by Lewis Teague;

The Dead Zone, directed by David Cronenberg; and *Christine,* directed by John Carpenter.

1984   *The Talisman* and fifth Bachman novel, *Thinner,* are published. *The Eyes of the Dragon* and *The Dark Tower: The Gunslinger* released in limited editions. Film adaptations released of *Firestarter,* directed by Mark Lester; and *Children of the Corn* (*Night Shift* collection), directed by Fritz Kiersch. King is invited as guest of honor at the International Conference for the Fantastic in the Arts, Boca Raton, Florida.

1985   *Skeleton Crew* published. Reveals the "Richard Bachman" pseudonym. NAL assembles collection of four Bachman novels entitled *The Bachman Books.*

1986   *It* is published. Underwood and Miller release a single-volume collection of King interviews entitled *Bare Bones: Conversations on Terror with Stephen King.* King makes his directorial debut in *Maximum Overdrive,* an adaptation of the short story "Trucks." Named the Lloyd H. Elliott Lecturer, University of Maine.

1987   *Misery* (originally intended as a Bachman book), *The Eyes of the Dragon, Silver Bullet, The Tommyknockers* and *The Dark Tower II: The Drawing of the Three* are published. Release of films *Stand by Me,* Rob Reiner's adaptation of *The Body* (from *Different Seasons*); and *The Running Man,* directed by George Pan Cosmatos. Delivers commencement address, University of Maine, Orono.

1989   *The Dark Half* (1.5 million copies printed in hardcover, the largest first-edition printing in the history of publishing) is published. Film release of *Pet Sematary,* directed by Mary Lambert.

1990   Revised and unexpurgated edition of *The Stand* and four novellas under the title *Four Past Midnight* are published. Film releases of "The Cat from Hell," King's contribution to *Tales from the Dark Side,* and "Graveyard Shift." Film adaptation of *Misery,* directed by Rob Reiner is released. *It* televised in two-part, six-hour mini-series on ABC.

1991–92 Scheduled release of *Dolores Claiborne, Needful Things,* and the third volume of *The Dark Tower* subtitled *The Waste Lands.*

1

Defining Stephen King's Horrorscape: An Introduction

TONY MAGISTRALE

In an interview conducted with Stephen King two years ago, I asked him to comment on the critical reception his work has received during the past decade. Befitting his personality and talent, his unassuming response was generous: "I think I could have been treated a lot worse. And I could have been ignored completely. . . . There has been a good deal more scholarship—or critical work—in the past six or seven years and some of it has been both more favorable and intelligent than I ever would have believed or expected" (Magistrale, ms. 22–23). King's observations are only partially correct: the last decade has indeed produced a proliferation of "favorable" books and articles about his fiction. On the other hand, very little of this critical work has been distinguished by the depth of its intelligence or the quality of its scholarship.

This book was assembled to rectify some of the existing liabilities in King scholarship; the essays in this collection consider King from a wide variety of intellectual points of view and orientations. Moreover, each of King's major novels, with the notable exceptions of *'Salem's Lot* (which has received more than its fair share of critical attention), *The Tommyknockers, The Dark Half,* and *The Dark Tower,* is represented by at least one chapter contained in this book. King's monumental 1987 novel *It* is significant enough to merit two separate chapters, and although Jeanne Campbell Reesman and Mary Jane Dickerson are the authors of the principal essays, King's novel is discussed extensively by at least three of the other contributors. A few of the authors reference several King texts in order to illustrate the pervasiveness of their theses—Douglas Keesey on occurrences of homophobia, Bernadette Bosky on food imagery and eating disorders, and Mary Pharr's wide-ranging analysis of King's female characters.

King's literary reputation among academicians and "serious" readers of literature continues to languish. Too often the mere inclusion of Stephen King's name in the company of contemporary American novelists requires elaborate qualifications and explanations. Some of King's loudest detractors have never read a sentence by the author and yet continue to slander his work; they base their judgments on generalizations and hearsay rather than empirical evidence. This book is not written to enlighten such narrow-minded individuals. Instead, it is offered to those who would continue to defy the condemnation by English teachers across America and maintain an intellectual curiosity about Stephen King, to those who have not denied his credibility as a writer or thinker, and to those, such as Andy Solomon, who have read King, but have not read him well.

By now, everyone knows Stephen King's flaws: tone-deaf narration, papier-mâché characters, cliches, gratuitous vulgarity, self-indulgent digressions. . . . We don't read Stephen King for common sense, originality or insight into the adult world. Many who wouldn't want the fact broadcast read this master of suspense to escape their helpless fear of the headlines and to re-experience the more innocent terrors of childhood, to be once again a preschooler whose heart pounds from a nightmare. (Solomon, 21)

Solomon's observations are not atypical; they reflect the type of misguided interpretation Stephen King's fiction has predominantly received from both the popular press and academicians for the past two decades. King is seldom appreciated as a writer capable of creating complex characters who live in complicated times. Solomon claims we read King to "re-experience the innocent terrors of childhood" and, as a corollary, to "escape the helpless fear of the headlines." Most reviewers similarly reduce his fiction to its basic plot line, with special attention provided to the new supernatural horrors presented in a particular book. The problem, of course, is that this orientation always overlooks the *real* horrors in King's novels because they are neither new nor supernatural. The "headlines" are ironically a major source of terror in Stephen King's world, and there is precious little that can be termed "innocent" about either these headlines or the manner in which they find their way into King's fiction.

The Dark Descent argues for the importance of examining King's art from two central perspectives: as a body of literature that is deeply influenced by the mainstream traditions of nineteenth- and twentieth-century American and European fiction, and as a commentary that profoundly illustrates the major political and social tensions shaping contemporary American life. Although this group of essays ranges widely over King's works and uses a variety of theoretical approaches – reader-response, mythic, psychoanalytic, structuralist, and so on – to shed new light onto King's fictions, most of the work in this volume reflects and embellishes these two core thesis points. Ron Curran's Jungian analysis of fairy-tale myths in *The Shining;* Mary Jane Dickerson's comparative treatment of Faulkner's stylistic and thematic influences on *It;* Len Mustazza's examination of *Pet Sematary* as classical tragedy; Gene Doty's symbolic reading of the simian toy in "The Monkey"; Ed Casebeer's essay on *The Stand* as a novel that assimilates several genres of popular literature; and Greg Weller's reading of feminine archetypes in *Carrie* supply further evidence of King's reliance on rich literary inheritances that include gothic prototypes from a century earlier as well as traditions not readily associated with King's genre of fiction (e.g., classical Greek tragedy).

As a collection, *The Dark Descent* posits that King has not only drawn deeply from various literary genres and traditions, but he has also embellished them by placing their fundamental archetypes, narrative structures, and thematic conflicts within a contemporary social milieu. No body of literature, even the literature of supernatural terror, can be understood as discrete from the culture from which it arises. At the heart of King's fictional microcosm is an acute awareness of the most emotional and deep-seated American anxieties. Under the supernatural veneer of vampires and telekinetic powers which remains acknowledged as one of the great popular attractions of his writing, King's world is a mirror to our own. Echoing a dominant concern of Christopher Lasch and many other contemporary social scientists, King's work highlights the ways in which American society undermines the morality necessary for love – of self and for others. Both Lasch and King depict a government and political system that remain unsupportive of human needs and efforts to sustain moral life in the community or workplace or within the intimacy of familial relationships.

Drug abuse; familial discord, particularly in the form of unresponsive and openly antagonistic parents; the absolute fear of technological advances beyond human means of comprehension, much less the ability to control; the zenophobia of small-town America; religious zealotry and its link to both societal and personal oppression; and the general inability of social institutions to maintain their viability in the face of changing values and needs; these remain the dominant issues in King's canon. And one or more of these concerns can be found in the interpretations of Michael Stanton, who writes about the political implications of *The Dead Zone;* Douglas Keesey's treatment of homophobia in King's canon; Mary Pharr's feminist evaluation of King's women characters; Bernadette Bosky's chapter on eating disorders and negative body imagery as symptomatic of social illness; and Jeanne Campbell Reesman's tracing of a polyphonic narrative structure as a means for group survival in *It.*

In addition to the extensive treatment afforded to King's significance as a post-modernist who incorporates a wide variety of sociopolitical sub-texts throughout his work, Lauri Berkenkamp's analysis of the multiple meanings associated with reading and writing in *Misery* and Arthur Biddle's awareness of the heroic-mythic journey as an inspiration for the production of art in *The Body* reflect the evolving importance King himself has attached to protagonist-writers who are struggling to adjust to their sudden fame. As King indicated in the 1989 interview he shared with me:

What I have written about writers and writing in the last five years or so has been a real effort on my part to understand what I am doing, what it means, what it is doing to me, what it is doing for me. Some of it has been out of an effort to try and understand the ramifications of being a so-called famous person, or celebrity. What does it mean when somebody who is a novelist is invited to appear on "The Hollywood Squares"? I am trying to understand these things. (Magistrale, ms. 16)

This biographical commentary can be seen fictionally encoded in characters as diverse as Ben Mears (*'Salem's Lot*), Gordie La Chance (*The Body*), Paul Sheldon (*Misery*), Bill Denbrough (*It*), and Thad Beaumont (*The Dark Half*), who possess some of the popular acclaim and financial abundance King has experienced personally in the past two decades. In addition to their wealth and fame, however, these characters are also depicted in struggles that challenge their capacities for survival, as both artists and moral beings. King's artist-characters emerge as some of the most heroic figures drawn in his canon.

This volume of critical essays seeks to address, then, the major novels and central thematic concerns that represent King's existing contribution to American letters. Less concerned with evaluating or judging the quality of King's literature (a dreary enterprise that most book reviewers and too many literary critics feel appointed to undertake when discussing King), the chapters that follow represent the best aspects of a scholarly tradition. They are more concerned with explicating the meanings of individual narratives and creating critical contexts – literary, social, historical – for interpreting them. *The Dark Descent* was assembled to establish a new level of critical discourse that will make King's prolific canon more accessible to his millions of admirers while simultaneously advancing the integrity of scholarship in this field.

REFERENCES

Magistrale, Tony. *Stephen King, The Second Decade:* Danse Macabre *to* The Dark Half. New York: Macmillan, forthcoming, 1992.
Solomon, Andy. "Scared but Safe," [Rev. of *Four Past Midnight*]. *New York Times Book Review,* September 2, 1990, 21.

2

The Masks of the Goddess: The Unfolding of the Female Archetype in Stephen King's *Carrie*

GREG WELLER

Role credits (over medium shot of teenagers entering a school building)

Masks of the Goddess: The Unfolding of the Female Archetype in Stephen King's *Carrie*

Starring:
Margaret White as the Witch in the Gingerbread House
Rita Desjardin as Artemis
Sue Snell as the Empath
And Featuring Chris Hargensen as the Bitch Goddess

With:
Tommy Ross, Billy Nolan and the Judeo-Christian God as the Chorus or Male Consorts

And: The entire population of Chamberlain, Maine as (innocent?) bystanders

Screenplay by Greg Weller
From narratives by Erich Neumann and Stephen King

Fade to Black

Just as they are about to embark on what is surely to be one of the most famous prom nights in contemporary American fiction, Thomas Ross and Carietta White pause to discuss a point of mythology:

He laughed and got out. She was about to open her door when he opened it for her. "Don't be nervous," he said. "You're like Galatea."

"Who?"

"Galatea. We read about her in Mr. Ever's class. She turned from a drudge into a beautiful woman and nobody knew her."

She considered it. "I want them to know me," she said finally.[1]

King's use of the Galatea myth at this crucial point in the novel is important for several reasons. For one, it shows the emergence of an ancient myth in a modern setting. The Galatea that Tommy refers to is the Galatea of Shaw's *Pygmalion* and the musical *My Fair Lady*. Tommy knows part of the myth, but only the part that has emerged into popular culture, and he is unaware of the deeper significance of the myth.[2] This use of the myth also underscores the tragic ignorance on the part of both Tommy and Carrie, and indeed on the part of all the major characters in the novel of the truly monumental forces that are shaping their lives. It is these forces that will be the focal point of this essay.

In this essay, I would like to discuss the mythic or archetypal aspects of *Carrie* and show how King uses myth and archetype to portray the tremendous societal and psychic forces at work on a young woman as she attempts to find her identity in late twentieth-century America.

I will begin by discussing the underlying structure of the novel, a structure based on the description of the female archetype as put forth by Erich Neumann, in his book *The Great Mother: An Analysis of the Archetype*.[3] In Neumann's schema, the female archetype consists of two basic character types—the elemental and the transformative. Each of these, in turn, is broken into positive and negative aspects. He goes on to break down the elementary character into its positive and negative aspects. The positive aspect he terms the "Good Mother" and associates it with such mythic figures as Isis, Demeter, and Mary. The negative aspect is the "Terrible Mother" and is associated with such figures as the Gorgon, Hecate, and Kali.

As with the elementary character, the transformative character also consists of two parts—the negative and positive transformative characters. The negative transformative is embodied in the figures of Lilith and Circe and in images of drunkenness and madness. In contrast, the positive transformative character is represented by Sophia or the Muse and images of wisdom and inspiration.

Now, this schema may seem vary static and lifeless, but Neumann goes on to show that this is far from the case. The archetype also has a "dynamic" as well as a "static" aspect, and it is in this context that conflicts are initiated and resolved, mysteries and rituals are entered into, Mother struggles with Daughter, Virgin fights with Whore, and from this cauldron emerges, if possible, a whole Woman.

I begin my discussion of the female archetype as it appears in *Carrie* with its static aspects, moving onto the dynamic after we see how clearly

Rita Desjardin, Margaret White, Sue Snell, and Christine Hargensen are manifestations of the positive and negative elementary and transformative aspects of the archetype.[4] As a somewhat more peripheral issue, one that comes into play in the dynamic aspect of the archetype, each of these female characters (with the exception of Ms. Desjardin) has a male analog or consort.[5] I will discuss each of these as we go along.

Perhaps the least obvious role of our four characters is Ms. Desjardin as the Good Mother; but, when we recognize her as a type of the Goddess Artemis, her role becomes much clearer. When we first encounter her, during Carrie's ritual humiliation in the shower room, she is described as their "slim, nonbreasted gym teacher." The description continues: "Her shorts were blinding white, her legs not too curved but striking in their unobtrusive muscularity. A silver whistle, won in college archery competition, hung around her neck" (King, 5). When we see her at the prom she is "dressed in a glimmering silver sheath, a perfect compliment to her blonde hair which was up. A simple pendant hung around her neck" (King, 152). The combination of the color silver with the archery medal connects her to the image of Artemis as "the Maiden of the Silver Bow," the eternally virginal goddess who is also the patroness of childbearing (Graves, 85). Additionally, the color silver is associated with the moon and links Ms. Desjardin to Artemis as Moon Goddess.

The description of her as being slightly masculine and "nonbreasted" as well as the somewhat condescending attitude that Chris Hargensen's father takes toward her by referring to her as "the young, ah, lady" reinforces her image as virgin goddess. At one point even Carrie sees her as "giggling and chuckling with rancid old-maid ribaldry" (King, 184). But along with this virginity, she is also a surrogate mother to Carrie, and as patroness of childbearing she is present when Carrie reaches puberty and "gives birth" to her psychic power. Throughout the novel, Ms. Desjardin takes a decidedly maternalistic attitude toward Carrie even when that attitude is tempered with the impatience that one would show toward a wayward child: "I'm living in a glass house, see, I understood how those girls felt. The whole thing just made me want to take the girl and shake her. Maybe there's some kind of instinct about menstruation that makes women want to snarl" (King, 10).

Ms. Desjardin also acts as a mother figure to the other girls, punishing them (in the positive sense of trying to correct their behavior) for their actions toward Carrie. Finally, we see her at the prom, acting out a role that mothers have acted out with their daughters for generations, a role that cannot, for obvious reasons, be fulfilled by Carrie's own mother – the role of mother as comforter and reassurer:

"I remember my own prom," Desjardin said softly, "I was two inches taller than the boy I went with when I was in my heels. He gave me a corsage that clashed with my gown. The tailpipe was broken on his car and the engine made . . . oh, an awful racket. But I've never had a date like it, ever again." She looked at Carrie. "Is it like that for you?" (King, 152)

Unfortunately for Carrie, Ms. Desjardin is not her biological mother. Carrie is destined to grow up with The Mother from Hell – Margaret White.

Any young person (and quite a few older ones) reading *Carrie* will instantly recognize Margaret White as every child's worst nightmare – a mother who is part Wicked Witch in the Gingerbread House and part raving lunatic, one who embarrasses one in front of one's friends. In short, a mother who is scarcely human. Margaret White is the mother as Wicked Witch. On her daughter's prom night, when most mothers would be anxiously awaiting their child's return to hear about the date, Margaret White anticipates Carrie's arrival, listening to the oppressive ticking of a Black Forest cuckoo clock, sharpening a butcher knife.

This image of Margaret White as not only a psychically oppressive figure but as an actual physical threat to her daughter's life climaxes when Carrie returns home. Mrs. White quite candidly confesses that her daughter never should have been born, that her conception was, indeed, the consequence of an act of weakness. This is truly the mother of our worst nightmares. And along with her physically destructive quality, Margaret White demonstrates what Neumann calls the "fixating" and "ensnaring" aspects of the archetype. Margaret White's favorite punishment, short of outright butchery, is to place her daughter in a locked closet, a closet that is described as the "home of terror, the cave where all hope, all resistance to God's will – and Momma's – was extinguished" (King, 54).

Margaret White's male accomplice in the torment of her daughter is not her husband, Ralph, whom she sees, like herself, as "weak and backsliding," but rather a particularly grotesque caricature of the Christian Trinity of Father, Son, and Holy Ghost. The Father and Son are represented by shrines in the White household. We see the Father as the eerily lit painting of a "huge and bearded Yahweh who was casting screaming multitudes of humans down through cloudy depths into an abyss of fire" (King, 57). The Son is represented by an especially gory crucifix. We encounter the Holy Ghost in one of Margaret White's mad rantings. He appears as a strange combination of Christian apocalyptic vision and some otherworldly horror out of H. P. Lovecraft: "in hollowed earth! We know thou brings't the Eye that Watcheth, the hideous three-lobed eye, and the sound of black trumpets" (King, 123).

It is surely axiomatic to say that it is easier to discuss evil than it is to talk of good, perhaps because good is more ambiguous, or that evil is more intriguing. So it is with Sue Snell as the positive transformative segment of the archetype. Part of the ambiguity in Sue's attitude toward Carrie, however, is what imparts to her an important aspect of the archetype – her wisdom and the sense that Sue has grown throughout the novel, from callousness tempered by pity, to mercy and understanding.

When Carrie suffers her humiliation in the locker room, Sue goes along with the rest of Chris Hargensen's "puppets." Even as she does so, however, she is forced to resort to a type of "psychic narcotic":

Sue was throwing [tampons] too, throwing and chanting with the rest, not really sure what she was doing – a charm had occurred to her mind and it glowed there like neon: there's no harm in it really no harm in it really no harm – It was still flashing and glowing, reassuringly, when Carrie suddenly began to howl. (King, 8)

And Ms. Desjardin, taking the measure of her "children," is surprised by Sue's actions: "And Sue Snell . . . You wouldn't expect a trick like that from Sue Snell. She's never seemed the kind for that kind of a stunt" (King, 20).

But as the novel progresses, Sue begins to acquire an intense awareness, an almost palpable knowledge of the consequences of her actions and the effect that they've had on Carrie and on her own place in the world. After making love to Tommy Ross she "felt low and melancholy, and her thoughts turned to Carrie in this light. A wave of remorse caught her with all emotional guards down" (King, 44). Believing, of course, that confession is good for the soul she tells Tommy about the incident in the locker room and then launches into an extended reverie on her own role in the high school community and her role to come in the "outside world" (King, 45–46). This passage, with its emphasis on the destructiveness of conformity, is some of King's finest social commentary. And, at the end of her vision, she realizes, somewhat grudgingly, that her newfound wisdom is owed to Carrie. Sue becomes the transformer and the transformed:

Carrie, it was that goddamned Carrie, this was her fault. Perhaps before today she had heard distant, circling footfalls around her lighted place, but tonight, hearing her own sordid, crummy story, she saw the actual silhouettes of all these things, and yellow eyes that glowed like flashlights in the dark. (King, 46)

Sue's growing awareness of Carrie's plight does not go unnoticed. At one point, Chris Hargensen "accuses" her of being "Joan of Arc" and tells her to go away, lest she be turned to gold by her presence (King, 75). Sue also recognizes what type of reaction her actions will generate: "She could never be quite the same golden girl in the eyes of her mates. She had done an unforgivable thing – she had broken ranks and shown her face" (King, 106).

She is finally able, through her growing awareness and subsequent sympathy toward Carrie's place in the world, to make the ultimate (to a seventeen-year-old girl) sacrifice: forgo her prom so that Carrie might go with her boyfriend. She discusses this with Tommy in a scene that shows that something has changed (even if she cannot fully articulate it) within her and she, in turn, wants to change Carrie:

But hardly anybody ever finds out that their action has really, actually, hurt other people! People don't get better, they just get smarter. When you get smarter you don't stop pulling the wings off flies, you just think of better reasons for doing it. Lots of kids say they feel sorry for Carrie White—mostly girls—and that's a laugh—but I bet none of them understand what it's like to be Carrie White, every second of every day. And they don't really care. . . . But someone ought to try and be sorry in a way that counts . . . in a way that means something. (King, 83)

And through her attempt to help Carrie, Sue will eventually gain the knowledge of death itself, and she will then use that knowledge to help the rest of the world understand the sad story of Carietta White.

Tommy Ross, Sue's male counterpart, appears as an Apollo figure: both athlete and scholar. He is a varsity baseball player and a poet. But more important, he seems to possess innately those qualities that Sue gains only through an intense personal struggle. The authors of *The Shadow Exploded* (one of the many books within the novel *Carrie*) state that "Ross's school records . . . form the picture of an extraordinary young man. . . . In fact, Thomas Ross appears to be something of a rarity: a socially conscious young man" (King, 90).

Tommy's social conscience leads him both to participate in Sue's transformation and be the agent of Sue's attempted transformation of Carrie. Tommy attempts to put Sue's and the other girls' actions into some sort of perspective. For her part, Sue, as one of the few survivors, attempts to put Tommy's actions in perspective for posterity: "There are lots of people—mostly men—who aren't surprised that I asked Tommy to take Carrie to the Spring Ball. They are surprised that he did it though, which shows you that the male mind expects very little in the way of altruism from its fellows" (King, 84).

If Sue had to go through a dark night (or at least dark twilight) of the soul to reach a positive attitude, Chris Hargensen was, to use a phrase of Sue's, "cat mean" from the word *go*. Chris, in her role as the negative transformative aspect of the archetype, is a master manipulator, both of the young girls to whom she plays ringleader—Mr. Morton refers to them as her "Mortimer Snerds"—and, perhaps most successfully, of men.

We first see Chris as a manipulator of men with her father. He is only too willing to storm into the principal's office and demand not only that his daughter be allowed to go to the prom, but that her perceived tormentor, Ms. Desjardin, be fired. Even when faced with evidence of his daughter's prior and extensive transgressions, he remains under her spell.

She is also spellbinding to young men, and she demonstrates an almost witch-like power to bind them to her will, transforming them, Circe-like, into animals:

[H]er boys had been clever marionettes with clear, pimple-free faces and parents with connections and country-club memberships . . . they began by treating her with patronizing good fellowship . . . and always ended up trotting after her with panting doglike lust. If they trotted long enough and spent enough in the process, she usually let them go to bed with her. (King, 128–129)

Chris is the ironic embodiment of Margaret White's vision: "After the blood the boys come. Like sniffing dogs, grinning and slobbering, trying to find out where that smell is" (King, 95).

Chris's effect on Billy Nolan is both inevitable and inescapable. Principal Grayle notes that "Chris Hargensen has [Billy] tied around her little finger" (King, 100); and Sue Snell notes in her book that "Chris Hargensen led him by the nose" (King, 106). But Billy's own admission of control by Chris is the most revealing. As he goes to kill the pig to obtain the blood for Carrie's ritual humiliation he realizes that he is doing it ". . . for Chris Hargensen, just as everything was for Chris, and had been since the day she swept down from her college-course Olympus and made herself vulnerable to him. He would have done murder for her, and more" (King, 112).

Chris and Billy's sexual relationship is also decidedly animalistic and serves to underscore further Chris's Circe-like transformative powers and to illustrate the type of savage sexuality that Margaret White, ironically enough, imagines her daughter and Tommy Ross are engaged in. While Chamberlain burns, Chris and Billy are in a roadhouse, starting their mating dance: "they stared at each other, panting, glaring" (King, 213). Ever the gentleman, Billy approaches Chris, "butting her in the stomach like a goat." He whispers gentle words of love to her, recalling the evening's earlier adventure: "I would have done it to you, you know that? I woulda dumped it all over your fuckin squash. You know it? Huh? Know it? Pig blood for pigs, right? Right on your motherfuckin squash." Chris returns the compliment by calling Billy a "creepy little one-nut low cock dinkless wonder." Their foreplay complete, "they descend into a red, thrashing unconsciousness" (King, 214). They are swallowed, literally kicking and screaming, by the power of the archetype.

Billy Nolan plays Dionysus to Tommy Ross's Apollo. He represents a dark, almost chthonic force. He is a hunter-killer, an apprentice demon who "went cruising for stray dogs" in his car at night only to return in the morning "with its front bumper dripping" (King, 137). Indeed, Billy's car is one of the clearest symbols of his power. Chris sees Billy's car as "old, dark, somehow sinister" (King, 129), and when Billy and his mates go cruising for pig's blood, the car appears positively demonic: "One head-

light was out; the other flickered in the midnight dark. . . . Three joints
were going, passing through the inner dark like the lambent eye of some
rotating Cerberus" (King, 110). Billy, himself, clearly grasps the demonic
symbiosis between a boy and his car.

But the car: the car fed him power and glory from its own mystic lines of force. It
made him someone to be reckoned with, someone with mana. It was not by accident that he had done most of his balling in the back seat. The car was his slave
and his god. It gave and it could take away. (King, 137)

And indeed, the car would take away his life, when control of it is relin-
quished to Carrie: "the car sprang forward like some old and terrible
man-eater . . . And Billy felt his car turn traitor, come alive, slither in his
hands" (King, 220).[6]

There is an interesting dynamic between the two transformative dyads
of Sue/Tommy and Chris/Billy. Whereas Sue was at first reluctant to let
her true feelings come out and was, to a certain extent, shamed into
action by Tommy, Chris begins to have second thoughts about what she is
about to do to Carrie and has to be goaded into action by Billy. Right before she pulls the rope that will release the bucket of blood, Billy tells her
that she "talks too fucking much" and she imagines punishing him by
withholding sex because "people did not speak to her in such a manner.
Her father was a lawyer" (King, 159). Both girls set forces into motion that
they ultimately cannot control, but whereas Sue, as the embodiment of
Wisdom, attains Wisdom, Chris, as the Bitch-Goddess, the mistress of
animals, is destroyed by the very forces that she seeks to control.

Now that we have delineated the various female archetypal figures
present in *Carrie,* as well as the dyadic couplings they form with their
male consorts or avatars, let us now examine the dynamic of the novel
itself and how these archetypal figures act in that dynamic structure.

In *The Great Mother,* Neumann discusses what he calls the "dynamic
and the polyvalence of the archetypal structure of the feminine":

Because the archetype fascinates consciousness and is dynamically very much
similar to it, the ego consciousness, when it approaches the pole, is not only attracted by it but easily overwhelmed. The outcome is seizure by the archetype,
disintegration of consciousness and loss of the ego. But since this fascination of
disintegration of consciousness means that at the polar points consciousness
loses its faculty of differentiation and in this constellation can no longer distinguish between positive and negative, it becomes possible for a phenomenon to
shift into its opposite. Helplessness, pain, stupor, sickness, distress, loneliness,
nakedness, emptiness, madness can, therefore, be forerunners of inspiration and
vision and manifest themselves as stations on a road leading through danger to
salvation, through intimation of death to rebirth and new birth. (Neumann,
75–76)

What we see here is the blueprint for a sacrificial ritual, a ritual that Carrie is destined to play out.

Carrie is the quintessential teenager in search of herself. When we first see her standing "like a patient ox" (King, 7), we know that we are in the presence of the standard victim found in high schools everywhere, the outsider: "She looked the part of the sacrificial goat, the constant butt, believer in left-handed monkey wrenches, perpetual foul-up, and she was" (King, 4). We soon come to see Carrie as a young person lacking all sense of ego, of self. She is not so much concerned with being Prom Queen, or, like Sue Snell, "Little Susie mix 'n match from Ewen High School, Head Cupcake of the entire Cupcake Brigade" (King, 49), she is not even concerned with college and a good job. Carietta White is concerned with finding *anything* beyond the utter emptiness that is her soul. She looks at herself in the mirror and sees only ugliness and then a void:

She caught a glimpse of her own face in a tiny mirror. . . .
She hated her face, her dull, stupid, bovine face, the vapid eyes, the red, shiny pimples, the nests of blackheads. She hated her face most of all.
The reflection was suddenly split by a jagged, silvery crack. The mirror fell on the floor and shattered at her feet, leaving only the plastic ring to stare at her like a blind eye. (King, 43)

The major force blocking Carrie from any self-actualization is, of course, her mother. Desperately, she tries to tell her that she has to "start to . . . to try and get along with the world," finally telling her "I only want to be let to live my own life. I . . . don't like yours" (King, 97). Ironically, the only way that Carrie can find her "own life" is in death.

This struggle for identity comes to the crisis point on Prom Night. The prom itself is a ritual with a magic setting. The gym has been transformed into something strange and wonderful. It is an enchanted place: "And she felt dusted over with the enchantment of the evening." Carrie realized that "if there was enchantment here, it was not divine but pagan" (King, 150–151). It is the kind of pagan throwback that fills the thousands of pages of Sir James Frazer's *The Golden Bough*. It is, indeed, the setting of a modern day version of the Eleusinian Mysteries. In an ideal world, Carrie would be chosen Queen, be taken through the darkness to the stage, the bright lights would be turned on, momentarily blinding her, and she would emerge as a new whole person. Carrie's world, unfortunately is not a decent place. It is the real world, a world made from flesh and blood and emotions and not constructed from papier-mâché, like the Venice of the Spring Ball.

On Prom Night, Carrie comes face to face with all the aspects of the female archetype and the various male counterparts of those aspects. In the interest of brevity, I will focus on two of those meetings – one positive, one negative – and conclude with Carrie's final encounter with Sue Snell. By doing this I hope to demonstrate the "dynamic" of Neuman's archetype and show that, if not for Carrie, then at least for Sue, there is some hope of positive transformation.

When Carrie first enters the transformed gymnasium on Prom Night, she is awestruck by the scene: "The first thing that struck Carrie when they walked in was Glamor. Not glamor but Glamor. Beautiful shadows rustled about in chiffon, lace, silks, satin. The air was redolent with the odor of flowers, the nose was constantly amazed by it" (King, 144). We should be careful to note the use of the word "glamor." It does not refer to mere fashion, but rather to one of the original meanings of the word – a magic spell or enchantment.

Not only is the gym transformed but, in Carrie's eyes at least, so are the people: "She did not really want to see them as her classmates. She wanted them to be beautiful strangers" (King, 144). Carrie's relationship with Tommy is also momentarily transformed. The scene could have been one out of "Teenage Heartthrob Comix," but due to the charged nature of the whole moment, King invests the transformation with a mythic quality: "While he held out her chair, she saw the candle and asked Tommy if he would light it. He did. Their eyes met over its flame" (King, 146). Carrie herself is transformed: "Her soul knew a moment's calm, as if it had been uncrumpled and smoothed under an iron" (King, 145).

In this scene, we see the dynamic of Neumann's archetype at work. Carrie enters a magical place, a place of coronation, of initiation, meets her consort as the emanation of an aspect of the archetype and, using Neumann's words, is "seized" by it. This seizure could have produced a lasting change in Carrie, a rebirth into the world. One of the survivors of the "Black Prom" sums it up perfectly: "It was as if we were watching a person rejoin the human race" (King, 168). Unfortunately, the ritual that could have effected this rebirth, the coronation of the King and Queen, turns out to be a ritual of humiliation. When the blood hits Carrie, there is a pause, and then the laughter begins.

Released from the positive transformative aspect of the archetype, Carrie reverts. She reverts to the broken state that she experienced earlier when the mirror shattered in her hands. She reverts to the frog-like state of the novel's opening scene of ritual humiliation in the locker room. She is sent spinning from the positive aspect of the archetype to its polar opposite and the people of Chamberlain are the victims of this abrupt reversal.

Carrie comes face-to-face with the dark half of the archetype in the depths of the Carlin Street Congregational Church, currently boasting a congregation of one: "She prayed and there was no answer. No one was there – or if there was, HE/IT was cowering from her. God had turned His face away, and why not? This horror was as much His doing as hers. And so she left the church, left it to go home and find her Momma and make the destruction complete" (King, 200). Once again, Carrie enters a ritual place and is transformed. She is seized by the negation of the "Abyss" that she finds there and is transformed into a type of Nemesis – the Goddess of vengeance:[7] "She paused on the church steps, looking at the flocks of people streaming towards the center of town. Animals. Let them burn, then. Let the streets be filled with the smell of their sacrifice. Let this place be called racca, ichabod, wormwood" (King, 200). Thus, things have come full circle. Carrie has been flung from one pole of the female archetype to the other, her thoughts even taking on the very cadence of her mother's rantings.

And so, we are left with the wreckage of Carrie, transformed in body: "Her body seemed to have become twisted, shrunken, crone-like" (King, 208), scarcely human: "Sue was reminded of dead animals she had seen on 95 – woodchucks, groundhogs, skunks – that had been crushed by speeding trucks and station wagons" (King, 228–229). Are we left, then, with the tragedy of a modern day Cinderella, who dies trying to flee her evil stepmother? Or do we see a cautionary tale about "instant karma": Carrie trapped in the role of an angel of death no less vicious than those contained in her mother's religious icons? To take either of these views would be a grave injustice to King as humanist.

At the end, after the carnage of Prom Night, after the blood, after the wailing and gnashing of teeth, there is a moment of calm. Sue senses "an essence of Carrie, a gestalt, muted now, not strident, not announcing itself with a clarion, but waxing and waning in steady oscillations" (King, 229). Carrie probes Sue's mind and they share "the awful totality of perfect knowledge" (King, 230). And in that joining, two human beings learn a great deal about each other:

> Books thrown open, flashes of experience, marginal notations in all the hieroglyphs of emotion, more complex than the Rosetta Stone.
> Looking. Finding more than Sue herself had suspected – love for Tommy, jealousy, selfishness, a need to subjugate him to her will on the matter of taking Carrie, disgust for Carrie herself, hate for Miss Desjardin, hate for herself. (King, 231)

Carrie has died, freeing herself from the control of the archetype, both negative and positive, but she has left a legacy imprinted on Sue's mind: the memory of what it was like to understand fully another human being, and the promise that she will know herself.

The story of Carrie, in essence, is not one of destruction, but one of going beyond: progressing beyond the bounds of family, school, even of mind, the self-imposed limits of the mind called "archetype" or "myth."

The final image that King presents us with is that of a young girl with the same telekinetic ability as Carrie. She is described as a "world beeter" (sic) (King, 245). By this, does King mean that she will beat the world into submission? No. After the carnage of Prom Night in Chamberlain, after Carrie's sacrifice and Sue Snell's transformation, the world has changed ever so slightly. A new force has been unleashed and people are being forced to work out their hopes and fears, both in their lives, and in the various texts cited within *Carrie*. The world has been somehow meliorated by Carrie's passage through it. We can see the girl beating the world in the same way we would see a goldsmith at work—beating a formless lump of ore into fine gold leaf.

NOTES

1. Stephen King, *Carrie* (New York: Signet, 1975), p. 134. All subsequent references to *Carrie* appear parenthetically in the text.

2. For a complete discussion of the Galatea myth, see Robert Graves's *The Greek Myths* (New York: George Braziller, 1957), pp. 211–212. All subsequent references to Graves appear parenthetically in the text. The Galatea myth is quite complex, consisting of at least three disparate versions, all three of which can be seen as functioning in *Carrie*. As an exercise in myth-crit, the reader is invited to consult Graves and filter Carrie's story through the sieve of the myth of Galatea.

3. For the complete particulars of Neumann's schema, see Erich Neumann *The Great Mother: An Analysis of the Archetype* (Princeton, N.J.: Princeton University Press, 1974), pp. 24–83, *passim*. All subsequent references to Neumann appear parenthetically in the text.

While there is no direct evidence that King consciously based the structure of *Carrie* directly on Neumann's archetype, there is evidence to suggest King's ongoing interest in myth, in both a practical and theoretical sense. In an interview conducted in 1989, for example, we read the following:

> TM: Has your work been influenced to any extent by mythic theories—Frazer, Campbell, Freud, Jung?
>
> King: Campbell. I was introduced to Joseph Campbell by Peter Straub several years ago, and I was particularly taken by the book *Hero with a Thousand Faces*. It is a wonderful book, and it definitely had some effect on me. . . .
>
> TM: Perhaps the other theorists—Frazer, Jung, Freud—have found their way into your fictional lexicon through other sources.
>
> King: Right. The trickle-down effect is absolutely there. . . . If I had to come down on one side or the other, I'd definitely be a Jungian rather than a Freudian. Jung's sense of myth and symbol is very provocative, very rich. (Magistrale, ms. 9)

With the type of background in myth that King displays and the added "trickle-down effect" that he notes, it is, of course, possible that King did have direct contact with Neumann's work at the time he wrote *Carrie*. So, while I am not suggesting that King had Neumann's text sitting next to his typewriter as he worked, I am inviting the reader to consider the very close parallels between the structure of King's novel and the structure of Neumann's archetype.

4. The astute reader will notice, of course, the absence of Carrie among these archetypal players. While Carrie is the focal point of the novel, she participates in the dynamic aspect of the archetype through the process of interacting with the four static elements of the archetype.

5. The best analogy that I can think of for the relationship between the female characters and their male counterparts is that of the Hindu concept of "sakti." Sakti is, in essence, a type of energy that is manifested through the consort of a deity. It represents Energy as opposed to Being. Although the sakti energy is usually conceived of as being feminine, Benjamin Walker in his *The Hindu World* (New York: Praeger, 1968) notes that "in many instances the female deity of the divine pair was regarded as the active principle of the universe and was often conceived of as having greater importance than the male" (Walker, Vol. 2, p. 336). Another approach would be to consider these pairs to be *dyads* in the psychological sense of "A pair, neither of whose members can achieve full reinforcement, or gratification, without collaboration of the other" (Benjamin Wolman, ed., *Dictionary of Behavioral Science*, New York: Academic Press, 1989, p. 101).

6. The reader who is familiar with King's work will, of course, recognize in Billy's car a prefiguration of the demonic '58 Plymouth of his later novel, *Christine*. One should pause to contemplate, given the age of the car and the age of Ms. Hargensen, the question of which came first – the Bitch-Goddess or the car?

7. The concept of the goddess Nemesis shows just how complicated myth-hunting can become. Graves cites a number of variations on the Nemesis myth: in one she is the moon-goddess as nymph who chases the sacred king and devours him; in a later version (after the patriarchy came to ascendancy) the roles are reversed. Complicating the matter further is the gradual shift in emphasis from that of a goddess playing out a role in a natural drama to that of an instrument of divine vengeance (Graves, pp. 127–130, 206–208). It should not come as a surprise that any or all of these interpretations can apply to this scene.

REFERENCES

Graves, Robert. *The Greek Myths.* New York: George Braziller, 1957.

King, Stephen. *Carrie.* New York: Signet, 1975.

Magistrale, Tony. *Stephen King, the Second Decade:* Danse Macabre *to* The Dark Half. New York: Macmillan, forthcoming, 1992.

Neumann, Erich. *The Great Mother: An Analysis of the Archetype.* Princeton, N.J.: Princeton University Press, 1974.

Walker, Benjamin. *The Hindu World: An Encyclopedic Survey of Hinduism.* New York: Praeger, 1968.

Wolman, Benjamin B., ed. *Dictionary of Behavioral Science.* New York: Academic Press, 1989.

3

Partners in the *Danse:*
Women in Stephen King's Fiction

Near the end of the preface to the Complete Edition of *The Stand,*
Stephen King declares, "I write for only two reasons: to please myself and
to please others" (xii). The pleasure of writing, not for the ages but for the
story, is seminal to an author whose genius lies in his accessibility. His
readers are his peers, and they never feel patronized. Harlan Ellison has
spoken of King's "invisible technique," something "so simply and
smoothly done that it's like Fred Astaire's dancing" (Beahm, 149). The
simile is apt, for King—like Astaire, an astoundingly hard worker in reality—never shows his effort in the ease of a finished product. For Astaire
that product was the dance; for King it is the *danse macabre,* the ritual
movement by which he takes us through his fictional universe.

By now, some twenty-five years into King's career as a published
writer, that universe has been explicitly defined as a place of both evil
and enlightenment. Tony Magistrale has noted that the "discovery of evil
is the central theme" that King shares with American Romantics like
Hawthorne and Melville (Magistrale, *Landscape,* 21). Magistrale further
notes that such discovery is sometimes overwhelming, sometimes regen-
erating: either "destructive of the central character or of others around
him" (21), or instructive of "the knowledge that moral maturity is a possible consequence from contact with sin" (22). In this sense, King's most
impressive characters are involved in a *rite de passage* that may end (as it
often begins) in horror or that may end in hope. Though the circumstances of a particular ritual may have enormous impact on its outcome,
the individual involved always has a choice: to cling to his inherent humanity or to give in to the despair that creates inhuman action.

The illusion of reality is critical here, for it is the credibility of the character that determines the impact that the choice has on the reader. In an interview with Douglas Winter for *Faces of Fear*, King has defined horror as "contrasting emotion to our understanding of all the things that are good and normal" (253). Working from this definition, King adds, "So in that sense, I think that if you can bring on characters that people believe, that people accept as part of the normal spectrum, then you can write horror" (254). This theory is most obviously embodied, perhaps, in King's fictional children, who may have special gifts but who almost always seem emotionally normal and appealing. But the response King seeks in his audience is found as well through adult characters like Ben Mears, Larry Underwood, and Paul Sheldon, all of whom appear very human in their flawed but fundamental decency. Equally credible are those characters whose flaws destroy their decency, who make the wrong moral choice: Jack Torrance, for example, or Harold Lauder. Whatever their choice, King's most memorable characters are always recognizable as people. Like their writer, these characters are their readers' peers.

They are also mostly male. King's female characters are plentiful enough, but they tend to lack substance. King has had trouble creating fictional women with the emotional dimensions so apparent in his children and men. In her article published in *Fear Itself*, Chelsea Quinn Yarbro points to a "lamentable flaw" in King's sensibilities: "It is disheartening when a writer with so much talent and strength and vision is not able to develop a believable woman character between the ages of seventeen and sixty" (49). It is a mark of King's integrity that when *Playboy* quoted Yarbro's charge to him, King called it "the most justifiable of all those leveled at me" (Underwood & Miller, 47).

The irony here is that women really matter to this man. Raised by his mother and his aunts after his father deserted the family, King himself has been married to his wife, Tabitha, for almost twenty years. Clearly, the women in King's life have been critical to his survival—both personal and professional. In fact, as most horror fans know, it was Tabitha King who rescued the manuscript called *Carrie* from the trash where her husband had consigned it. King had thrust it there in frustration after finding its female-oriented theme difficult to handle. Once rescued, *Carrie* went on to hard-cover publication and its author, to phenomenal fame. But his frustration with fictional females has remained.

At the beginning, however, King wrote *Carrie* as a deliberate attempt to break away from American chauvinism:

A lot of my efforts in writing about women were made because I wanted to understand women and try to escape the stereotyping that goes on in so much male fiction. I read Leslie Fiedler's book *Love and Death in the American Novel* . . . . Fiedler argues that in American fiction all women are either bitches or zeroes.

And I decided I want to do better than that. And this was a motivating force behind the writing of *Carrie*. (Magistrale, *SK*, ms. 10)

Written about women for the purpose of breaking stereotypes, *Carrie*
(and Brian de Palma's attendant movie) attracted plenty of attention to
the subject; but instead of refuting Fiedler's arguments, the novel perpet-
uated them. Douglas Keesey calls *Carrie*'s title character "patriarchal society's worst nightmare concerning women and their bodies" (11). Harlan
Ellison says that the novel's shower scene taps into "basic cultural mythology" (Beahm, 148). In 1983 King himself described Carrie as a character "who starts out as a nebbish victim and then *becomes* a bitch goddess"
(Underwood & Miller, 47). In spite of himself, then, at the beginning at
least and through much of his most famous fiction, King does type
women. Despite his best efforts, King's women are reflective of American stereotypes, just as their author is himself reflective of the male
American perspective explored in Fiedler.

Of course, on occasion King has created credible female characters.
The fact that most of these credible females are either juvenile or elderly
is a point worth noting not only as a confirmation of Yarbro's criticism
but also as an indication of just what King's cultural heritage has brought
him. In *Love and Death* Fiedler writes of Mark Twain, observing, "For a
good American like Twain, all offenses are offenses against the woman;
to be born is to rack the mother with pain; to be married is to blaspheme
against purity; to have a child is to set a seal on such blasphemy" (295). A
century after Twain, King has cast off the Victorian guilt that led men to
such a perverse view of the male–female relationship, but he–like other
American writers–has retained its impression. A loving son and faithful
husband, a compassionate father and successful professional, King is
himself the very model of a good American male. And his most convincing female characters are precisely those who are the least threatening to
men: little girls like Ellie Creed and old women like Stella Flanders. By
reason of their youth or their age, such females are defined not so much
by their sex as by their idiosyncrasies. This focus on personality rather
than on sex neatly avoids that sense of guilt about women that Fiedler
finds embedded in the male subconscious.

Yet such individualized characters spin out of gender-neutral situations, and by narrative necessity, many of King's fictional females cannot
be angled away from their femininity. That femininity ought to add extra
dimension to these characters; instead, it seems to limit their development as prescribed by cultural conventions. Fiedler's book refers repeatedly to the male myth of the Pale Maiden and the Dark Lady: "one is
'spotless,' which is to say, sexless; the other charged with blood and ready
to break through all bounds" (206). Working out of his American *menta-
lité,* King occasionally uses this dichotomy (most notably – color aside – in

The Drawing of the Three). More often, however, it serves as a backdrop to his perspective on women. On the one hand, King has dropped the emphasis on virginity as a synonym for purity in adult females; on the other, children and old ladies have replaced pale maidens in their chastity. Meanwhile, King's mid-life females have the right to express their sexuality so long as it is also an expression of their love. Sex without love, however, inevitably leads to trouble.

In effect, King's sexually active females are defined by the integrity of their womanhood—as perceived by men. Limited by this definition, many of these women can be classified as female stereotypes, as monsters, helpmates, and madonnas, in particular. These types are based on narrative circumstances, of course, but also on the characters' level of adherence to conventional ideals. The classifications are neither mutually exclusive nor all-inclusive, and every now and then a fantasy-goddess sneaks in (witness Ophelia in "Mrs. Todd's Shortcut" [*Skeleton Crew*]); but even then, the frame of reference for this fantasy begins at home. King never consciously writes against independent females, but he does make such females especially vulnerable to evil, far more likely to end up villains or victims than heroines.

In this respect, King's women are judged by the same rules that determine the fitness of romance-novel heroines. Kay Mussell has described a "domestic test" such heroines must pass to prove their worthiness. This test conforms to "the three traditional and interrelated roles of female socialization: wife, mother, and homemaker" (89). Those who pass the test are those who exhibit "the innate traits of good women—sexual control, modesty, intuition, selflessness, caring—but who use those qualities actively to benefit others" (90). Mussell could be describing King's most familiar female characters, the ones who may not be distinct or complex enough to be realistic, but who are easy to judge by their success or failure when their feminine virtues are put on trial.

In King's universe, the difference between monstrosity and normalcy is determined for women by their ability to care for others on a regular basis. This traditional role of woman as supportive helpmate or loving mother is critical to the well-being of both society and individuals. Children carry wisdom and wonder in this universe, and adults need these traits to survive the periodic assaults of evil on humanity. Like it or not, men must be ready to bear the brunt of these cosmic assaults; and both children and men need shelter from the rigors of their lives. Ideally, women provide such a respite for their mates and their young. This role is enormously important and never intentionally patronizing. Its defect, however, is also enormous: it determines a woman's worth exclusively by her domestic success or failure rather than by any achievements she may have as an individual. The domestic test is, finally, a very narrow, very tough way to judge any human being, even fictional ones.

That judgment is easiest to pass on King's dark ladies, those monstrous creatures with no feminine virtues at all. These insidious females are as dangerous as any of the dark ladies described in Fiedler's book, but not so much for blatant sexual activity as for their social dysfunction. Although King distrusts institutions of all kinds, he admires traditional social virtues, particularly in women. Of his mother he has said, "She was a wonderful lady, a very brave lady in that old-fashioned sense, [who] went to work to support us, generally at menial jobs because of her lack of any professional training" (Underwood & Miller, 34). When King speaks of his wife, he talks in a similar vein, describing his gratitude for "the unremitting commitment that she's made to me and the help she's given me in living and working the way I want to" (Underwood & Miller, 46). The strength of these traditional virtues is what separates exemplary women from ineffectual ones, and the absence of these virtues altogether is what creates dark ladies, who are fundamentally incapable of caring for others or feeling for anyone beyond themselves.

In origin and form these monsters vary greatly, but the one deficiency they share is so critical to the traditional concept of femininity that it types these females more than a uniform background or appearance ever could. In essence, the dark ladies lack the ability to nurture other beings. As females, they are charged with the passion that Fiedler ascribes to the type, but that passion is directed only toward the self. Obsessed with self-gratification, King's female monsters are unable to respond to either individuals or society. In almost every instance, these women refuse either their social role as wife or their biological right to be a mother. And though these dark ladies sometimes begin in pathos and often act with a notable lack of conscious control, they are always destructive in the end and always isolated from humanity by that destruction.

Even excluding Christine, the mean machine–bitch on wheels, a list of such dark characters would include increasingly inhuman females. It begins with Margaret White, whose fundamentalist fanaticism makes her more a monster than Carrie ever is. In *The Stand* Nadine Cross is a different kind of fanatic. Frustrated with her status as an old-maid schoolteacher, Nadine nurses a monomaniacal sense of her own importance that leads her away from her initial decency into the embrace of a demon. Then there is Susan Norton, who metamorphoses from a sweetly inept helpmate to an equally inept vampire in the town of 'Salem's Lot. A far more frightening metamorphosis occurs in "Nona" (*Skeleton Crew*), where a violently disturbed youth sees an exquisite girl become a savage graveyard rat. Nona may be only a metaphor for the youth's own psychosis, but real or not, she is the very image of woman as predator. Hungry for control, Nona dazzles her victim, first turning him against other men, then devouring him sexually and emotionally. More recently, the character Bobbi Anderson has had an alteration of her own, from a strong-willed writer to a tentacled Tommyknocker. Bobbi is a career woman who considers herself both tough-minded and independent, but for all her supposed strength, she never really has a chance against the alien force that engulfs her. She loses her humanity, but in a sense, she is never as inhuman as is Annie Wilkes, the monstrous nurse in *Misery*.

Annie's monstrosity lies in her singularity: she is a brilliant caricature of the nurturing female so favored by her author. In his review of *Misery*, John Katzenbach calls Annie "a single-dimensional hulking horror" (20), but the dimension in which Annie exists, despite King's disavowal of the type, is the vast realm of the bitch-goddess. *Misery* has a remarkable protagonist in Paul Sheldon, a popular novelist who, in the most classic of King's rituals, finds himself by losing his way. In this version the traveller loses his way by drinking himself into a car accident that cripples him and leaves him under Annie's dominion. Registered nurse, Colorado resident, and serial killer, Annie thinks of herself as Paul Sheldon's "number-one fan" (6), but Paul soon comes to associate her with the awful Bourka Bee-Goddess he creates for the novel she forces him to write. And what he fears most is that "The goddess is immortal" (293).

This one is not, of course, and she is eventually killed in a fight with Paul and his typewriter. Nonetheless, as Katzenbach points out, "Nurse Wilkes is seen only through [Paul's] eyes" (20), a point of view that makes the reader quite capable of sharing Paul's terror. Nor can Paul be termed paranoid: he loses more than his way when Annie makes him a drug addict, then slices off a couple of his body parts after he disobeys her. For Annie, such action is justified by her own world-view, which divides everyone alive into three groups: "brats, poor poor things . . . and Annie" (177). As the only Annie on the planet, the goddess must punish the "brats" for misbehavior and eliminate the "poor things" for pity's sake. So she burns and mutilates and murders, not at random nor even for pleasure, but as the duty of the divine handmaiden of death.

Moreover, Annie's deific duties require her to be lover and mother to her chosen bard. Early in the novel she resuscitates Paul after he stops breathing. By using the kiss-of-life on his unconscious body, she becomes, metaphorically at least, not just Paul's saviour but his lover as well, a lover quite completely in control of this affair. For Paul, the metaphor is very different: he feels that Annie has "raped him full of her air" (5), a feeling that goes beyond revulsion as he realizes that his clinical death must have come from an accidental overdose at the hands of his "rapist." For though occasionally a careless nurse, Annie is always a demanding god. When Paul uses profanity in a work, she makes him both wash out his mouth with dirty rinsewater and burn the offending manuscript. Thus, she is given a sacrifice while she gives Paul a grotesque version of the kind of lesson most mothers have to give recalcitrant sons. Great goddess, life-giving lover, and wise matriarch, Annie is a legend in her own dimension.

Outside herself, in the space where Annie cannot go, she is seen by a decent but damaged man as the psychotic she surely is. Paul hates her as readers hate her, this grotesque-looking woman who kidnaps and kills without compunction. It's difficult not to hate Annie, particularly when she says, "I love you, Paul" (280), a remarkable confession to the man she has turned into a drug-enslaved amputee. Yet she literally lives, and lets Paul live, for the return of Misery Chastain, the romance-novel heroine who would make a perfect score on the domestic test (not even Frannie Goldsmith could do that). Annie's obsession with this character is at the root of her love for Paul, who quickly comes to understand that his goddess has cast him in the role of Scheherazade. Like the rape-resuscitation, this roleplaying simultaneously weakens Paul's masculinity and increases Annie's power. In particular, it gives her a private conduit into the life of her most treasured alter ego, not the Bourka Bee-Goddess but the delicate and passive fantasy that is Misery. Annie is drawn toward Misery, her polar opposite in femininity, perhaps because Misery's passivity makes her a very different kind of goddess from the kind Annie imagines herself to be. Literally brought back from the grave, Misery seems to spend most of her time unconscious in the book Paul writes for Annie. All she has to do to be worshipped by both men and women is to remain a sleeping beauty—honey for the bees, in effect. As the perfect Gothic heroine, Misery is a housewife's fantasy; as a goddess, she's a dark lady's dream as well.

King does not try to rationalize Annie's sociopathology. He chooses not to delve into the physical defects, psychological stress, and social restrictions that create serial killers. It's not Annie's girth or society's mistreatment of nurses that is on trial here. In fact, the scrapbook Paul finds in her parlor proves that Annie had some professional success and was once attractive enough to find a man to marry her. Even so, she has always been a monster, a thing beyond rational explanation or moral boundaries. Only once in this story, when Paul sees in Annie's tears "the woman she might have been if her upbringing had been right or the drugs squirted out by all the funny little glands inside had been less wrong" (282), does this darkest of King's ladies really evoke compassion. Elsewhere, she's the psycho-goddess, and the reader is as likely as Paul to weep for joy when she dies from his authorial attentions.

In Annie's world, everything traditionally feminine has been reversed. Most of King's women exist in a far more conventional dimension, one still dominated by the domestic test. Indeed, it may well be the constricting nature of this test that causes so many of King's characters to fail it at a critical moment and so fall short as helpmates and madonnas. Often, those who fail the test are good-hearted women who function quite well during periods of tranquility, but who lack the skill and perception needed to sustain their mates and dependents in or after an extended crisis. Still, they generally try to help as best they can. Leigh Cabot, for example, loses one boyfriend to the demonic force that lies within the car Christine, but assists another boy in defeating this monstrosity. Yet the memory of that experience is enough, eventually, to come between Leigh and this boy, too, while Roland LeBay's implacable fury is apparently on the move again at the novel's close. For the mothers in King's universe, failure can be even more catastrophic. After cheating on her husband, Donna Trenton tries to save her child's life in *Cujo,* but she isn't strong enough to kill the rabid dog before Tad dies. King never suggests that Tad died for his mother's sins, but the sins are there and Tad is not.

In fact, throughout King's universe, the job of rescuing others is essentially a man's job. In *The Shining,* Danny Torrance is a fount of wisdom compared to both his parents, but at least Jack Torrance is tragic; Wendy Torrance is pathetic. Always dependent on men, she is brought into danger by the actions of one man, and she is brought out of it by the actions of another. Without Dick Hallorann, who literally carries Wendy and Danny to safety, she would lose her son and herself when she loses her husband. Even Liz Beaumont, the intelligent wife and mother who is kidnapped with her babies in *The Dark Half,* becomes essentially an onlooker in the end. At one point, the policeman who is also George Stark's prisoner gazes at Liz and wonders "if Stark had any idea of how dangerous this woman could be to him" (380). Dangerous Liz goes so far as to hide a knife as a potential weapon, but at her husband's request, she throws the knife away and lets him handle his psychic twin. She knows enough to let her man rescue his family.

In *Firestarter,* Vicky McGee is not rescued. Tortured and then murdered at the hands of government agents who want her daughter Charlie, Vicky dies unable to protect either herself or her child. When her husband finds her body, it is stuck beneath an ironing board, a grotesque parody of a housewife with "a cleaning rag stuffed in her mouth" and "a thick and sickening smell of Pledge furniture polish in the air" (142). Eventually, Andy McGee dies as well, but his death gives Charlie the strength she needs not just to escape her kidnappers but to incinerate their lair as well. Afterwards, eight-year-old Charlie McGee is no longer a little girl. At the end of her story, she is a goddess, with "a kind of serene, calm glow" (371), a dazzling smile, and the potential to create a nova that could crack the planet Earth. Charlie is unlikely to end up like her mother.

Leigh, Donna, Wendy, Liz, and Vicky all fail to one degree or another to protect their loved ones, but none fails so utterly as Rachel Creed. Early in *Pet Sematary,* Rachel is described as another version of her five-year-old daughter, Ellie: "Even the expression was the same – set and a bit sullen on top, but wounded beneath" (39). The comparison of mother to daughter rather than the reverse is ironically appropriate since throughout the novel Rachel is manipulated like a child and yet is far less perceptive than Ellie. Traumatized in her own childhood by the horrible death of her sister, Rachel is too neurotic to accept Ellie's natural interest in why things die. She is also a highly dependent wife, who as a young girl exchanged a domineering father for a rationally minded husband. A decade later, Louis is the one who answers Ellie's questions and saves baby Gage from choking while Rachel collapses, on both occasions, in hysteria. In no sense is she her husband's full partner, and so he never even considers confiding in her about his nocturnal treks to the Micmac burial ground. Inevitably, when Gage makes his fatal run for the road, Rachel quickly falls behind Louis as they try to catch their son, but this time Louis misses.

That miss is catastrophic, not the least so because it destroys Louis Creed's ability to care for anyone but the dead baby. Rachel cannot help anyone, and Louis helps neither his wife nor surviving child, leaving Ellie to "swim in her grief as best she could" (253). For a kindergartner, Ellie swims quite well, better than her mother, who lets her husband send his wife and daughter away the day after their baby's funeral. Rachel tells Louis that leaving "feels wrong" (269), a feeling based on Ellie's dream of doom, a dream Rachel understands to "have a quality of prophecy" (269). But she leaves anyway. Only when Ellie's shine is so strong that it illuminates her mother's own intuition of evil does Rachel set off to save her husband. Bernadette Bosky finds this intuitive juncture of mother and daughter "an inspiring but ultimately weak and ineffective counterpoint to the influence of the Wendigo-blighted burial ground" (248). Bosky is right, but the inspiration has Ellie at its origin, while the ineffectuality belongs to Rachel. She becomes Ellie's champion against the Wendigo, but a champion prone to neurosis, hysteria, and ineptitude. Nor has she any idea of what she's about to face.

So Rachel Creed dies, after being toyed with by the Wendigo on her way home, after weeping in frustration at the thought of Louis, the thought that "Something is trying to keep me away from him" (333). It never occurs to her that something is sending her to Louis at its own pace. After losing Gage, then leaving Louis in one place and Ellie in another, Rachel is slaughtered in utter confusion while embracing the Gage-thing. Brought back by her insane husband (who never stops trying to justify himself), Rachel returns as a monster herself at the story's close. In what is really her only effective scene in the entire novel, she leaves domestic failures far behind to croak out *"Darling"* to a madman. Her success as a monster is left to the reader's imagination.

Rachel is domestic failure *in extremis,* and she ends by degenerating into monstrosity. There are, however, a few women in King's universe who begin by taking the domestic test and end by evolving beyond it. These are the rarest of adult females in King's canon: women who closely resemble their creator's male protagonists, women who are able to fashion a limited victory out of defeat. These are also the women who survive their men just as King's men so often survive their women. By that survival, these few females move past their initial role of helpmate or madonna. And though they may reestablish that role, if they do so it is with a bittersweet awareness of the world outside the home.

Among these female protagonists is *Carrie's* Susan Snell, who cannot save her lover, her friends, or the town of Chamberlain. Even her pregnancy proves to be false at the very moment when she most needs a last gift from her dead lover. Rather than breaking her, however, her role in Chamberlain's tragedy changes Susan from a naive girl into a mature woman, albeit a woman with an almost preternatural understanding of the hardness and brevity of existence. In *The Dead Zone,* Sarah Bracknell loses John Smith to the vagaries of life, and not even a good husband and a healthy baby fill the void in her soul. Yet like Susan, Sarah goes on, an adult who believes what Johnny often said: "We all do what we can" (426). In "The Reach" [*Skeleton Crew*], the aged Stella Flanders cannot go on. With her husband long dead, her children grown, and her body riddled with cancer, she has already done all a woman can do. So she walks out on the ice to die, but in dying she rediscovers the bond of love that humans extend one unto the other even into death. For her the *danse macabre* becomes a sacred celebration.

Still, for most of King's women, the *danse* is more horrific than celebratory. Yet it can confer an almost sacred stature on those women who fulfill their nurturing roles to perfection. Frannie Goldsmith is one such woman. Perhaps the most popular of all King's female characters, and the one who most easily passes his version of the domestic test, Frannie is a model madonna and helpmate. Like Wendy Torrance and Vicky McGee, Fran is destined to become the mother of a special child. Like Liz Beaumont, she is as well the worthy mate of an exceptional man. Unlike these lesser females, however, Frannie is blessed with extraordinary gifts that secure the safety of her family. It's not that Fran is perfect; she does err, but even her errors reflect her femininity, symbolized by her accidental but inevitable first pregnancy.

Only twenty-one when the superflu decimates the world, Fran is the daughter of an indifferent mother and a compassionate father. She is also pregnant. In fact, she is pregnant for virtually the entire novel. Although the pregnancy is unplanned and she doesn't really love the baby's father, maternity completes her as a woman. Even before the catastrophe of Captain Trips, she wants to have this child. Apparently, her parental instincts are based on her father's, not her mother's, example. More accurately, Fran's natural instincts as an earth mother find practical support in her father's example. Soon enough, the plague rips that support away from her, but it also confirms her instinctive need to protect her child at all costs.

From the beginning of the apocalyptic struggle that is *The Stand,* Frannie's baby has a unique importance to both sides. Long before she knows who he is, Frannie dreams of the Walkin Dude approaching her unborn child with a twisted coathanger. From then on, she feels a "fierce protectiveness" seep over her at the thought of "the baby in her belly" (256). And this girl is uniquely qualified to protect her baby. Unlike many other women, Fran retains her spirit, sexuality, and strength during a pregnancy that occurs amid what can be described (without fear of overstatement) as trying times. She rides across the country on a Honda 250, becomes the center of a romantic triangle that ends in tragedy, and serves as a founding member of the Free Zone's first governing body, all before she delivers. Of such stuff are heroines created.

Nonetheless, traditionally at least, heroines depend on heroes, and Frannie is no exception. During the course of her pregnancy, she is first associated with Jess, who doesn't want responsibility; then her father, who already feels responsible for his little girl; then Harold, who wants Fran for everything she represents; and finally, Stu, who accepts her unconditionally. For the women of the post-plague world, women's lib— "nothing more or less than an outgrowth of the technological society" (527)—is gone. Its departure has left Frannie Goldsmith, who only weeks before had dumped the ineffectual Jess and even planned to leave her loving father, acutely aware that "she badly needed a man" (528). In Stu Redman, she finds one. As his mate, she becomes the conscience of the Free Zone Committee (also its secretary), voting against the return to society's old ways of spies and deception. When the men, including Stu, override her objections, she defers to their judgment and changes her vote, until the Committee's attention turns to the nomination of her man as the Zone's first marshal. The margin there is 6–1, "and this time Frannie would not change her vote" (790). To do so would be to fail the helpmate portion of the domestic test. Stu takes the job anyway, of course.

Frannie's feminine sensibility does not allow her to override male thinking, but it does form a critical part of her heroism: the intuition that saves most of the Committee from Harold Lauder's bomb. No one else, not even the other female Committee member, senses danger before the explosion, but Fran can feel it within her, a warning, perhaps, from her unborn child: *"Get out of here,* the voice inside suddenly cried. *Get them all out!"* (888). She doesn't quite get them all out (among others, the lesser committeewoman dies), but her premonition saves enough lives for the struggle to continue.

The most important of those lives may well be that of her baby. When Mother Abagail (who serves as God's helpmate in the post-apocalyptic world) sends Stu and three other men to meet Randall Flagg, Frannie rages against her man being "sacrificed to your killer God" (917). Nonetheless, Stu goes, not so much for Abagail or God as for Fran's unborn child, whose life, so often threatened in dreams by Flagg, is now "in Stuart's hands, and in God's" (916). Abagail tells Frannie her child "will have four fathers" (916), but by the time baby Peter is born, he "belongs to the entire Free Zone" (1137). The son of many men, Peter is also God's son, the first baby to survive the plague and the rock on which the older survivors' hopes are built. And God rewards Peter's mother with the return of her man alone among the four who journeyed out to meet evil incarnate. With that evil abated though not destroyed, Frannie (pregnant again) and her family are soon on their way back to Maine, where their Edenic life will, for a while at least, be free of interference from God, the devil, and society. It's no wonder readers love Frannie; she really is an epic figure.

Frannie's stature is critical to the continuation of all mankind in a world that is tottering on the brink of extinction. As earth mother and companion, she is the high priestess of heroism itself. In *It,* King's compendium of his own Romantic philosophy, Beverly Marsh Rogan is high priestess of the Ritual of Chüd, the life-confirming rite by which the otherwise all-male Losers' Club destroys a cosmic evil. King dedicates this book to his children, noting that his mother and wife taught him "how to be a man," while his children taught him "how to be free" (v). Within the novel proper, Beverly is the resource material for both lessons. Child-woman, she becomes what King himself calls "the symbolic conduit between adulthood and childhood for the boys in the Losers' Club" (Magistrale, *SK,* 12). The domestic test is not sufficient to describe such a vessel: Bev is not just a romantic heroine; she is King's *femme eternale.*

This living icon is also a battered wife whose husband keeps her "in emotional, spiritual, and sometimes physical bondage" (1119) before the Losers call her back to them. Tom Rogan understands that Bev, though beautiful and talented, needs male protection, the kind of protection her father (possessed by It) never gave her. Tom turns Beverly's need into a sadomasochistic relationship, but inevitably, It possesses him as well, leaving his wife in the care of the men who need her as much as she needs them. In returning to her childhood Beverly becomes an adult, an archetypal pattern of maturation for King's protagonists. For Beverly, however, maturation is not independence but merely a transfer of dependence, from the perversity of sadomasochism to the purity of feminine inspiration. As a child and then again as an adult, she accompanies the Losers to It's lair, where she stands and inspires them to fight. They strike the physical blows with Beverly behind them, the Jeanne d'Arc of the Losers big and little.

As priestess, moreover, Beverly is not just inspirational; she is also physically vital to the Ritual of Chüd itself. In 1958 eleven-year-old Bevvie Marsh soothes her frightened fellow Losers when they are lost near It's lair. She does so by pulling each boy aside and making love to him in the dark. For each boy Bev is his first sexual experience, his first encounter with physical love as the "essential link between the world and the infinite, the only place where the bloodstream touches eternity" (1082–83). And however improbable this orgy of flesh and spirit may seem for these fifth-graders, it is the eucharistic part of the Ritual, each Loser finding grace and courage and manhood through Bev's body. Bonded through her, they find their way home.

Twenty-seven years later, they are called back to finish this sacred *rite de passage,* which moves not just from childhood to adulthood but back again, back to the wonders of an age when anything can be imagined, including monsters and the magic needed to destroy them. The Losers need their childhood's imaginative strength to defeat It, the Monster, the only other significant "female" in this book. The novel's title defines the asexuality of this universal glamour that exists only to feed off humanity; in effect, It can use any physical form or sexual valence it prefers. But Its final illusion is that of a giant female spider, laying its eggs in the tunnels beneath Derry, Maine, trying to hatch itself into infinity. In this respect at least, It is female when it is most dangerous to mankind.

It is still female when the male Losers destroy it with their fists and faith. Bill Denbrough (whose wife is a pale copy of Beverly) delivers the final blow to the Spider-It, literally breaking Its heart between his hands as he cries, "Try this, you bitch! TRY THIS ONE OUT! DO YOU LIKE IT? DO YOU LOVE IT?" (1093). Meanwhile, Ben Hanscomb, the Loser who loves Bev most of all, is busy grinding Its eggs and infant spiders under the heels of his boots. In an assault on a universal bitch, the Losers have freed mankind of Its tyranny and aborted Its fiendish spawn. By killing the evil female, they have proved themselves worthy of the good female who made them men.

And so King comes full circle, back to his dedication where women bring manhood and children free the soul. Still, something is askew here. Beverly may be awesome, but she is no one's peer. Like heroic Frannie, weak Rachel, and despicable Annie, Bev fits a male-designed mold that has produced a set of female characters who are physically striking but who have no more depth than a collection of dolls. (Even Annie, the evil goddess who is the exception to the beauty found in most of King's women, is simply the nightmarish antithesis of that beauty.) Too often, in a universe of transcendence and choice, King's women are predictable fantasy figures who do as their men would have them (or fear they will) do. As fantasies, they are sometimes intriguing, but they are seldom full partners in the *danse macabre* that whirls across King's universe.

Several years ago, King said of the difficulties he had in creating believable women, "I recognize the problems but can't yet rectify them" (Underwood & Miller, 47). Today, King believes he has modified this situation, by means of a forthcoming novel:

It has changed a little bit in the sense that I've written a novel called *Dolores Claiborne* that I think is a good, strong piece of work where not only is the protagonist a woman, she's also an older woman who is *the* major character. . . . And I feel that I did a good job with her and that readers are going to be pleased with the woman they find there. (Magistrale, *SK*, ms. 10)

Elsewhere in this interview, King says that *Dolores Claiborne* "is not a horror story" (17). Whatever its genre, this novel's title character will be welcome as a partner in the new dance her creator sets in motion. It's time a woman led the steps.

REFERENCES

Beahm, George, ed. *The Stephen King Companion*. Kansas City: Andrews & McMeel, 1989.

Bosky, Bernadette Lynn. "The Mind's a Monkey: Character and Psychology in Stephen King's Recent Fiction." In *Kingdom of Fear*, edited by Tim Underwood and Chuck Miller, 241–276. New York: New American Library/Signet, 1986.

Fiedler, Leslie A. *Love and Death in the American Novel*, rev. ed. New York: Stein & Day, 1966.

Katzenbach, John. Review of *Misery*, by Stephen King. *New York Times Book Review*, May 31, 1987, 20.

Keesey, Douglas. "Telekinesis and Menstruation in Stephen King's *Carrie*." Paper presented to the International Conference on the Fantastic in the Arts, Ft. Lauderdale, Fla., March 1990.

King, Stephen. *The Dark Half*. New York: Viking, 1989.

———. *The Dead Zone*. New York: Viking, 1979.

———. *Firestarter*. New York: Viking, 1980.

———. *It*. New York: Viking, 1986.

———. *Misery*. New York: Viking, 1987.

———. *Pet Sematary*. Garden City, N.Y.: Doubleday, 1983.

———. *The Stand*, rev. and unexpurgated ed. New York: Doubleday, 1990.

Magistrale, Tony. *Landscape of Fear: Stephen King's American Gothic*. Bowling Green, Ohio: Bowling Green State University Popular Press, 1988.

———. *Stephen King, the Second Decade:* Danse Macabre *to* The Dark Half. New York: Macmillan, forthcoming, 1992.

Mussell, Kay. *Fantasy and Reconciliation: Contemporary Formulas of Women's Romance Fiction*. Westport, Conn.: Greenwood, 1984.

Underwood, Tim, and Chuck Miller, eds. *Bare Bones: Conversations on Terror with Stephen King*. New York: Warner, 1988.

Winter, Douglas E. *Faces of Fear: Encounters with the Creators of Modern Horror*. New York: Berkley, 1985.

Yarbro, Chelsea Quinn. "Cinderella's Revenge – Twists on Fairy Tale and Mythic Themes in the Work of Stephen King." In *Fear Itself*, edited by Tim Underwood and Chuck Miller. San Francisco: Underwood-Miller, 1982.

4

Complex, Archetype, and Primal Fear: King's Use of Fairy Tales in *The Shining*

RONALD T. CURRAN

If fiction had birthdays as do people, days on which the positions of heavenly bodies could be reckoned, then the fairy tales in *The Shining* would be the stars whose divining would cast the novel's horoscope. For in King's book they provide an archetypal infrastructure of meaning. They point the way to determine the destiny and the general temperament of the characters, a form of divination that guides both its readers and the Torrance family in their mutual experience of primal fear.

King uses fairy tales in *The Shining* to take advantage of archetypal symbols that reflect our common experience. He employs them to take the reader back into the archaic world of childhood where magical thinking precedes ego defense, when parental power was both fantastic and absolute. There King uses fairy tales to conjure again those anxieties in childhood, the times when we felt the threat of being overwhelmed, abandoned, and annihilated. His comments in both *Danse Macabre* and *Bare Bones* (Underwood & Miller) acknowledge a "myth pool" from which fairy tales come and argue for the existence of an archetypal dimension that they occupy. In *The Shining* these narratives put us in touch with a fear that precedes our ability to articulate it. Our total vulnerability to each parent's dark side faces us with the possibility of nonbeing in the time before the presence of an ego secures the boundaries of our individuality. King's use of fairy tales in *The Shining* puts us in touch with the negative mother and the negative father complex.[1] They deepen and focus our experience of the mother who devours and the father who anni-

hilates. In so doing they connect us with an archetypal dimension to evil
that is located in the Overlook Hotel.

In fact, Stephen King's *The Shining* can be read in a Jungian perspective
as a dramatization of both the negative mother and the negative father
complex. But let's look first at King's own comments on the novel and his
attitudes toward fairy tales. He is aware that Jack Torrance's unresolved
problems with his abusive parent, his identification with his father's infantile rage, impotence, and sadism surface again in the generation he
has himself fathered. The Greek concept of psychic determinism, so evident in the Atreus family line, finds popular expression in the House of
Torrance. Danny's broken arm is the physical signifier of a destructive anger that psychically cripples, an anger with archetypal roots more transpersonal than its domestic origin suggests. These deeper roots King
himself acknowledged in his criticism of Stanley Kubrick's direction of
the movie version of *The Shining,* saying that "Kubrick just couldn't grasp
the sheer inhuman evil of the Overlook Hotel. So he looked, instead, for
evil in the character and made the film into a domestic tragedy with only
vaguely supernatural overtones" (Underwood & Miller, 29).

The evil, destructive rage in *The Shining* does, indeed, have a transpersonal dimension in King's mind. The intensification of Jack's homicidal
anger towards Wendy and Danny coincides with his control by and eventual absorption into the all-encompassing evil represented by the Overlook Hotel. To personify this process King develops a diabolic and
destructive death energy, an archetypal dimension to human evil. In *The
Shining* it takes on an aspect even more powerful than the creative psychic energy both Freud and Jung (and Plato before them) referred to as
Eros, an energy that was self-realizing in nature, more a pull from ahead
than a push from behind (May, 88). In the Overlook Hotel, however, we
encounter the bipolar aspect of this psychic energy, this dark side, an evil
dimension fueled by both its archetypal nature and its historical past in
the novel. In personifying this energy King moves from the conventional
domestic image of the Gothic castle or family mansion to the collective
one of the Overlook Hotel, one with an *archetypal resonance.* This resonance includes both its sleezy personal (the woman in Room 217) and
professional (Mafia) past as well as the timeless dimension to the evil
force it represents.

In its timeless, archetypal aspect, this destructive rage moves a step beyond its personal and collective dimensions. It isn't simply the dark side
of individual and group behavior. It is an inherent mode, like an instinct,
that drives toward the destruction of ourselves and others. The archetypal resonance of the Overlook Hotel takes the reader into the obses-
sional, possessive, and autonomous nature of the destructive rage that
menaces everyone in the novel. The level of fear intensifies accordingly
and is experienced as coming from a negative force that is split off from

the personal and social worlds of any of the characters. This negative energy drives both Jack and the Colorado hotel. Archetypal in character, it suggests mythic personifications like the devil, Beelzebub, and Loki.

The Overlook Hotel's evil, then, comes not from its historical past alone. It stems from a "chemistry" (the huge storage battery) with omnipotent power that is sustained by the waters of the "myth pool."[2] King felt that many haunted houses stored this energy and got the "reputation of being Bad Places," and he felt those reputations "might be due to the fact that the strangest emotions are the primitive ones – rage and hate and fear" (King, *Danse*, 265). This kind of malignant energy was so attractive to King that he compiled a scrapbook of the activity of the serial killer Charles Starkweather in whom he found a "big-time sociopathic evil, not the neat little Agatha Christie-style villain but something wilder and darker and unchained" (Underwood & Miller, 41).

King's comments reinforce his intention to dramatize the archetypal and collective dimension to evil in *The Shining*. With no background in Jungian psychoanalysis and with a reputation for acute gastritis in the face of psychological interpretations of his fiction, King does a creditable job of Jungian psychoanalytic thinking. He even manages a few words of its theoretical jargon in the bargain. His essays in *Danse Macabre* point out that readers of his work will know that he's dealt with the archetype of the Bad Place at least twice, in *'Salem's Lot* and in *The Shining* (King, *Danse*, 264). In these essays King makes references to archetypes and to mythic patterns, and he identifies an aspect of horror fiction by depicting characters as both identified with and eventually absorbed by the archetypal dimension of evil. He recognizes its personal (Charles Starkweather), collective (Nazism), and archetypal (Overlook Hotel/"Bad Place") dimensions (Underwood & Miller, 48). In fact, although he eventually changed the ending to *The Shining* in order to add its optimistic conclusion, his darker vision of total possession by archetypal evil guided his original plan. His initial scenario was "for them all to die up there and for Danny to become the controlling force of the hotel after he died. And the psychic force of the hotel would go up exponentially" (Underwood & Miller, 121).

In his own language King argues a dynamics of horror that can be elucidated from a Jungian psychoanalytic perspective. He sees the regressive possibilities in the dramatic constellation of archetypal patterns: how the representation of a primal, *a priori* deterministic organization to human behavior is compelling in a way that engages our unconscious and puts us in touch with fears powerfully evocative of our childhood experiences with them. King uses fairy tales in *The Shining* to make us children again and to position us to feel things adults cannot. He uses them in this text to do what he claims the horror film achieves. It knocks, King says, "the adult props out from under us and tumbles us down the slide into childhood. And there our own shadow may once again become that of a mean dog, a gaping mouth, or a beckoning dark figure" (King, *Danse,* 101). King argues that we give fairy tales to children "almost instinctively understanding on a deeper level, perhaps, that such fairy stories are the perfect points of crystallization for those fears (drowning, abandonment, kidnapping, enslavement, homicide, cremation, cannibalism)" (King, *Danse,* 103–4). This effect is both primitive and obvious, he maintains, as he refers to "the old equation of the fairy tales, each symbol as big and easy to handle as a child's alphabet block" (King, *Danse,* 106).

The first mention of a fairy tale in *The Shining* comes when Hallorann takes the Torrances on their tour of the Overlook Hotel, which he begins with a visit to "the most immense kitchen Wendy had ever seen in her life" (King, *Shining,* 72). Thus the reader's introduction to the Bad Place, King's image of archetypal evil, begins in what is conventionally thought of as a feminine space. Coincidentally Wendy introduces the fairy tale most relevant to her experience of the Overlook Hotel, "Hansel and Gretel." She said that the kitchen "was more than just big; it was intimidating" (King, *Shining,* 72). She remarks that "there was a breadboard as big as their Boulder apartment's kitchen table" (King, *Shining,* 72). Wendy is dwarfed by the sheer Brobdingnagian magnitude of this maternal space; its huge proportions put her in the position of a Lilliputian child in the huge world of adults. Her first response is to identify with the emotions of this space, saying, "I think I'll have to leave a trail of breadcrumbs every time I come in" (King, *Shining,* 72).

Before we explore this narrative identification, however, let's first look at Stephen King's personal feelings about the same fairy tale. In his *Danse Macabre* section on the modern American horror movie, King begins section eight by quoting the introductory paragraph from "Hansel and Gretel." He follows this long, evocative passage remarking that "now, with this invocation from 'Hansel and Gretel,' the most cautionary of nursery tales, let us put out even this dim light of rationality [linking real anxieties to the nightmare fears of the horror film] and discuss a few of those films whose effects go considerably deeper, past the rational and into those fears which seem universal" (King, *Danse,* 175). King's own investment in this fairy tale causes it to appear more than any other in his published commentary on his own work or on horror in other media and genres.

There seems to be some good reason for this. King's own father, Donald Spansky, abandoned the family in 1949, when Stephen was two years old. So Mrs. King governed the household for the majority of her son's life. She was, as Stephen described her, "stubborn, intractable, grimly persevering and nearly impossible to discourage." He felt that she "had gotten a taste for captaining her own life" and therefore "went out with guys, but none of them became permanent fixtures" (King, *Danse,* 98). In

The Shining, Wendy, too, had a powerful mother. Danny's access to Wendy's unconscious thinking lets us know how she experienced her own mother. On their trip to the Overlook Hotel, Danny tells Wendy that he knows how she feels about her mother. "Bad. Sad. Mad," he says. "It's like she wasn't your mommy at all. Like she wanted to eat you" (King, *Shining,* 201).

Both Freudian (Bruno Bettelheim) and Jungian (Hans Dieckmann) readings of "Hansel and Gretel" acknowledge the figure of the devouring mother in the gingerbread house (Bettelheim, 161). Dieckmann says that "she embodies an archetypal mother figure who possesses a superior knowledge and superior powers, who can approach humans in part helpfully and generously, in part demonically and destructively. She has her mythological parallels in the great nature goddesses of pre-Christian religions and thus personifies a deeper more powerful natural force that far surpasses the human conscious ego" (Dieckmann, 36). She is, in other words, an archetypal figure. Dieckmann sees the oven in both form and function as corresponding "to the symbol of the nurturing womb furthering the process of maturation." It stands, he feels, "at the border of the magical realm of the 'Great Mother' " (Dieckmann, 51).

Wendy, however, experiences the multiple ovens in the Overlook Hotel much as Goldilocks did the parental furniture in the house of the three bears. Her response to the kitchen and its ovens is archetypal in nature; it resonates with a numinosity more powerful than her personal and cultural memory could have generated. Everything is disproportionately large; this space of the Great Mother is experienced by Wendy as both "immense" and "intimidating" (King, *Shining,* 72).

Of course, neither Dieckmann nor Bettelheim is arguing for maternal cannibalism in any literal sense. Both simply call attention to the extreme and prolonged dependence of the child on the mother, a relation that quite often leads to fantasies of being devoured by her. Nor is it unusual for parents to tell their children affectionately that they are so lovely that they could just eat them up. No wonder, then, that the chain of association set in motion by the huge, overwhelming kitchen and Brobdingnagian ovens leads Wendy to recall the infamous Donner party. Although it is not the cannibalism they practiced that is uppermost in her mind, surely the gingerbread house that was nothing but food must linger in her thoughts from her earlier use of "Hansel and Gretel" to frame her experience and to put her sense of primal fear into a familiar narrative pattern. Her predominant feelings are of abandonment and dangerous isolation. "They would sit up here," she said, "in this deserted grand hotel, eating the food that had been left them like creatures in a fairy tale and listening to the bitter wind around their snowbound eaves" (King, *Shining,* 73).

The witch aspect of the all-powerful figure of the mother appears in

"Hansel and Gretel" in her tempting gingerbread house where she presents both siblings with the challenge to escape the devouring mother or become dinner on her kitchen table. From a developmental perspective, the challenge is one that all children face. Danny's awareness of Wendy's devouring mother locates the Gretel in Wendy, and Wendy's response to the Overlook kitchen affirms her son's judgment. Danny's "shining" ability intensifies his response to his mother's anxieties and makes him literally aware of the concrete forms that they take. Thus Wendy's reaction to the gingerbread-house/Overlook-kitchen parallel pulls Danny into the same fairy-tale narrative that his mother uses to understand the design of her own experience. There he can find his own role (Hansel) and feel anxious himself about the inherent potential of the hotel to devour them all. In this way Wendy involves Danny not only in her own personal mother complex, but she also makes him aware of the archetypal dimension of this fear. The destructive rage of the Overlook Hotel has its devouring side as well, and Wendy puts her son in contact with it. "Hansel and Gretel" allows King to suggest a sibling relationship between mother and son. They are two persons menaced by the same threat. Like Hansel and Gretel, they will have to cooperate to survive. So the narrative also signals a change in status for Danny who must function more independently than a child his age would normally be expected to. The roles of brother and sister must be added to those of son and mother if they are to escape.

Early on in *The Shining,* then, a well-known fairy tale helps to structure the landscape of primal fear that symbolically resonates for Wendy and the identifying reader. We and Wendy are in the land of the devouring mother, a projection that the Overlook Hotel carries for Wendy. This is Wendy's archetypal Bad Place symbolizing all the evil energy of the relationship with the negative aspect of the Great Mother archetype. This is the side Hindus represent in their devouring goddess Kali Ma, the Dread Mother, she who rules over all the dark elements of Nature, wears the necklace of human skulls, eats her consort Shiva's entrails while her vagina devours his penis, and feeds her own children and fattens on their corpses. She represents the dark aspect of the Great Mother goddess, the looming menace behind nature and nurture (Walker, 488–493). Wendy experiences this archetypal dimension to the Overlook Hotel; she responds to its matriarchal dimension, because her complex stems from her own devouring mother.

For Jack, however, it is the patriarchal dimension of the hotel that stands out. Wendy's access to the Overlook Hotel's malevolent constellation of primal fear—of "death" at the hands of the devouring mother—is through its distaff side. But for both Jack and Wendy the narrativizing and archetypal aspects of fairy tales contain and symbolize the primal fear each is experiencing. At this early juncture in the novel, then, King begins to use the archetypal dimension of a fairy-tale narrative to both frame and evoke levels of infantile fear that he associates with the best efforts horror fiction can arouse in its audience. However, given the patriarchal structure of the Overlook, as well as its former connection with the Mafia, the masculine dimension of the hotel stands out, more so than that of its devouring-mother qualities. Jack, not Wendy, is shaped by its malevolent influence.

Soon after Wendy's reference to "Hansel and Gretel," Danny introduces the second fairy tale text—"Bluebeard" (King, *Shining,* 87–88). His father read this story to him when Danny was a small child, and "Bluebeard" carries the negative father archetype for both of them. By mentioning this tale King begins to counterbalance the devouring mother-witch image in "Hansel and Gretel" with that of the homicidal father. The "Bluebeard" narrative calls attention to this duality. It is the psychological counterpart to the Book of Tobit in the Old Testament.[3] In the Book of Tobit the husbands who die on the wedding night are the "queen's" roomful of corpses; whereas in *The Shining* it is the wives who are the "king's" victims. Each text points toward the destructive role of the opposite-sexed parent. These negative mother and father images are rarely separate from one another. Jack's toss of the Janus-faced coin of complex formation turns up heads every time. Both his mother's enervating weakness and his father's tyranny dethrone his ego position and influence his aggressive acting out.

In this perspective the fairy tale is not only a cautionary one about the perils of curiosity, wifely obedience, or husbandly forgiveness. It is also the story of the projected anger and homicidal acting out of the mother-identified man in its most pathologized form. It is against this background that Danny's reaction to Room 217, deepened and amplified by his "shining," can be fully understood.

When Hallorann tells him the story of the hotel employee's (Delores Vickery) spooking and subsequent firing over her experience with Room 217, Danny begins immediately to experience its parallels with the fairy tale his father read to him when he was three. As Wendy did with "Hansel and Gretel," Danny recalls the fairy tale most pertinent to the dimensions of *his* primal fears, the one roughly analogous to both the popular history of the Overlook Hotel and to his clairvoyant images of REDRUM scrawled on a mirror. It functions to structure, symbolize, and focus the affective tone of his feelings and to narrativize his amorphous sense of dread. "Bluebeard" allows Danny to write himself into the story that his "shining" tells him is unfolding before him. It helps him to connect with collective and archetypal dimensions to his experience. Both the existence and content of "Bluebeard" argue for Danny's part in a scheme of things larger than his terrifying personal feelings.

Hallorann misunderstands the validity of Danny's fear telling him that his "shining" talent gives him images "like pictures in a book . . . that scared you" (King, *Shining,* 87–88). He doesn't know the prophetic nature of the story and picture Danny immediately recalls to mind "where Bluebeard's new wife opens the door and sees all the heads" (King, *Shining,* 88). Nor is Hallorann aware for all his shining talent that the image resonates with archetypal energy, because it symbolizes for Danny destructive psychological fate expressed in his father's negative mother complex.

In part, like Bluebeard's wife, Danny, too, is drawn to Room 217 "by a morbid kind of curiosity . . . He remembered a story Daddy had read to him once when he was drunk. That had been a long time ago, but the story was just as valid now as when Daddy had read it to him" (King, *Shining,* 169). Danny recalls further that "the story was about *Bluebeard's* [sic] wife, a pretty lady that had corn-colored hair like Mommy. After Bluebeard married her, they lived in a big ominous castle that was not unlike the Overlook" (King, *Shining,* 169). Danny then relates the entire plot of the fairy tale, a full page of text; King seems less willing to trust the reader's memory or his capacity for analogy than he did in his earlier reference to "Hansel and Gretel." "The old fairy tale book," we are told, "had depicted her discovery in a ghastly, loving detail. The image was burned on Danny's mind. The severed heads of *Bluebeard's* [sic] seven previous wives were in the room, each one on its own pedestal, the eyes turned up to whites, the mouths unhinged and gaping in silent screams. They were somehow balanced on necks ragged from the broadsword's decapitating swing, and there was blood running down the pedestals" (King, *Shining,* 170). Danny then recalls a happy ending that "paled to insignificance beside the two dominant images: the taunting, maddening locked door with some great secret behind it, and the grisly secret itself, repeated more than half a dozen times. The door locked and behind it the heads, the severed heads" (King, *Shining,* 170).

Immediately after this elaborate recollection of the fairy tale with a rich index of motifs supplied by King, Danny strokes the door knob of Room 217 and twirls the passkey on its chain before deciding not to enter despite his curiosity. "Bluebeard," the most elaborate and sustained fairy-tale reference in the novel, calls conspicuous attention to itself. In it Danny identifies with his mother because each is equally threatened. However, Mrs. Massey lies on the other side of the door to Room 217, not the corpses of seven wives, and she is a suicide. It would appear that King has missed somewhat with this analogy. Unless, of course, the reference to "Bluebeard" also includes the many deaths, particularly those of women, that have occurred throughout the hotel since it was built. But King is only using Danny's capacity to "shine" to characterize the experience of other family members. Wendy is facing a similar situation of threat, and, through Danny's recollection, King wants to suggest that an archetypal pattern is repeating itself in the form of the Torrance family's psychological fate.

If "Bluebeard" is the way Danny frames his psychic experience *before* opening the door to Room 217, then Lewis Carroll's *Alice in Wonderland* works in a similar fashion to locate Danny's personal experience in both its cultural and archetypal dimensions *after* he decides to enter.[4] Like a dream, Alice's "wonderland" symbolizes her unconscious experience of family and society. The White Rabbit is her guide. Danny's guide is Tony. Danny's "shining" gives him access to his own inner world while he functions in everyday life. Alice's "shining" — the symbolic landscape of Wonderland — reveals itself in its dreamlike images. Alice's "little golden key" (Carroll, 8) fits the unique lock she encounters after her initial fall, and it allows her to enter into her mythopoetic, imaginal inner world. Danny's passkey, on the other hand, more general in its symbolic implications, opens one door of many in the Overlook Hotel. But Danny also uses another key to wind up the clock at midnight in the Colorado ballroom. With this key Danny opens up the whole world of the Overlook in the same way that Alice's key admits her to the world of Wonderland.

Symbolically, King's choice of *Alice's Adventures* to signal by analogy a context of similar experience and meaning makes good sense. But in terms of style and tone, it offers an ironic contrast to Danny's experience. Danny is emotionally in the grip of overwhelming terror and overcome with fears of abandonment, separation, and annihilation by a parent caught in a psychosis with its central core located in the archetypal Bad Place. Alice, on the other hand, tends to approach her experience in Wonderland with an almost pedantic English reserve. She is never completely intimidated by the adult figures whose rude and nasty behavior always seems counterbalanced by their seeming a bit daft to begin with.

Having no ironic distance, Danny is full of anxiety, dread, and fear of annihilation, while Alice only seems to get a little wet from time to time. Perhaps King intended this contrast and wants *Alice's Adventures* to counterpoint the abusive, homicidal world of *The Shining.* Perhaps the cute rabbit's "white kid-gloves" (Carroll, 35) that Alice puts on at one point may insulate her from the sensations with which Danny must deal directly. By analogy, then, Alice provides a form of emotional distance unavailable to readers of *The Shining.* Some dimensions of the fear that Danny experiences, however, are present in *Alice's Adventures.* That very distance, in combination with the presentation of analogous images of primal fear, relieves the unbearable tension somewhat.

Like a dolphin's sonar, the echo-resonance of *Alice's Adventures* in *The Shining* images forth in the reader's mind a similar landscape of primal fear. Despite the influence of authorial projection and national character, *Alice's Adventures* raises the same anxieties that striate Danny's experience. The White Rabbit fears the loss of his head if he keeps the homicidal Red Queen waiting (Carroll, 16), and Alice's visit to the Dutchess' home convinces her that she must rescue the baby she finds there, because they will kill it in "a day or two" (Carroll, 69). Her world beneath its ironic defenses is equally as dangerous as Danny's, for annihilation lurks everywhere. In fact, ironic exaggeration may even intensify the reader's awareness of threat in the manner of whistling in the dark. "We're all mad here," the Cheshire cat exclaims (Carroll, 73). It's a wonder Jack Torrance didn't turn up for tea like the character in a later Barth novel.

Alice's Adventures may be playfully menacing as they reflect the child's sense of threat in an abusive adult world. But the same issues that Danny faces surface more coolly and are echoed in Carroll's text. The world of the Red Queen serves as a counterpoint to the one of Bluebeard. King conflates both as he pairs two children with burning curiosity to enter forbidden territory. Each text has a homicidal monarch to symbolize the displaced image of the parent, and both have a fondness for decapitation: "queens" sever with a sword; "kings" smash with a mallet. Together these two fairy tales carry the dynamics as well as the images of the primal fears of children living with both the mother and the father complex. Like Alice and Bluebeard's wives, Danny, too, has two keys that unlock the chambers that will reveal the terrible secret of a child's experience of adult intention. In making his transition from king to queen, from father to mother, King borrows the pattern of language play from the Mad Tea-party (King, *Shining,* 78) as Danny stands outside Room 217 again with the passkey in his pocket. Eventually his musings will lead to his conflation of the scene with *Alice's Adventures,* but as a preamble to that analogy he says "what big teeth you have grandma and is that a wolf in a BLUEBEARD suit or a BLUEBEARD in a wolf suit" (King, *Shining,* 215).

The compression King achieves here is exceeded only by the density of the implication of his linking "Little Red Riding Hood" with "Bluebeard." In doing so he gives the reader in symbolic form an image of the Janus-faced nature of the reciprocal complexes in operation in *The Shining.* Jack's father complex is the psychological fate he inherits from his abusive father. Intimidated himself by his father and made to feel paranoid in the face of authority, Jack attacks the childlike vulnerability he cannot allow himself to feel (Danny's). He either cowers in the face of or identifies with the omnipotent authority he locates in the Overlook's management.

But there is another side to the father complex, and it has ties with Jack's mother as well as Wendy's. We have already seen how Wendy's mother was experienced as devouring and aligned with the witch in "Hansel and Gretel." But we need to keep in mind also that Jack's mother in a more passive way was perceived as an equal threat to undercut masculine potential. Describing his own and his father's experience in the projective identification he offers, Jack says that his dad was "handcuffed to a dead man in a wasteland," that he "had tried to do right as he dragged her rotting corpse through life" (King, *Shining,* 379).

Danny's experience of both the paternal and maternal aspects of the complex are reflected in both "Bluebeard" and "Little Red Riding Hood."

In the former the decapitating king symbolizes the threat of the father Danny feels toward himself and Wendy. In "Little Red Riding Hood" it is the devouring aspect of the "grandmother"—the Great Mother—that the child experiences in the bedroom scene. In the German version it is the wolf in grandmother's sleeping costume who devours Little Red Riding Hood as the litany of the "grandmother's" aspects—eyes, ears, mouth, and teeth—are recited before the child is devoured by the parental imago in the fairy tale. The wolf-grandmother symbolizes the devouring aspect of the mother herself.

This pairing of the two fairy tales heralds the upcoming visit to Room 217, which calls forth the analogy to *Alice's Adventures* in order to use its Red Queen and her croquet game to frame Danny's experience of terror. As he touches the passkey in his pocket, then turns it in the lock, Danny equates himself with the White Rabbit "on its way to . . . the Red Queen's croquet party storks for mallets hedgehogs for balls" [Carroll, 216]. And when he turns the key he repeats the Red Queen's punishment, the one that aligns her with Bluebeard and puts Danny in touch with his fear of death as his father prepares to wield the roque mallet. After bolting from Mrs. Ramsey's corpse, Danny makes the connection, which joins his tale with Alice's for "his eyes [are] starting from their sockets, his hair on end like the hair of a hedgehog about to be turned into a sacrificial (croquet? or roque?) ball" (King, *Shining,* 298).

Siblings in their mutual fear, however differently dramatized, Danny and Alice each face beheading at the hands of a parent or parent surrogate. In either case the child views itself as literally or symbolically annihilated, either murdered or "beheaded" and made a "hedgehog," struck by the whim of the parent and within the arbitrary rules of the game of life. The children are propelled through arches according to patterns not their own. In many ways the Overlook Hotel is the ice palace of Danny's "wonderland." In it Danny experiences evil in its personal and transpersonal dimensions. He, too, like Alice, fears the loss of his spirit, fears his "going out altogether, like a candle" (Carroll, 11).

King uses the archetypal dimension to fairy tales in *The Shining* as a way of dramatizing and organizing prototypical life patterns. The symbols and narrative structure in the fairy tales King retells in *The Shining* fuse the personal dimension of the relationships, actions, and feelings in the Torrance family with larger, a priori patterns that structure human behavior. Fairy tales provide him with a relationship to myth, and that tie, in turn, conjures a dimension of ahistorical time, of *timelessness,* in King's popular Gothic fiction that it would not otherwise have, nor resonate with so powerfully. Whether this is conscious literary artifice on King's part or unconscious recognition of the transpersonal reality he is depicting is a moot point. For in forming this analogical bridge between fairy tale and popular fiction, King argues an intertextuality that causes the highly personal, and therefore reductive, events in the Torrance household to vibrate sympathetically as a chord struck from an archetype. Fear of abandonment, annihilation, and engulfment take on affective dimensions far larger than the personal ones in the domestic, timebound life of the Torrance family. They link Danny, Wendy, and Jack to Oedipus, Atreus, and Kali, to Tantalus, Daedalus, and others.

These fairy tales help to mythologize and ritualize the dramatic action in *The Shining*. They provide a link with the sacred for King's secularized modern text, suggesting its ties with the ancient and the archetypal. The fairy tales are signifiers of meaning. They act as containers for feelings and actions that otherwise would have less of a sense of function and universal implication within an overall context – the archetypes of the collective unconscious. They provide a sense of the *telos* toward which all the events aim – toward health and transformation or toward pathology and psychosis as Jack's ego is overwhelmed by his unconscious. What we participate in as we read *The Shining* is the process within which a child's archetypal predispositions make him vulnerable to the personal flaws of his parents. We experience the ambivalent mix of what is supportive and what is lethal as Danny Torrance makes his own archetypal journey toward individuation, just as did his brothers and sisters in all the fairy-tale texts in which King chooses to suggest his relation with all children beyond history and throughout all time.

NOTES

1. For the basic sources of Jung's complex theory see: Carl G. Jung, *Collected Works*, Vol. VIII, "A Review of Complex Theory," 92–104; Vol. II, "On the Doctrine of Complexes," 598–604; Vol. II, "The Associations of Normal Subjects," 3–39; and "The Association Method," 439–465 (New York: Bollingen Foundation, Princeton University Press, 1974). Two other very helpful interpretations of Jung's complex theory are Jolande Jacobi's "Complex," in *Complex/Archetype/Symbol in the Psychology of C. G. Jung* (New York: Bollingen Foundation, Princeton University Press, 1974), 6–30, and John Hill's "Individuation and the Association Experiment," *Spring* (1975), 145–151. According to Jung, parental complexes are characterized by a common emotional tone and exert a compelling influence on behavior. The father complex in particular enables us to be powerfully influenced by our relation to this figure. Because of this complex, we can realize and incarnate the father imago in ourselves. It is, however, important to differentiate between the real father and the father imago. Jung explains that it is an "error in judgment" to make the "assumption (which is only partially correct) that the real parents are responsible for the parental complex. In the old trauma theory of Freudian psychoanalysis, . . . this assumption even passed for a scientific explanation. (It is in order to avoid this confusion that I advocated the term 'parental imago.') The simplest soul is of course quite unaware of the fact that his nearest relations, who exercise immediate influence over him, create in him an image

which is only partly a replica of themselves, while its other part is compounded of elements derived from himself. The imago is built up of parental influences plus the specific reactions of the child; it is therefore an image that reflects the object with very considerable qualifications" (*Collected Works,* Vol. VII, 184–185).

2. King employs the metaphor of a car battery saying that "so-called 'haunted houses' might actually be psychic batteries, absorbing the emotions that had been spent there, absorbing them much as a car battery will store an electric charge. . . . And the fact that many haunted houses are shunned and get the reputation of being Bad Places might be due to the fact that the strangest emotions are the primitive ones—rage and hate and fear" (*Danse,* 265). While somewhat crude, this image suggests his awareness of the archetypal nature of these emotions. King seems to recognize that they have an archetypal dimension, that these emotions are biogenetic in nature, part of man's evolutionary inheritance, passed on from generation to generation and not extinguished in the death of a person, family, or nation. "Storage-battery" houses personify for King the omnipresence and continuing quality of these emotions. Unacknowledged and unintegrated in human consciousness, they accumulate an intensifying "charge" that can manifest itself personally in family and society or collectively in warlike acts of aggression. When shadow projections are not withdrawn, the possibilities for their acting out increase dramatically. This is probably why King in the Forenote to *Danse Macabre* said that the "myth pool" is one "in which we all bathe communally" (King, *Danse,* xvi).

3. C. G. Jung, "The Significance of the Father in the Destiny of the Individual," in *Collected Works,* Vol. II, 321–323.

4. Frances Wickes, in *The Inner World of Childhood* (Englewood Cliffs, N.J.: Prentice-Hall, 1966), remarks that "the ego of the child is still too unformed to be able to set up barriers against the invasion of forces that move in the unconscious of the adult to whom he is still bound in an identification which is only broken as his ego achieves a degree of conscious integration" (42).

REFERENCES

Bettelheim, Bruno. *The Uses of Enchantment.* New York: Vintage, 1977.

Carroll, Lewis. *Alice's Adventures in Wonderland.* New York: Random House, 1964.

Dieckmann, Hans. *Twice-Told Tales: The Psychological Use of Fairy Tales.* Wilmette, Ill.: Chiron Publications, 1986.

Hill, John. "Individuation and the Association Experiment." *Spring* (1975), 145–151.

Jacobi, Jolande. *Complex/Archetype/Symbol in the Psychology of C. G. Jung.* New York: Bollingen Foundation, Princeton University Press, 1974.

Jung, Carl G. *Collected Works.* New York: Bollingen Foundation, Princeton University Press, 1960.

King, Stephen. *Danse Macabre.* New York: Berkley, 1983.

———. *The Shining.* New York: New American Library, 1977.

May, Rollo. *Love and Will.* New York: W. W. Norton, 1969.

Sale, Roger. *Fairy Tales and After: Snow White to E. B. White.* Cambridge, Mass.: Harvard University Press, 1978.

Underwood, Tim, and Chuck Miller, eds. *Bare Bones: Conversations on Terror with Stephen King.* New York: McGraw-Hill, 1988.

Walker, Barbara C. *The Woman's Encyclopedia of Myths and Secrets.* New York: Harper & Row, 1983.

Wickes, Frances. *The Inner World of Childhood.* Englewood Cliffs, N.J.: Prentice-Hall, 1966.

5

The Three Genres of *The Stand*

EDWIN F. CASEBEER

In *The Stand,* Stephen King once again uses the horror novel as a literary metaphor to explore dark contemporary psychological and social realities. His first published novel, *Carrie,* explored the diurnal horror of the unadapted adolescent in the American educational system; then, *'Salem's Lot* mythologized the horror of individual isolation and meaninglessness in small-town America; the literary tools wielded in *The Shining* revealed, a decade before its topicality, the impact of alcoholism in the co-dependent family system.

The Stand is much more clearly programmatic than its predecessors. For King, at the time of writing *The Stand,* apocalypse seemed inevitable:

There was a feeling — I must admit it — that I was doing a fast, happy tapdance on the grave of the whole world. Its writing came during a troubled period for the world in general and America in particular. (King, *Danse,* 400)

Clearly, biochemical warfare is for King no metaphor. It exists. He fears its existence. He fears the power structure of politicians, scientists, and technicians who currently shape consensus reality. His novel thus posits that the current power elite has released a biochemical plague that has eliminated the bulk of the population. Merging with the science-fiction novel, the characters, situations, imagery and tonality typical of the horror novel, he presents to us then in *The Stand* a powerful metaphor for the nature and consequences of modern warfare — the most frightening horror story of the twentieth century. Then by transforming Gothic science

fiction into Gothic epic fantasy, he provides in imaginative and visionary
terms an alternative to the power concerns of rational materialism that
lead us so inexorably to Armageddon. The result is an apocalyptic novel
that provides a nexus for three mainstreams in popular fiction: science
fiction, epic fantasy, and Gothic horror.

The text of reference here will be the 1978 edition of *The Stand* (henceforth *S1*), for I believe that the circumstances of its publication urged
King into some artistic decisions that produced a compelling generic fu-
sion. I grant that the second edition changes little of an essential plot
summary such as now follows. Yet although much of the difference between the two editions is in degree, a true difference in kind exists. In the
1990 edition, King flags the tonality and intent of fantasy much sooner;
the 1978 edition keeps the generic lines separate at the outset, then transforms them into a unique form that artistically expresses the interface between science fiction and fantasy, both epic and horror.

A READER'S RESPONSE

A narrative of my experience with *The Stand* will clarify my perspective. A popular culture scholar for some years when I began reading
King, I had – through teaching, editing, academic research, and personal
reading – become immersed in both epic fantasy and in science fiction;
horror literature had a limited imaginative draw for me in the pre–New
Wave days. When I first read *The Stand,* I naively began it with some en-
thusiasm as an apocalyptic science-fiction novel (with much the same en-
thusiasm I read its contemporary Niven and Pournelle's *Lucifer's Hammer,*
to which it seemed close kin). But by Part Three, I found myself reading
hard-core horror fantasy with the strong Christian undertones that,
at the time, I was finding unappealing in such literature; that it had a
Tolkienesque inflection toward epic fantasy seemed more confusing
than admirable. Much influenced theoretically by David Ketterer,[1]
my first reaction was to assume that King – a beginning novelist – was out
of his depth in this abortive experiment with science fiction: he knew
how to begin the process, but as is often the case with apprentice novelists, did not know how to finish it.

Later, as I read *The Stand* more deeply to prepare the book for a course
on King, my initial reaction reversed: I began to admire the novel's
unique evolution from one generic mode to another to still a third in development of a subtype common to all three. King had found in the apocalyptic novel a point at which science fiction, epic fantasy, and horror
fantasy could converge. He had found a literary and political situation
common to the trinity (and one much in the air then and now), pounded
out a new synthesis of the three, which displayed the highest quality of
artistic craftsmanship in all genres, and created an illuminating and
evolving metaphor for our era from three of its most popular literary

genres. Uniting these is the dramatic question: can humanity survive itself? Posed in the realistic mode of Parts One and Two, the question is answered in the fantastic mode of Part Three: "if rationalism is a deathtrip, then irrationalism might very well be a lifetrip" (*S1*, 473). To put the issue thematically, King's traditional suspicion of the rational receives validation and demonstration in Parts One and Two; his veneration for the dark and romantic empowers the evolution to Part Three.

The 1978 edition's Book One still is for me clearly science fiction in genre, style, tonality, characterization, setting, theme – a realistic extrapolation from the actual circumstances of our present military technology: the mapping of the course of a biochemical plague. Book Two is transitional between science fiction and the purer fantasy of Book Three. Despite the initial prominence of Mother Abagail, the fantastic character who motivates its central situation, Book Two is the customary development of extended apocalyptic narrative: a *gedankenshrift* (i.e., thought process) dramatizing the utopian options ensuing the cataclysm. Certainly there were the visionary dreams, the growing telepathy among the new citizens of Boulder, but some science-fiction novelists regard such psychic phenomena as quite possible, and such seems King's attitude. Only Flagg's possessed weasels and the dog Kojak's memory of his wolves suggest Tolkien. The actual presentation of Flagg and Las Vegas in Book Two is so much inflected by the deranged perspective of the Trashcan Man that it fits comfortably in the dominant material mode of the Book. I mark the surfacing of fantasy to be the point in Book Two where Flagg's possession of Harold and Nadine and his inducement of them to terrorism becomes the main plot. Only then the two bands of spies and heroes march on Las Vegas and Flagg begins clearly to resemble Sauron.

But in the 1990 edition of *The Stand* (henceforth *S2*), the novel is much more clearly a fantasy from the beginning (Collings, *Gauntlet*, 179). The allusions to and manifestations of fantastic literature are more prominent from the beginning of the novel. When King edited *S2* to produce *S1*, he deleted most of the references to Tolkien: The journey doesn't begin until Mother Abagail sends out the two groups, the spies and the heroes, against Flagg. But in Chapter 35 of *S2*, the most intricately revised chapter of the two editions, Rita sees the analogy of the situation to *The Lord of the Rings* at the outset of her exodus from New York City with Larry:

" 'The way leads ever on' . . . It's a line from Tolkien," she said. *"The Lord of the Rings.* I've always thought of it as sort of a gateway to adventure." (*S2*, 307)

Larry meditates upon the analogy:

He found himself thinking that she hadn't been so wrong to quote Tolkien at that, Tolkien with his mythic lands seen through the lens of time and half-mad, half-exalted imaginings, peopled with elves and ents and trolls and orcs. There were none of those in New York, but so much had changed, so much was out of joint, that it was impossible not to think of it in terms of fantasy. (*S2*, 308)

In *S1* the Tolkienesque epic fantasy doesn't begin to emerge until the last section of Book Two, but here we find at the outset of a major plot line (Larry) in the last quarter of Book One an explicit analogy between the adventurers and the hobbits, between the mad and the deformed of New York City and Tolkien's "mythic lands." It is clear that King saw himself in this earlier draft making connections from the beginning between a favored model and his current undertaking. But in *S1*, the marker shrinks to a simile: "It was a walk that Larry never forgot. So much had changed, so much was out of joint that New York seemed almost a fabled city in a Tolkien story" (*S1*, 194).

A second difference is the character of the demonic antagonist, the Antichrist, Flagg. In his first appearance in *S1*, Flagg *could* be a mad man; but in *S1* Flagg actually performs magic: he psychically elevates himself from the ground, and as the diabolical and hilarious maniacal figure we later come to know in a deleted anecdote, he magically makes a victim disappear. In both books it is only when Flagg meets Lloyd Henreid that we realize he really is magical and demonic in nature as well as in character. As in *'Salem's Lot*, where the author opted to leave the nature of his monster much to the reader's imagination until the novel's culmination, so does King seem to have decided under the pressure of the order to reduce his novel's size to leave its fantastic character more implicit until much later.

Third, Flagg's other antagonists and the reality of the Dark Man's threat are more fully fleshed out. In *S2*'s Book Two, Trashcan is more the deranged Kid's sympathetic victim than a madman himself; through him *S2* gains a clearer, saner perspective and accordingly a much more developed account of Las Vegas that establishes the fantastic nature of its circumstances. In short, to produce the truncated *S1*, King greatly reduced (in addition to other categories of material) the fantastic elements, both epic and horror, of Books One and Two to produce a much more realistic mode.[2]

BOOK ONE: THE APOCALYPTIC NOVEL

King's "Christian commitment is generally circumscribed, . . . sometimes treated with sardonic humor" (Reino, 511). The sources of his apocalyptic vision are provided instead by contemporary popular fiction and film, both Gothic and science-fictional. At the core of the former is a dramatization of some of the prophesied moments of Revelations (e.g., the emergence of an Antichrist and the last conflict between the powers of good and evil or, as King puts it, the Apollonic and the Dionysian); in

Danse Macabre (401) King compares the novel at length to the film version of *The Exorcist*. While King cites George R. Stewart's *Earth Abides* as an immediate science-fictional influence (398), Larry Niven and Jerry Pournelle's *Lucifer's Hammer* (1977) provides even a better contemporary analogy: their novel translates the same cultural anxieties into extrapolative science fiction that is very nearly identical in structure to Books One and Two of *The Stand*. In the first section of *Lucifer's Hammer* a comet causes cataclysm, and in its second, a possible utopia (a much-reduced population equipped with nuclear power) arises. Part of the reader interest in this novel and cataclysmic literature in general (*The Poseidon Adventure* and its clones) is in the theme of the survivor: the presentation in believable terms of such skills and physical and psychological abilities that one might need to survive cataclysm. As usual, King intuitively senses and employs the most popular *and* most successful structures in *The Stand:* the Gothic Antichrist and the last battle, the nuclear cataclysm and the possible utopia, the technology of survival.

King is a capable science-fiction novelist. Here his ability with realistic characterization, demonstrated from the outset of his publishing career, places him in a strong position, for it is through character that he presents apocalypse: Stu Redman tells us of the inception and the collapse of rural Texas and the subsequent medical coverup; Fran shows us small-town New England, Nick Andros' Arkansas, Larry Underwood's New York City. And through a series of powerful vignettes (much expanded in *S2*) King presents the impact of Captain Trips upon the rest of the nation. Here is his pattern: first we see the world as it is, and it is not pretty (the Old Jerusalem, to use the Christian metaphorical framework everywhere evident in the novel). Then we see the horror of a very possible plague; here he develops the horror novel in terms in which he has been reconceiving it and not in terms of Gothic fantasy (Apocalypse). This accomplished, King presents the natural world as it once must have been (Eden returning) and proceeds, in Book Two, to the political issues confronting the founding of a New Jerusalem.

The Stand presents familiar issues in its readers' world. The people in charge are military, political, or professional figures, generally more motivated by maintaining their positions and systems than by serving society. When the plague hits, the main effort of those in power is to deny its existence – by mass executions if need be. The society that they have created is oblivious to human value. The current power elite disenfranchises those who will emerge as the most valuable contributors to humanity's salvation: "in nearly every instance . . . there is the same sense of divorcement from life, of loss of purpose" (Collings, *Discovering,* 87). Stu Redman, the archetypal hero, is an unemployed factory worker in an economically depressed Texas town. His beloved cofounder of the new world to come, Fran, suffers on the personal level from sexual exploitation and a dysfunctional family. Larry Underwood, who willingly undergoes martyrdom to save society, suffers psychological immaturity in a world that offers few passages into a richer life. Mother Abagail, God's own vessel on earth, is an elderly black woman deserted in her shack by friends and family. The politically central figure of the new utopia, Nick Andros, is a deaf-mute drifter; its central theoretician, Glen Bateman, an eccentric professor shunned by his colleagues. And Tom Cullen, whose innocence and purity will be key in confounding the Antichrist himself, is a retarded adult hidden away by his family. The current power elite is impervious even to the negative ranges of human value. Villains go as unnoticed as heroes. Like Tom, the Trashcan Man, Antichrist's weapon, is a retarded car-wash attendant, once innocent child, now mutilated by his history in the power elite's society. Antichrist's right-hand man, Lloyd Henreid, is a small-time hood barely aware of his crimes. And the Antichrist himself is an outdated and discarded countercultural revolutionary of the 1960s hitchhiking on a lonely road in the Idaho sagebrush desert. The world in which these people live simply doesn't work very well: it is undramatically falling apart at the seams and totally lacks the resources to survive cataclysm. Sometimes, as in the lives of Lloyd Henreid and the Trashcan Man, it can produce horror, but the counter-arc of its pendulum swing ends in the mundane and dreary.

The apocalypse as handled in this novel, then, is a remarkable piece of science fiction in quality, mass, and depth. Had King written it today, it easily could have been marketed, as is his current *Dark Tower* fiction, as the first in a sequence of novels. King has carefully worked out the symptoms and progress of his super-flu, graphed its spread from source to planet, choreographed a timetable that carefully tracks the multiple perspectives in space so that there is a strong sense that *all* of America has been represented. He maintains crisis peak intensity throughout: assaulting all senses, images of death, mutilation, and decay abound as do bizarre characters and violent incident–all rendered with close-focus detail. Imbedded within this surreal canvas is a powerful narrative: the intense suspense of Stu's escape from the hospital and Larry's journey through the Lincoln tunnel; the pathos of Fran's loss of her father and Larry's loss of Rita; Nick's complicated struggle to preserve the lives of both his jailor and his prisoners in a dying town.

In the recovery phase of the apocalypse, the dynamic is journey: all leave the old world and, after some aborted movements, orient to the West, to the Dark Mother and the Dark Father, to the last Cataclysm. Here are anecdotes of convergence and meeting. Except for the dream visions, the style remains realistic, though sometimes lyrical, as King presents us a natural world soon recovering, not only from the plague but also from the depredations of humanity: the growth of plant and animal life. The events are generally positive, the people encountered benign and helpful though cautious or traumatized (deleted is *S2*'s extended and bloody account of Stu's band's encounter with brutal ex-soldiers murdering survivors to capture women for their drugged "harem"). Even the story of the Trashcan Man is pathetic; he is a victim, not a persecutor – the alter ego of Tom, the Innocent, the mystified new Frankenstein, puzzled and hurt, beset by strange impulses. The incidents are tinged with comedy and warm human interest – the deaf-mute Nick learning how to relate to the retarded Tom; the banter of Stu and Glen Bateman; Larry's maturation upon adopting the wild boy, Leo. The implicit message is that the natural man and the natural world are enough. People are good enough to people and good enough to the world that they live in that Eden could exist without effort.

It is the effort, and its agency – the organized community, society – that destroys. Douglas Winter makes the point clearly:

[The] sociopolitical subtext poses difficult questions about the nature of order and authority. Humans need companionship, but companionship produces a society, which in turn seemingly requires some semblance of order. As King's sociologist, Glen Bateman, argues: "Show me a man or woman alone and I'll show you a saint give me two and they'll fall in love. Give me three and they'll invent that charming thing we call 'society.' . . . Man may have been made in the image of God, but human society was made in the image of His opposite number and is always trying to get back home." (Winter, 69–70)

Thus, at the outset, when we learn that there is to be a gathering, we soon learn that Mother Abagail does not intend to found a new society in Boulder but to create against Flagg a weapon for the Lord. Unlike the founding fathers of the Free Zone, she faces the last cataclysm, not the New Jerusalem. Although King makes the utopian issue his dramatic question for the bulk of Book Two, "a final visionary experience by Mother Abagail rouses the Free Zone from the comfortable sleep of socialization, provoking 'the stand' " (Winter, 71). To follow King to his final conclusions, then, it is necessary to understand that Boulder finally fails: there will be Eden again but no New Jerusalem. Finally, the organized community is at the root of the evil that destroyed the world. Humanity survives best in the dyad or the family and in no larger unit than the ad hoc band, which dissolves upon achieving its purpose, such as to find Mother Abagail or to destroy Flagg.

Thus from the beginning, under the surface plot of a utopian *gedankenschrift,* the subtext of Book Two prepares for a cautionary and horrific tale of destruction. The mode in which King poses his problems may be realistic science fiction, but that is not the mode in which he will present his answers. This is not to say that King doesn't consider seriously how a small group of people might practically go about restoring the technical operations of a small city and thereby recreate an ordered society. He does. He gives us a detailed account of the personal and political processes operative, the kinds of material problems and solutions encountered and provided. But Boulder is to end in disaster, for there is no political and rational answer to the question "How shall man survive upon the earth?" For there is no material question to be asked; it is a spiritual problem.

Thus as soon as it is organized, Boulder implodes. Its materialistic and rational politics cannot bar from its center its worst enemy: Flagg's terrorists destroy Nick Andros, its first and best leader. Nor can politics retain its leaders: Mother Abagail sends them out as martyrs in the Cataclysm. The only survivor of the Band, Stu Redman, turns his back on Boulder and takes with him Fran and her child to live the only viable social life, that of a small family surviving within a rural setting—the New Eden. The New Jerusalem is not the answer.

BOOK TWO: THE TRIPLE PLOT AND THE PROTAGONIST BAND

The novel has three plot strands that merge in Book Two: the plots of Nick, Stu, and Larry. Nick's plot is presented essentially in the mode of science fiction. His is one of the more developed realistic perspectives through which we see the Apocalypse; he is the key figure in the founding of the Free Zone, and with his assassination the utopian plot ends. The core plot presents Stu and Fran. Long a realistic adjunct to the Nick plot, theirs is finally the story of the recreation from Fall to Eden of the new Adam and Eve. As the novel emerges from materialistic and realistic science fiction to become epic fantasy, characters like these (and unlike Nick or Bateman) become archetypal. Larry's plot measures for the novel's dynamic: it is to him and his dark alter ego Harold that the novel *happens,* for they are the two developing characters responding to the novel's dynamic in all three phases. Like Stu and Fran, they evolve from the realistic to the mythic, Abel and Cain, Christ and Judas. The point where the projections of writer and reader intersect, their fates sort out the values and realities of the work.

The surviving characters of these plots sort themselves out into a "protagonistic band." To clarify the term, I will quote from a paper that I delivered on *'Salem's Lot* in which I found useful a cognitive model expressed by James Hillman (30–38):

[C]onsciousness emanates not from an individual but from a community of personae *within* the individual, an inherent configuration that has been much interrupted by the pathology of "single-minded" contemporary materialistic and rationalistic culture. (1–2)

What we witness in *The Stand* is a gathering of such personae: each of the central characters is an aspect of a psyche. The psyche is the novel itself (its characters, settings, dynamic) and that psyche, like Brahma, is reintegrating. In its first phase the apocalypse is mythic essentially as a dynamic, the extinction and scattering of humanity, the fall of Babel, the flood, the first phase of the apocalypse. Otherwise, the literary mode is the realistic mode of science fiction.

Next, the mode's segue from realistic to mythic through the Journey is empowered by reintegration. The Journey has two phases: the Gathering and the Final Conflict. As the novel moves into the Gathering, the characters begin to slim down into personae, members related in a protagonistic band, itself an overarching psyche. It is this phenomena that provides the subtext to the surface *gedankenschrift* of Book Two. As the novel begins with Stu, so does the process of mythologizing. Stu is the band's Ego, a literary stereotype, Gary Cooper, the strong and silent Westerner, the Sheriff, the Hero, the New Adam, the Survivor. He first meets Super-Ego: Glen Bateman, teacher, thematic character, just before he encounters two characters of the unconscious: Anima, Fran, the New Eve, the First Mother, Stu's cofounder at the end of the novel of the New Eden; and an avatar of Shadow, Harold, Cain, Judas the first murderer and traitor in the New Jerusalem. The agendas raised by super-ego, anima and shadow manifesting, the course to the underground becomes evident and the journey west to the Land of the Shadow begins: to Boulder the land of the Benign and Nurturing Dark Mother Abagail and the Malign and Destructive Dark Father Flagg; Abagail is of music and intuition and vision, Flagg of the superrational and hyperrational. Within Boulder, a comfortable merger of ego, super-ego, and anima is achieved. A mastery achieved over the more destructive impulses of the local avatar of the Dark Man (Harold), oriented by the Mother (Abagail), Stu is ready to set out to preserve a New Eden threatened once again by the Father engaged in the excesses of rational materialism wielded as political power.[3] Nick and Larry do not properly belong to this mythic plot, though they have mythic inflection: Nick is foremost among the inheriting meek, for the deaf-mute vagrant becomes the God-appointed king, the first magistrate of the New Jerusalem. And Larry's mythic role is dictated by the history of European plot: the archetypal Christian protagonist, Everyman, upon whom act the history of the Earth and the will of the Lord. He is rounded out by Harold, the other developing character at the center of the psychomachia enacted by Abagail and Flagg, finally. Harold is Man Fallen, Larry, Man Saved, perhaps finally Man as God, the new Messiah crucified.[4]

BOOK THREE: THE RESOLUTION

In the last phase of the novel is manifested its major conflict – the Last Battle – and there are casualties. But one of the features of the protagonistic band is that personae don't disappear when they die; they combine. In *'Salem's Lot,* as each of the members of the band falls to the vampire, the protagonist Ben Mears gains that much in power and perspective against the antagonist until, at the end of the novel, he literally becomes St. George hacking at the universal dragon. I have already traced the beginning of that process by designating as protagonist the character of the first plot, Stu Redman, and observing the archetypal underside of the characters whom he meets and who enable him. He meets super-ego and is educated, meets anima and loves, meets shadow and moves clearly into the light. But he is not a developing protagonist. His encounters empower rather than change him. He becomes quite simply the novel's hero. But King is transforming Stu from the more typical hero, the Gary Cooper warrior society hero of the first book, into an archetype more fundamental to the species: the first man, the new Adam. Thus, unlike Larry and Nick, his direction is toward dyad, the merging with Fran, with Eve, hero as first husband, first father. King ends with the development of family, a new race of humans, living in abundance and through telepathy and prophecy harmonized with time and space.[5]

Certainly a major aspect of Book Three is to provide a climax to the Final Conflict, to bring the band of heroes into the presence of the antagonist and to defeat him. My classroom experience has made clear, however, that many *Stand* readers wonder that if this is the point of the book, we have gone a long way for little. The heroes make the journey with little incident, other than Redman's injury separating him from the band, are immediately captured and prepared for execution, get some spirited last words before crucifixion, and are witness to the Trashcan Man's accidental immolation of the New Babylon and the revelation of Flagg's nature: he is nothing, nothing at all, empty clothes. Like Barlow of *'Salem's Lot,* evil is distant from a good that is all being and reality. Its metaphor is the zombie rather than the demon.

The resolution provides completion of the Larry/Harold plot, the Everyman plot so far underpinning and sorting out the values of the novel: Harold dies ("a waste") while Larry puts behind him the last of his selfishness and, for love of man, the artist mounts the cross, a second Christ confronting Antichrist, bringing by his mere presence all his antagonist's evil to a pure focus so that it can effectively destroy itself. And Bateman watches and clarifies Flagg's nature:

"You're *nothing!*" Glen said, wiping his streaming eyes and still chuckling. "Oh pardon me . . . it's just that we were all so frightened. . . . I'm laughing as much at our own foolishness as at your regrettable lack of substance." (*S1,* 749)

But while King achieves that resolution, he interweaves in it the situation of Redman, abandoned in the desert. And after the Las Vegas destruction,

King energizes the novel with another dramatic question: "Will Stu survive?" He does, but not on his own. The merging continues. By his presence in the band, nominally its chief, he engages with Larry, the novel's ego, and enforces with his presence as archetypal hero its impulse and direction toward self-transcendence. But further merging must continue: rather than saving himself, the hero is saved by a dog and a retarded man, emblems of the natural world and the natural man. Throughout this section, as Magistrale (37) has suggested, the merging is empowered by love. A childlike human, Tom, himself merging with the consciousness of the dead Nick, the lost leader, who adds to the efforts of the dog Kojak to preserve and bring back Stu to his wife and his future. The love intrinsic to child and dog, to all that is natural, empowers Stu and moved by his own love he returns to Fran. Returning to even more fundamental archetypes, the spiritual warrior finds his empowerment and orientation in the love intrinsic to the child and to the animal world.

And now a last dramatic question impels the novel. Will man survive, first, the apocalypse, and, second, himself? Yes and yes. After cliffhanging, Fran delivers the first healthy child. And after mature thought, she and Stu leave Boulder. Generally speaking, humanity committed to city and society seems capable of little more than recreating its own problems. Out of Boulder will come no New Jerusalem, just another apocalypse. But there is hope. Stu and Fran leave Boulder for Maine. Humanity as dyad, man and wife, producing child and family in its own garden will continue strong and healthy. The New Jerusalem was never promised. But Eden was.

Saved by the miraculous, the other world having manifested itself in both the destruction of Sodom and the preservation of Adam in the desert, the final generic position of *The Stand* is in fantasy. Before Stu and Fran lie the possibilities prophesied by the dead saint Glen:

And suppose . . . that when rationalism does go, it's as if a bright dazzle has gone for a while and we could see. . . . Dark magic. . . . A universe of marvels where water flows uphill and trolls live in the deepest wood and dragons live under the mountains. Bright wonders, white power. "Lazarus, come forth." Water into wine. And . . . and . . . just maybe . . . the casting out of devils. . . . The lifetrip. (*S1*, 473)

NOTES

1. Holding that the "apocalyptic imagination . . . finds its purest outlet in science fiction," Ketterer observes that the apocalyptic novel is less a tale of ending than of beginning. He sees three categories: "sociological science fiction" that extrapolates the "future consequences of present circumstances"; "modification of an existing condition" by scientific or technological innovation or by disturbance;

a startling discovery that places humanity in "a radically new perspective." Certainly King's novel is a good example of types one and two, until Book Two evolves out of the science-fictional mode. Incidentally, Ketterer was well aware that apocalyptic concerns found "expression in the gothic mode" but the example available to him of the combined modes, Lovecraft's stories, he found "oscillating uncertainly between the gothic and science fiction" (16–19).

These issues lie outside the scope of this chapter, but Ketterer's "Edgar Allan Poe and the Visionary Tradition of Science Fiction" (50–75) illuminates *The Stand*. The arabesques of Poe's visionary and the dark magic of Bateman's irrationalist share King's psychic terrain.

2. He had an array of tactics. Sometimes there is simply less: we see less of Fran's parents and town, less of Nick's problems in Shoyo and Shoyo's problems with the plague. We have less of the brilliant and powerful anecdotes exemplifying the plague's impact. Stylistically, he tones down the 1978 version by deleting some of the more graphically gruesome passages and reducing didacticism, especially Glen Bateman's. The impact of a certain kind of revision is to recast humanity as more innocent, more a victim of omission rather than commission, even in Las Vegas. *S2*, in contrast, presents a more morally complex picture with its restoration of the characters the Kid, the soldiers' harem, and so on. Most significant is that the reduction overall seems to have been done with great discrimination, often by the word.

3. In a more truncated form, a similarly antagonistic band forms about Flagg, much more so than in *'Salem's Lot*. I find suggestive Reino's observation that Flagg is "a mere symbolic abstraction" in contrast to Lloyd Henreid and that "Lloyd Henreid and the . . . Trashcan Man . . . are psychopathic embodiments of his . . . Antichrist spirit . . . the right and left sides of Flagg's demonic kingdom" (60–61). Trash is id (Magistrale, 44), Henreid is ego, and Nadine is anima to Flagg's self.

4. According to Winter (63–64), Larry's situation dramatized for King his own psychological dilemmas at the time of composition, particularly with reference to the impact upon his psyche of sudden wealth and fame. But the sixteen-year-old Harold also very closely fits King's description of himself at the time: he is a tall, overweight adolescent with straight black hair and a vision of himself as a talented author. I suspect that both developing figures give King (as mask and shadow) psychological access to the novel's dynamic – it works on him as it works on them, enabling and transforming one of his psyche's personae, the young artist, and putting the quietus to the other, the adolescent self.

5. In *S2* the vision is bleaker. At its close, we see Flagg resurrected. The snake eternally challenges man.

REFERENCES

Casebeer, Edwin F. "The Communal Psyche of *'Salem's Lot*." Paper presented to the International Conference on the Fantastic in the Arts, Ft. Lauderdale, Fla., March, 1990.

Collings, Michael R. "Considering *The Stand*," *Gauntlet* 2 (1991): 179–185.

———. "*The Stand*: Science Fiction into Fantasy." In *Discovering Stephen King*, edited by Darrell Schweitzer. Mercer Island, Wash.: Starmont, 1985.

Hillman, James. *Re-Visioning Psychology.* New York: Harper & Row, 1975.

Ketterer, David. *New Worlds for Old: The Apocalyptic Imagination, Science Fiction, and American Literature.* New York: Anchor, 1974.

King, Stephen. *Danse Macabre.* New York: Berkley, 1982.

———. *The Stand.* New York: New American Library, 1978, 1980.

———. *The Stand.* New York: Doubleday, 1990.

Magistrale, Tony. *Landscape of Fear: Stephen King's American Gothic.* Bowling Green, Ohio: Bowling Green State University, Popular Press, 1988.

Reino, Joseph. *Stephen King: The First Decade,* Carrie *to* Pet Sematary. Boston: Twayne, 1988.

Winter, Douglas E. *Stephen King: The Art of Darkness.* New York: New American Library, 1986.

6

Some Ways of Reading
The Dead Zone

MICHAEL N. STANTON

It is dangerous to speak of Stephen King's novels in superlatives, especially now that what was once his longest novel has been reissued, expanded by some 350 pages. Nonetheless, many readers have found in the quiet achievements of *The Dead Zone* some of King's finest work. Coming between the apocalyptic destruction of *The Stand* and the pyrotechnic madness of *Firestarter, The Dead Zone* seems to strike a softer note than either. It is a richly human novel, and it is the more so for its relative compactness. In what is for him a mere 370 pages, King has managed to write both a narrative of one man's personal ordeal and an inquiry into the nature of American government. Still, read as I propose to read it here, *The Dead Zone* is one of King's most disturbing novels, for although John Smith's famous ability is to see the future, much of the novel concerns what has already happened in America, or to America.

The keynotes that King strikes in *The Dead Zone* are fear, inadequacy, and loss of faith, nerve, and integrity, and they are sounded in the reactions to John Smith's strange mental power and in the reactions to Greg Stillson's political aspirations. *The Dead Zone* can be read on at least four levels, or in four aspects: the symbolic, the historical, the personal or psychological, and the political. These aspects of the novel are richly intertwined, and separating them for examination necessarily creates a distortion: but it does enable us to see how and why John Smith dies for his country, and why it may already be too late.

On the symbolic level, we can begin with an apparently inconsequential vignette that seems almost an interpolation into the narrative line. On a hot summer day about two years before Johnny Smith comes up out of his coma, a travelling salesman stops at Cathy's Roadhouse near the Maine-New Hampshire border. This man is not the travelling salesman of smutty anecdote; he sells lightning rods. He manages to quench his thirst; he does not manage to sell the owner of the roadhouse his quaint product. What the man sells is continually emphasized; again and again King calls him the "lightning rod salesman," or, with curiously formal diction, "the seller of lightning rods" (King, 78–80). He is an anomalous figure, since the commodity he vends was obsolete long before 1973. He is in fact more a prophet than a pedlar, for as he drives away, he thinks that "Maybe someday he [the owner] would be sorry" (King, 80). And he will be, when lightning strikes his building and fire consumes a fair fraction of the Durham High School Class of 1977, celebrating its graduation there.

The episode of the seller of lightning rods is a fairly obvious bit of plot foreshadowing, and if his appearance were only a plot device it would be almost painfully transparent. But it is more than that: it symbolizes the function or position of characters in the novel.

Johnny Smith, for example, is a lightning rod.

The mind of John Smith is a conductor of energetic flashes of information from the anywhere to the here and now. His psychic power operates without respect to time, drawing from the past (the fate of Sam Weizak's mother), the present (the fire in Eileen Magown's kitchen), and the future (the roadhouse tragedy). And like lightning striking, John's power is almost everywhere associated with burning:

"Two rubber tires burned sootily" (King, 1) at the edge of the pond where Johnny had the boyhood skating accident that brought into being his psychic power, and although he scarcely remembers bumping his head, the association remains. Just before the accident that renders him comatose, his run of luck at the county fair has "the strangest goddam associations for me . . . burning rubber" (King, 42). That heavy smell of burning lurks always just below the surface of Smith's life.

For example, when Johnny pulls in the information that Dr. Weizak's mother is still alive, he gets images of the Nazi invasion of Warsaw: the refugees are fleeing, "the city's on fire" and "Poland has fallen before the lightning warfare" (King, 107).

In his next revelation, Johnny sees his therapist's kitchen curtains afire miles away. In the face of Eileen Magown's disbelief, he summons help and her home is saved.

Fire and lightning seem to surround John Smith. Even Dr. Strawns, his first attending physician, later dies of burns when his house catches fire (King, 81). When John gets a job tutoring young Chuck Chatsworth, who has a reading problem, he thinks of the verbal disability of the man who could not shout "Fire!" in a burning theatre; the high-impact fiction he sets Chuck to reading is Max Brand's *Fire Brain*. And of course the rod-less Cathy's Roadhouse burns on the night of Chuck's graduation, the fire "caused by a bolt of lightning" (319); one "cannot buy off the lightning" (319) as Chuck's father observes, but as the seller of lightning rods might have observed, one could have.

Enough actual fire and lightning are associated with John Smith to be worth noting, but the lightning rod is symbolic in another way too. Johnny is an emotional lightning rod, through whom is discharged the fear in those whose lives he touches. It is a universal ironic fact that whenever John Smith's psychic power enables him, or forces him, to do a good deed, the general reaction to him is one of dread and loathing (when it is not outright disbelief). When John tells Eileen that her curtains are on fire but that her house will be all right, she blesses him and kisses him but "the expression on her face was very much like superstitious dread" (King, 41). Meanwhile the nurses at the duty station where Johnny has called in the fire are "lined up . . . staring at him" like "crows staring at something bright and shiny, something to be pecked at and pulled apart" (King, 41).

When Johnny predicts the fire at Cathy's Roadhouse during a lawn party at the Chatsworths' earlier in the day, Chuck's girl friend faints and her mother screams at Johnny, "What's *wrong* with you?" The other guests stare "like crows strung out on a telephone wire . . . looking at him as if he were a bug, a freak" (King, 312). That evening when the radio carries the news of the actual fire, Chuck's girl friend again becomes unstrung and screams at Johnny (in what seems to be a paroxysm of self-referen-tiality): "It's his fault, that guy there! He made it happen! He set it on fire by his mind, just like in that book *Carrie*. You murderer!" (King, 320).

Despite the girl's accusation, Johnny's power is of course purely pas-sive, not kinetic, and it is not solely predictive; but it sets him apart from the bulk of mankind. He flees it but it seems to pursue him (Roger Chatsworth's reference to "The Hound of Heaven" [321] is not unapt). He hates what his mind can do, but always his refusal or reluctance to use his power when he has that option, as when Sheriff George Bannerman asks for his help in finding a serial killer, puts him in a dilemma where refusing to act is ethically worse than acting, whatever the cost to himself of action (and it always is costly). Drawing upon himself the fear and ha-tred of the community by his power, John Smith becomes both a scape-goat and an exile. His gift is indeed rather a "curse" as Dr. Vann observes much later (King, 367).

There are exceptions to this pattern, of course; it is not merely mechan-ical. Johnny's very first exercise of power is such an exception. Unlike all the visions that follow, it brings a piece of good news. He tells his nurse

Marie that her son's eyesight will be restored after an operation on his im-
pacted cornea. The tiny episode is a pleasant introduction to a trouble-
some gift, perhaps because its subject is the gift of sight itself.

Johnny Smith's early revelations are not just news flashes from nowhere meant to disturb and dazzle their hearers. At the level of history,
one at least is significant not merely in its own right, but also as creating a
historical matrix for events that develop later in the novel.

The importance of the circumstances in which Sam Weizak became
separated from his mother seems to escape Johnny himself. It is not just
"the Nazi invasion of Warsaw" that estranges mother and child; that invasion belongs in the larger context of the very beginning of World War II.
The German invasion of Poland in September, 1939, marked the opening
of a great conflagration and also marked the end of an era of uneasy and
waning peace littered with promises broken, treaties breached, and
faiths betrayed. Hitler and Stalin had signed a nonaggression pact that en-
abled them to divide Poland between them like a wishbone; a year later,
Hitler broke that pact and invaded Russia. All of this, and more, is implied in Johnny's vision of a burning city and fleeing people.

Several years after this remarkable reach into the past, John Smith has
Hitler on his mind again, as he considers what to do about Greg Stillson.
Johnny has had an oddly blurred, but not ambiguous, vision of Stillson's
presidency and consequent nuclear war. The more Johnny researches
Stillson's background and studies Stillson's present actions, the more he is
convinced that his vision is accurate and that Stillson is a fascist in popu-
list's clothing.

King's account of Stillson's political behavior may be heightened (for effect) but for Johnny the question of how to deal with the man remains.
He takes a kind of informal survey: "just suppose you could hop into a
time machine and go back to the year 1932. In Germany. And suppose
you came across Hitler. Would you kill him or let him live?" (King, 306–7).
The responses are interesting. One old man, who served in World War I
and lost a son in World War II, would kill Hitler without hesitation. Roger
Chatsworth, the successful businessman and deal-maker, would not: "I
think I'd join the party instead. Try to change things from within" (King,
308). Roger, who fancies himself a realist, thinks Johnny's question is
"pointless but interesting" (King, 308). His 17-year-old son Chuck asks
questions of his own which are closer to the bone: Would they catch me?
Could I escape in my time machine back to 1977? To both these inquiries,
Johnny must posit a no. "Well, it wouldn't matter [says Chuck] I'd kill him
anyway" (King, 309).

These responses provide only ironic guidance. Johnny is in the moral
equivalent of 1932, with his own potential Hitler, and must act on his
own to prevent a tragic future. (Still more ironically, perhaps, as Johnny

compares Stillson to the Hitler who began World War II, Stillson's future war will begin with nuclear weapons – the means by which World War II was ended.) At all events, historical analogues and the sense of history, which subsumes issues of war, politics, and the presidency, loom over the consciousness of John Smith and the progress of events in *The Dead Zone*.

Large historical events, both past and future, are by no means the only concerns of this novel. As in every King novel, personal history matters greatly. The surface topics of politics and war are richly underlain by the humus of ordinary lives. The implication of rot is unpleasant but it is not inaccurate: lives decay through the novel in an atmosphere of fear, fanaticism, and irrationality, and each life contributes its mite to the rank social and political air of the mid-1970s, which John Smith and others must breathe.

To say that John Smith and Greg Stillson are the twin poles of *The Dead Zone* is to state the obvious; they are everywhere juxtaposed. Still, in the opening pages, King shows us more of Greg Stillson. Of Johnny, we learn little more than that a rather odd power has been made manifest in his mind. By contrast, King paints the young Stillson with fairly broad strokes; he is a flimflam artist travelling the roads of Middle America, selling a dishonest product (the Bible), arrogant in his assumed superiority, a coward, and a bully – a perfect little demagogue in embryo.

Greg Stillson did not acquire these unlovely traits by happenstance. One strongly implied contrast between the two opening scenes of the novel is in the nature of Johnny's and Greg's boyhood. Johnny's, while not vividly realized at the outset, is at least normal: two loving parents (Vera Smith's religious fanaticism not yet having surfaced) with whom he has an affectionate relationship in a stable small-town setting. Greg's, by contrast, is nomadic; his father, a roughneck oil-field worker, shows only contempt for the runty little kid, a contempt that Greg returns, with interest, as hatred; the mother is a nonentity. "The domineering father and the laxly approving mother," is King's description of this charming couple (King, 304). It seems clear that even as he hates his father (who, as it happens, dies by fire) Stillson seeks the dead man's approval by emulation: his campaign gimmick of wearing a hard hat "cocked at a rakish angle" (King, 267) on his head reproduces the father's "hard hat cocked jauntily back" (King, 296) in the photograph of father and son that Johnny sees.

In fact, even though it is the one King novel that does not have a child as a major figure (although children are important in it), *The Dead Zone* is greatly concerned with relations between parents and children, and the keystone of many of these relationships is fear or hatred.

Frank Dodd's mother, for example, that crazy reptilian woman, teaches her son to hate and fear his own sexuality. Her punishment of his inno-

cent presexual interest in his body contributes largely to Frank's fear and
loathing of women and to his subsequent career as a rapist and serial
killer. Frank's father, a drunkard, died many years ago, and for whatever
kind of substitution it might imply, Frank never wanted to be anything
but a policeman. And his boss, Sheriff Bannerman, refuses to believe that
Frank is the killer, because, as Johnny points out, he is the "man you
think of as your own son" (King, 226).

Chuck Chatsworth's fear arises from a very different source: he wants
to please and fears failing his successful father, whom he idolizes; his
reading disability is a symptom of that fear: he is overanxious to succeed
and thereby please Roger Chatsworth. He is "overswinging" as his tutor,
Johnny Smith, puts it (King, 254).

Just these three examples show that in *The Dead Zone* the relationships
between parents and children are a network of fear and inadequacy. Parents fail their children; children fear failing their parents. Living fathers,
for example (like Herb Smith or Roger Chatsworth), get fairly high marks
for caring, while dead ones, blameable by their very absence, are seen as
mean or weak. Mothers, living or dead, are usually neutral figures (Shelley Chatsworth), or weak (the late Mrs. Stillson), or strangely warped
(Vera Smith, Henrietta Dodd).

Moving beyond questions of characters' intrafamilial relations with
each other to questions of their own value systems, we see the same
kinds of shortcomings and failings at work. People ask themselves, What
can I believe? or, How can I make sense of my life? and their answers are
inadequate to the extent that they arise from ideology or dogmatism.

The litmus test for such dogmatism is John Smith, or rather two events
in his life: his unlikely recovery from a years-long coma and the revelation of his psychic power. We see at once that those characters who respond most inadequately to the phenomena presented by the existence of
John Smith are those whose beliefs are most fixed. Such rigidity shows
the mind, constrained by its own belief-sets, unable to handle actuality.
Dr. James Brown, for example, is a scientific materialist. Because he cannot explain Johnny's peculiar power according to his own principles, he
refuses to admit that it exists. As Brown's colleague Sam Weizak explains
to Johnny, "He thinks you are having us on. . . . His cast of mind makes it
impossible for him to think otherwise. . . . He is a mechanic of the brain.
He has cut it to pieces with his scalpel and found no soul. Therefore there
is none" (King, 119). Brown dislikes Johnny Smith because the fact of him
threatens Brown; John possesses something that Brown's medical training cannot explain or deal with, that training having been wholly within
the rational order.

Quite irrational, but equally rigid and inadequate, is Vera Smith's belief
that her son is specially marked by God. Herb and Vera know nothing of
Johnny's psychic power ("neither of them had any idea," says Johnny

[King, 150] on the night of Vera's stroke), but Vera firmly believes that an interventionist God brought Johnny out of his four-and-a-half-year coma to do *something*. During that period Vera has been moving toward cultic, fundamentalist beliefs, and now she has arrived at the lunatic fringe. If Dr. Brown's view of reality has essentially only one dimension, Vera's has two—good versus evil. On the one side are the rapture, the miracle-working God, the *deus ex* flying saucer, and the apocalypse; on the other are the agents of Satan who run this world (doctors mostly). It is easy to make fun of Vera and her beliefs, but that is only because she has taken her rejection of human will and human responsibility to an extreme. She refuses to take her blood pressure medicine because if God wants her to live He will see to it, and if He wants her to die He will see to that: "It was a seamless argument and Johnny's only possible rebuttal was the one that Catholics and Protestants alike have rejected for eighteen hundred years: that God works his will through the mind of man as well as through the spirit of man" (King, 133).

Poles apart as they are, Vera's views and Dr. Brown's view are alike in the inadequacy of their response to complexity. Still, Vera's views at least have consequences for Johnny: her last words to him are "Do your duty, John" (King, 158), and soon enough John finds the duty he must do. In a secular sense, Vera's command continues to haunt the novel and John Smith's life.

Discovering what John Smith's duty is brings us to the political aspect of the novel, and closer to its core. Many things have been established at this point in *The Dead Zone*. For the character of John Smith, these are established: his essential decency and humanity; the pain he suffers whenever he must use his gift or power; and the loss of other, purely human, satisfactions (such as the rewards of his skill as a teacher) his power brings with it. As to the power itself, it has been established that it is unpredictable in its appearance, accurate, verifiable and always verified, and almost without exception takes as its subject matter loss, crime, and disaster. John Smith's gift does not change in character or quality as the novel proceeds, but the scope of its operation does: from dealing with individual matters like the fate of Sam Weizak's mother or the whereabouts of Sarah Hazlett's ring, to dealing with the problems and concerns of entire communities such as Castle Rock, Maine, or Durham, New Hampshire. In its final manifestation, Johnny's vision rises to the national level in predicting the career of Greg Stillson.

Equally well-established is the social context in which John Smith's power is operating. The America of 1975 into which John reawakens is seriously wounded. We have seen this in the physically disabled characters who haunt the novel, and in the absurd belief systems to which individuals cling. We have seen deformity of personality or character, and craziness of tenet, as expressions of a pervasive atmosphere of loss, fear, and inadequacy manifested in a variety of ways (not least against John Smith himself).

All this malaise sets the stage for the emergence of Greg Stillson as a major figure. Our memory of him has been refreshed periodically throughout, but he emerges as the chief architect of evil only in the last one hundred pages or so of the novel. Still, the convergence of John Smith and Greg Stillson is fated or destined in an almost Hardyesque way (not for nothing do we find Chuck Chatsworth, once he has graduated from Max Grand, reading *Jude the Obscure*). An unsympathetic observer might find the collision of protagonist and antagonist almost mechanically arranged, but it is the most significant if not the most poignant encounter in the novel. By it, King raises the focus of Smith's power, as well as the ethical questions surrounding its use, to the highest levels of public life. He thus forces us to ask ourselves what makes a Greg Stillson possible. Can fears, doubts, and inadequacies previously shown in individuals and communities be operating at a national level? Will a diseased nation embrace a would-be dictator as its savior and future president? In illustrating how such a situation can come about, *The Dead Zone* becomes a shrewdly observed and thoroughly pessimistic novel.

To make his point about national loss of faith, King skillfully times the events of his protagonist's life. He puts John Smith to sleep in October of 1970 and reawakens him in May of 1975. The world around Johnny has changed immensely, as he keeps learning to his dismay. Much is new besides Flair pens and hair styles. For example, Johnny's coma began a few months after students at Kent State University, demonstrating against the war in Vietnam and its extension into Cambodia, were shot and killed. It ended a few weeks after the fall of Saigon and the takeover of all of Vietnam (and Cambodia, too) by a Communist government. John's sleep encompassed the beginning of the troubles in Northern Ireland, the publication of the Pentagon Papers, the massacre of Israeli athletes at the Munich Olympics, Wounded Knee, the Yom Kippur war, the bizarre adventures of Patty Hearst, and a great deal more. None of these events gets so much as a passing mention, and even Vietnam is treated as a background event.

This is not a sin of omission on King's part; it is rather an act of selection. Foregrounded, thrown into high relief, brought to Johnny's attention at once, is the fate of the American presidency. When Herb Smith says that Richard Nixon has resigned because he was about to be impeached, "Johnny suddenly realized that there had been some great and fundamental upheaval in American politics. . . . How much had things changed? He was almost afraid to ask" (King, 111).

Johnny begins to learn the extent to which Nixon had failed and abused his trust (a few days later we find him reading Woodward and Bernstein's

All the President's Men); he learns about Watergate, the tapes, the Saturday night massacre. He learns that for the first time in our history men never elected nationally are serving as president and vice president. He learns, in short, that while he lay comatose the United States had undergone its worst constitutional crisis since the Civil War.

In the relative stability of 1990, it is hard to remember how dreadful an ordeal the American Constitution went through in 1973-74.[1] But King was working on *The Dead Zone* only a couple of years after those events. The memory of constitutional crisis barely weathered was still fresh; the betrayal still hurt. Johnny's intuition that this fundamental upheaval was "almost surely a result of the war in Vietnam" (King, 111) is almost surely right. As the veteran observer of the Presidency, Theodore White, writes, in 1968 "Americans were confronted with a new reality – they were engaged in the first major war they would not win. By the time Nixon came to power, that realization had split the country at every level, and resentment at . . . Vietnam had spilled out . . . in . . . violence and . . . bloodshed" (White, 330). Nixon's betrayal of his obligation to lead and heal a divided nation, his betrayal of his office, and his forced resignation from that office "left a nation [whose] faith was shattered" (White, 324).

I do not mean to suggest that all of the fear and inadequacy portrayed in *The Dead Zone,* all of the lack of belief and rigidity of belief and madness of belief shown there springs from the trauma of America's belief in its leadership having been destroyed. I mean to suggest only that King's presentation forces us to look in the direction of the White House. The soiling of the presidency took place during Johnny Smith's long sleep; when he awakens, the greatest menace he must confront is a man who would be president – Greg Stillson – one who manipulates people's fears and hopes and inadequacies to further his presidential ambitions, to whom things such as constitutional guarantees seem elegant trifles, and who, according to Johnny's oddly occluded vision, is capable of destroying his country entirely.

"His ruthlessness, vengefulness, nastiness were the characteristics of a man who has seen himself as underdog for so long that he cannot distinguish between real and fancied enemies, a man who does not really care whom he slashes or hurts when pressed, who cannot accept or understand when or what he has won." This description of a political figure of a certain kind could be Stephen King's, or any reader's, of Greg Stillson. It is in fact Theodore White's description of Richard Nixon (White, 333).

Once again King operates selectively: he keeps our attention focused on the intermingled fate of the presidency and Vietnam by concentrating on the presidential campaign of 1976 (only incidentally mentioning the concomitant Bicentennial) and Greg Stillson's parallel congressional campaign, and by providing a commentator on the political scene in the person of a Vietnamese refugee, Ngo.

The substance of Ngo's comments is in two stories he tells Johnny, both about tigers. One is about a game children in his village played, in which one child dressed up in an animal skin and "the other children tries to catch him as he runs and dances. The child in the skin laughs, but he is also growling and biting because that is the game" (King, 273). Johnny feels later "as if Stillson might have taken the game of the Laughing Tiger a step farther: inside the beast-skin, a man, yes.

"But inside the man-skin, a beast" (King, 277).

In his second tale, Ngo tells about a real tiger that "went bad near my village. He was . . . [an] eater of men. . . . And one day this tiger was found in a pit that had been baited with the body of a dead woman. . . . I am thinking that this Stillson is like that bad tiger" (King, 293).

What separates Ngo's story of the child's-play tiger from that of the man-eating tiger is the rally in Trimbull, New Hampshire, where Ngo and Johnny see Greg Stillson in action, and Johnny actually shakes his hand. Greg Stillson the campaigner is magnetic, attractive, energetic, has a way with words, knows all the right buttons to push. He, like Johnny, is a lightning rod and through him is discharged all the fear, disgust, and desire for change, any change, of a politically disillusioned people. And (metaphorically at least) it is a terrifying thing when one lightning rod touches another: the rally was "all mass confusion. Excitement was humming through the crowd like a series of high-voltage electrical cables" (King, 282). When Johnny and Stillson actually shake hands, Johnny's vision of a nightmare future, with Stillson at its center, is the strongest he has ever had. It was "like burning high-tension wires," a "sweet, coppery scent" (King, 284), and then Johnny blacks out.

One of the underlying paradoxes of the novel is that while John Smith is essentially a good and honest man, his mysterious power of knowing attracts fear, distrust, and even hatred; by contrast Greg Stillson is essentially an evil man whose quite unmysterious power of communicating attracts popularity, affection, and something not far short of idolatry. John Smith accurately perceives that each of Stillson's campaign stops is not so much a political gathering as "a love feast . . . or a group grope" (King, 278). With uncanny prescience King portrays in Stillson's highly orchestrated love-ins that appearance of spontaneity without the reality of it, which has increasingly characterized America's encounters with its politicians over the last decade-and-a-half.

Greg Stillson appears to be the type of politician America can produce, and lovingly endorse, once its faith in its own constitutional system has been breached. People like Roger Chatsworth—people who are steady, sensible, and above all comfortable—tend to laugh off Stillson. Roger tells Johnny that Stillson might serve one term, but then will lose his seat because he hasn't learned the lesson: "Don't fuck the people over for too long" (King, 271).

But Johnny's horrible vision of the Stillson presidency shows that in post-Nixonian America the people have apparently forgotten that this lesson is in their power to teach. As frightening as any element of Johnny's vision of Stillson as president are the "scared fieldmouse eyes" (King, 283) of the chief justice administering the oath of office. Those eyes show that Stillson has trampled law, custom, and constitutional process to gain his high office. Johnny's vision shows that the corruption and betrayal of America by those who govern it, a process begun during his sleep, is now complete.

The meeting between John Smith and Greg Stillson at the Trimbull rally is in a sense the climax of *The Dead Zone*. Every subsequent happening flows from it: John Smith has found the duty his mother said he had, and he must do it, even knowing he will pay the ultimate price. And when his brain tumor appears, he knows that his responsibility is no longer years in the future, as he had once thought.

And yet, although John himself dies, he is spared the crime of murder he had thought he must commit. Greg Stillson's character as a self-interested bully has been so carefully and thoroughly built up through the novel that it comes as no surprise to see him grab a child in a blue-and-yellow snowsuit to shield himself from John's bullets. In that act, the final puzzling detail of Johnny's vision falls into place — the blue or striped filter across it is explained. Stillson's impetuous act is highly characteristic, and, thanks to the photographs of it (another sort of vision), finally ruinous to his career. Stillson lives but the would-be dictator dies along with John Smith.

Johnny had nearly died several years earlier, but instead he fell into the deep sleep of coma, and we can now see that his coma had two functions: it not only activated his dormant psychic power, but it also preserved his innocence. He is the only man in America capable of having the actual vision of a Stillson presidency, and, thanks to his preservation in sleep from the corruption of American constitutional government, he is the only man in America capable of acting to prevent it. The rest of us were awake and gave our assent in a fashion to the breach of faith that was the Nixonian presidency; Johnny slept and was absent from our fall from grace.

All the many facets of *The Dead Zone* that we have examined bear the imprint of the character of John Smith. Except for his one extraordinary gift, he is an ordinary (hence his name) decent man, and with his decency he has courage — courage not only to bear the burden of his power, but more importantly, to act upon the implications of his vision. Unlike Greg Stillson, who is a self-made man, John Smith is a destined man. Stephen King is careful not to specify whence John's destiny comes (although we can probably rule out the irate Father of Vera's zealotry), but he is equally careful to show us John Smith fulfilling it admirably.

NOTE

1. As I write this, on July 19, 1990, the Nixon Library in Yorba Linda, California, is being dedicated with great fanfare and praise for the now-statesman-like, unindicted co-conspirator.

REFERENCES

King, Stephen. *The Dead Zone.* New York: Viking, 1979.
White, Theodore, H. *Breach of Faith: The Fall of Richard Nixon.* New York: Atheneum, 1975.

7

Fear and Pity: Tragic Horror in King's *Pet Sematary*

LEONARD MUSTAZZA

In his review of Stephen King's *Firestarter* for *The Wall Street Journal*, John Podhoretz observes that "the fun of Mr. King's novels rests in the ability to read them with delight and then put them aside without a thought" (Podhoretz, 26). This assessment of the effects that King's books are likely to produce is based not so much on King's talent as it is on the nature of the horror genre itself, which Podheretz calls "trifling," an "odd literary subfield." I suspect that King himself would concur, at least in part, with this view of the horror novel. In his own overview of the genre in *Danse Macabre*, King admits that entertainment, diversion by means of a good story, is often the only goal of what he terms "fearsomes," and, to be sure, that goal carries with it a good deal of ephemerality.

At the same time, however, King also cogently argues in *Danse Macabre* that the work of horror does at times become more than mere entertainment, that, in fact, it becomes art, when it manages to touch our "phobic pressure points" (4), our very real fears, the stuff of shocking nightmares. "What it's looking for," King writes, "is the place where you . . . live at your most primitive level. The work of horror is not interested in the civilized furniture of our lives. Such a work dances through these rooms which we have fitted out one piece at a time, each piece expressing—we hope!—our socially acceptable and enlightened character. . . . It achieves the level of art simply because it is looking for something beyond art, something that predates art" (4). King's strength as a writer (and, I would add, a good deal of his popularity as well) lies in his ability to touch our "phobic pressure points," and by so doing he manages to achieve more than mere entertainment. In his biography of King, Douglas Winter suggests that *Pet Sematary* makes clear that horror fiction at its most important moments "is not make-believe at all. It is a literature whose essence is our single certainty—that, in Hamlet's words, 'all that live must die' " (Winter, 136). Although Winter never explores the connection he implies here between classic tragedy and King's horror fiction, such a link does exist and it is a powerful one indeed. King does make us feel a sense of the tragic in life—of paralyzing fear, of unmerited suffering and death, of desperate unhappiness—and the effects produced by watching his good characters pass through such torment are comparable to those evoked by the world's great tragedies, these effects being the Aristotelian emotions of fear and pity. Although many works in the King canon manage to evoke these effects, none does so more memorably than *Pet Sematary.*

Since its birth in ancient Greece, tragedy has remained an enduring art form, though its contours have continually changed in accordance with the outlooks, values, and tastes of the varying societies in which the genre has appeared. These changes primarily have concerned the role of character in the tragic action. For the ancient Greeks, character flaw (*hamartia*) and fate conspire in the undoing of a person of high station. Renaissance tragedy, too, involved the suffering and death of an aristocratic person, though that outcome was the result not of fate but of human agency, both internal and external; that is, tragedy is the result of the protagonist's character defects and the pernicious actions of a malefactor. Although it was somewhat popular in the Renaissance and again in eighteenth-century Britain, modern America, owing perhaps to its democratic leanings, has shown a preference for the form known as "domestic tragedy" or "tragedy of the common person." In this particular permutation, the aristocratic or historical personages who had acted as protagonists in earlier forms of tragedy were replaced by common people, and the tragedy resulted from the collision of character and dire circumstance.

With these generic descriptions in mind, let us consider two questions: how, if at all, are these tragic visions related to one another despite their differences, and, more important, how, if at all, does *Pet Sematary* qualify as a tragic vision? While the social station of tragic figures differs from one historical period to another, what remains constant is our feelings for character, feelings that result from watching the spectacle of an admirable though flawed person undergo sufferings out of all proportion to any error he or she may have committed. Aristotle long ago defined these effects as fear and pity. Fear, Aristotle wrote in his *Poetics,* is aroused by watching the misfortunes of a person like ourselves, and pity results from our recognition of his or her unmerited misfortune (Aristotle, 75–76). Although the descriptions of tragedy found throughout the *Poetics* apply, of course, only to Greek tragedy, Aristotle's assertion about tragedy's effects are widely applicable to a variety of forms.

Accordingly, if we judge by such effects, King's *Pet Sematary* well qualifies as a tragic vision, involving as it does the unmerited misfortune of a
man not unlike ourselves, a man we come to love and admire. "You have
got to love the people," King has said speaking of characters in horror fiction. "There has to be love involved, because the more you love . . . then
that allows the horror to be possible. There is no horror without love and
feeling" (Winter, 47). In a sense, though he uses the term "horror" rather
than "tragedy," King is saying the very same thing here—fear and pity derive from love. After all, if we hate a character, we tend to regard his or
her undoing as mere poetic justice. However, there is more than favorable sentiment involved in producing the tragic effects. If we watch the
helpless sufferings of sympathetic people, we tend to regard them as *pathetic* rather than tragic figures. Tragedy must also involve choice and
struggle. In other words, a truly tragic figure must be caught in a bad situation not of his or her own doing, must make certain moral choices in the
struggle against large forces or formidable opponents, and must fall as a
result of the other's greater potency *and* his or her own flawed judgments
and character defects. Accordingly, Sophocles' Oedipus and Shakespeare's Othello and Miller's Willie Loman lose to the powerful forces
that oppose them—respectively fate, a human antagonist, and a vicious
economic system—but their own character traits and choices conspire
against them as well. Such is precisely the case with King's Louis Creed, a
man we come to love and admire, a man who does not choose evil but is
chosen by it, but also a man whose flaws in character and judgment will
bring about his and his family's ruin, which, in turn, will evoke the Aris-
totelean tragic emotions of fear and pity in those who behold this sad
spectacle.

Before he can make us sympathize with the dire circumstances in
which Louis Creed finds himself, however, King must establish a context
for that sympathy. Interestingly, a large part of that context comes about
through his deft manipulation of the novel's narrative structure. *Pet Sematary* is divided into three parts of unequal length titled, respectively,
"The Pet Sematary," "The Micmac Burying Ground," and "Oz the Gweat
and Tewwible." The first of these parts is by far the longest, running some
213 pages in the paperback edition or half the novel's total length. Curiously, moreover, this disproportionately long first part contains little that
is horrible or frightening, little of the kind of action that one might expect
in, as the blurb writers scream, "the most frightening book Stephen King
has ever written!" Rather, it is taken up with what is arguably the longest
exposition in fiction. Slowly, patiently, and with masterful skill, King
brings the reader into the life of the typical American nuclear family in a
small American town. Apart from the scenes involving Pascow and the
revival of Churchill, the first section of *Pet Sematary* is hardly "fearsome"
at all. Deborah Notkin, regarding King's *The Shining* more as a
story about a disintegrating family than one about ghosts and haunted

houses, writes that "it may well be the only horror story ever written where the ghosts could be entirely excised and the story not significantly changed" (Notkin, 154). Practically the same can be said about the long opening section of *Pet Sematary,* where the focus is upon character.

Of course, the character who dominates our attention is Dr. Louis Creed, a thirty-five-year-old physician. King takes special pains to show that Louis is a good and decent man, one who cares deeply about his family and friends. In scene after scene of what might strike one initially as entertaining but fairly mundane occurrences, King does that which every tragedian must in order to make the fiction work: he makes us love and admire the central character by making that central character someone like us. In this regard, King's work is closer to contemporary tragedies of the common man than it is to classic Greek and Renaissance models, where the tragic figures are typically of high social station and where, therefore, the fall from greatness to adversity is at least part of the reason we regard their fates as tragic. Although the field in which Louis works, medicine, is accorded great prestige in our society, the gulf between a man like Louis Creed and the reader is not as great as it would be, say, between the "groundling" who paid his penny to watch Shakespeare's tragedies and the aristocrats like Hamlet and Lear whose lives he watched come apart on stage. To the contrary, Louis is kind and approachable. He chooses to work at a university infirmary rather than in a private practice in a large city because he values his family life, and he places wife and children above career and fortune. Ironically, even as we grow more and more materialistic in response to life's demands, we continue to admire idealism in our fictional characters, and Louis's values make him a perfect candidate for our admiration.

It would be a mistake, however, to regard Louis as an overly sentimental person. Rather, as one might expect from a man who practices science, he is rational, intellectually controlled, and scientifically empirical not only in his work but also as much as possible in his personal life. Human responses that lie outside this outlook, that smack in any way of the irrational, he dismisses as cant. He is, in short, a thoroughly modern man. There are many scenes in the first part that illustrate Louis's modern sensibilities even as they confirm our essential liking for his values, but I want to focus on the best example which occurs after his initial visit to the pet cemetery. His daughter, Ellie, begins at that time to question him about death generally and the death of cats specifically, the questions reflecting, he knows, her concern for her own cat, Churchill. Although she tries to frame her questions as indirectly as a five-year-old can, Louis sensitively recognizes what is on her mind, and he tries to address her very real fears. In keeping with his practical sensibilities, his scientific "bias," he decides that honesty is the best policy: "See, there's this thing called *metabolism,*" he explains, "and what metabolism seems to do is tell time. . . . Dogs have a fairly rapid metabolism. The metabolism of human beings is much slower" (49–50). As might be expected, that very sound, very rational answer fails to comfort a little girl. She begins to cry, and her tears bring home to Louis the terrible truth that Ellie's young mind has just grasped, the kind of truth that no amount of scientific explanation can diminish. Hence, Louis is forced to put aside, at least momentarily, the logic of nature and to accept the logic of fear:

He held her and rocked her, believing, rightly or wrongly, that Ellie wept for the very intractability of death, its imperviousness to argument or to a little girl's tears; that she wept over its cruel unpredictability; and that she wept because of the human being's wonderful, deadly ability to translate symbols into conclusions that were either fine and noble or blackly terrifying. If all those animals had died and been buried, then Church could die . . . and be buried; and if that could happen to Church, it could happen to her mother, her father, her baby brother. To herself. Death was a vague idea; the Pet Sematary was real. In the texture of those rude markers were truths which even a child's hands could feel. (51–52)

What can he say at this point? How much will his commitment to rationality allow him to say? "Honey. It happens," he asserts in humane simplicity. "It's part of life" (52). Even this answer, though it does not yield an inch to the irrational, shows his love for her.

This entire scene does not, in itself, depict anything extraordinary; in fact, it is all too ordinary — a father trying to deal with his child's emergent awareness of death. But, then again, King is not really concerned in this first section with the extraordinary of any stripe — realistic or supernatural. Instead, by showing us Louis Creed's mind and heart, King sets us up for the tragic action to follow.

The beginning of that tragic action occurs in the second part, The Micmac Burying Ground, where we watch the painful transformation of Louis Creed from loving father and capable physician to madman. The unhappy descent is prefaced by the narrator's commentary on "horror":

It's probably wrong to believe there can be any limit to the horror which the human mind can experience. On the contrary, it seems that some exponential effect begins to obtain as deeper and deeper darkness falls — as little as one may like to admit it, human experience tends, in a good many ways, to support the idea that when the nightmare grows black enough, horror spawns horror, one coincidental evil begets other, often more deliberate evils, until finally blackness seems to cover everything. And the most terrifying question of all may be just how much horror the human mind can stand and still maintain a wakeful, staring, unrelenting sanity. (229)

Of course, the "horror" to which he refers here is not in the least synonymous with the literary genre of the same name. Rather, it has to do with the very real horror of dealing with the death of a loved one, in this case,

Louis's young son, Gage. Can we feel this sort of horror vicariously in this novel? I think we do, and it is because King has taken his time to acquaint us with the Creeds and thus allow us to feel the weight of the family's suffering. Such suffering is, King suggests, the very stuff of *horror*—the kind that we see in great tragedies, the kind to which none of us is immune.

As Part Two progresses, we watch the painful mental unravelling of Louis Creed, and, because King has laid the emotional groundwork so well, we feel the fear and pity he wants us to feel—pity for a good man's heartbreaking suffering; fear that he will do precisely what we expect him to do, try to resurrect his dead son, try to possess again the child he loved beyond reason. Even though the return of Churchill should have taught him better, even though his former attitude toward death was cool resignation, he now desires to undo again death's victory, to choose a qualitatively altered life over the pain and loss.

In sharp contrast to the slower progress of the first section, Part Two, which begins with Gage's funeral and culminates in Louis's reclaiming of his son's body, moves with rapid fury. In short, violent thrusts, King takes us through Louis's nightmarish experiences: his initial fear that Gage's head is gone; his grief at seeing the little boy dressed so formally; his renewed rage over the boy's death; his solicitous undoing of nature's and the mortician's work, wiping away the moss that covers Gage's face and plucking the cotton from his mouth; and his heartrending speeches to the lifeless child. More important, in an action that clearly recalls his rocking of Ellie earlier to comfort her in the face of death, Louis, who has come a long way from the days when he could so confidently speak the scientist's language, rocks his dead son in his arms and reassures him: "Gage, it will be all right, I swear, Gage, it will be all right, this will end, this is just the night, please, Gage, I love you, Daddy loves you" (343). Earlier he claimed to love Ellie, too, and that was why he could not lie to her about death. Now he lies to himself and to Gage's lifeless ears. Louis knows that things will not be "all right," and that lie is a measure of how much he has changed. As Bernadette Bosky succinctly puts it, "the tragedy of *Pet Sematary* is that Louis Creed begins to follow his intuitions only when he should begin to doubt them" (Bosky, 268).

At this point we must consider a question that is central in any discussion of tragedy: to what extent is the protagonist responsible for the dire circumstances in which he finds himself? Put another way, are Louis's choices primarily responsible for his tragedy? Several commentators have attempted to address this issue, though, interestingly, all of them have expressed ambivalence of some kind or another about the matter. Natalie Schroeder, for instance, writes that "King leaves the ultimate causes of Louis's behavior ambiguous. Either he is completely controlled by the supernatural powers of the burial ground . . . or, in his overwhelming grief at the loss of his child, Louis reaches for any possible way to get his child back – even to committing what he knows is blasphemy, by playing God knowingly this time and resurrecting Gage" (Schroeder, 137). Likewise, Tony Magistrale argues that most of King's characters retain a good deal of free will in their encounters with evil; indeed, "the majority of his protagonists are like Louis Creed: they choose their own course of action" (Magistrale, 62). And yet, in his comparison of *Pet Sematary* with many of Hawthorne's works, Magistrale also admits that Louis, like so many of Hawthorne's youthful idealists, finds evil far more than a mere abstraction. "Instead, he finds his own confrontation with evil to be overwhelming, and like Hawthorne's Eathan Brand and Goodman Brown, he surrenders to its vision of chaos and corruption" (Magistrale, 17). Tim Underwood suggests that, lacking emotional and intellectual resources, Louis will finally become unhinged by grief. He goes on: "Responsibility for the disaster in store for Louis may be laid fairly at his own doorstep, but King has created a character with whom it is easy to identify and sympathize, a basically good man in a bad situation" (Underwood, 309). Finally, Douglas Winter has suggested that Louis Creed was deliberately so named, "his creed – rationality – [being] the flaw that pushes him along the path to destruction" (Winter, 134).

The issue that these critics raise – the matter of choice, of willed human action – is very important. Does Louis, in fact, choose evil, and, if so, does this choice reflect a character flaw? The Greeks called such a flaw *hamartia*, and, as Aristotle pointed out, the flaw was more in the nature of some error or frailty than some great vice or depravity, which would stand in the way of our admiration for the hero (Aristotle, 75–76). This flaw does not cause the circumstance or the eventual catastrophe; it merely conspires with the forces the hero opposes. Oedipus's irascibility, for instance, does not place him in his dire predicament, but it does hasten the tragic revelation in Sophocles' play. In the Renaissance, the tragic flaw came to take on greater and greater importance. In Shakespeare's mature tragedies, for example, coincidence or fate plays a very small role in the cause or outcome of the action while character flaw is all important. In a contemporary domestic tragedy like Miller's *Death of a Salesman,* character defect is all that stands between the tragic and comic visions.

Curiously, although *Pet Sematary* contains much that is familiar to the modern sensibility and is therefore closest to domestic tragedy, its sense of determinism, fate, shares much with classic Greek tragedy. Northrop Frye, Sheridan Baker, and George Perkins provide a useful definition of the form:

Greek tragedy was strongly influenced by the conception of a contract of order and stability in which gods, human society, and nature all participated. An act of aggression (Greek *hybris*. . .) throws this cosmic machinery out of gear, and hence it must make a countermovement to right itself. This countermovement is usually called *nemesis,* and a number of words often translated "fate" . . . also refer to this recovery of order, which makes the tragic action seem inevitable. The conception of a contract is a moral conception, but the particular action called tragic that happens to the hero does not depend on moral status. Aristotle spoke of a tragic *hamartia,* usually translated "flaw," as essential to the hero, but this flaw, despite the fact that *hamartia* is the ordinary New Testament word for sin, is not necessarily a moral defect, but rather a matter of being in a certain place exposed to a tragic action. (Frye, 465)

Like Oedipus, Louis does nothing to cause the tragedy that will grip him—in his case, the death of Gage, the event that sets the tragic machinery in gear. For this reason, I cannot agree with Douglas Winter's suggestion that Louis's rationality "pushes him along the path to destruction." At best, his excessive rationality plays him false in the end, but it is no more responsible for his catastrophe than is Oedipus's irascibility the cause of his woes. If we apply the passage above to his circumstances, Louis's "sins," such as they are, do not cause his sorrows. Rather, that outcome is the result, in part, of being in the wrong place, "exposed to a tragic action." As Victor Pascow's warning to Louis early in the novel suggests, evil will not wait for Louis to choose to act; instead evil will choose him, and, when it does, he will have little opportunity for refusal. Although Pascow entreats Louis not to pass beyond the barrier in the burial ground, the dead student knows that neither his warning nor Louis's free will have much to do with the matter. The deterministic nature of this summons to tragedy is underscored in Pascow's sad prediction, "Your destruction and the destruction of all you love is very near, Doctor" (87).

By the same token, however, the crossing of the barrier to restore Gage's life is the violation of the "contract of order and stability" referred to above, and in this violation Louis's *hamartia* does play a role. What pushes him beyond that barrier, however, is not reason, as Winter suggests, but an emotion that flies in the face of reason—love. In his article on the grotesque in King's fiction, Vernon Hyles maintains that love "becomes distorted in the modern gothic. . . . It is an attempt to create order out of chaos and strength out of weakness, but instead it creates monstrosities" (Hyles, 59). So it is in *Pet Sematary.* The love that Louis earlier showed for his children becomes an obsession to restore Gage's life at any cost; the love that he felt for Jud Crandall has turned into mad suspicion; the love he once had for his wife is subordinated to his dreadful "mission." One of the most disturbing moments in the novel occurs when Louis sits on the ground beside Gage's opened grave and tells his dead son, "Daddy loves you." To be sure, Gage's daddy does love him, but the love he now shows stands in frightening contrast to the feelings that led us to admire

Louis in the first place and in anticipation of the last perversion of love in the novel – Rachel's gravel-voiced "Darling" to her mad husband. As Clive Barker maintains, "in [King's] fiction, even love's power to outwit the darkness is uncertain; the monsters will devour that too, given half a chance" (Barker, 61).

The last part of *Pet Sematary* contains much that King calls "gross out" material – the blood and guts for which the horror novel is infamous. Although the homicidal child-corpse inspires fear in us, it is also the stuff of which Podhoretz speaks when he says that King's books can be enjoyed and then put aside without a thought. What cannot be put aside so easily, however, what lingers in memory long after the gory details have faded is the artist's rendering of the human mind's capacity or incapacity for dealing with death, which Winter calls "the vision of the mindless chaos – indeed malevolence – awaiting at the end of life" (Winter, 135). If *Pet Sematary* can be called art, that is only so because King manages to show us that chaotic vision stripped of all the consolations of philosophy, science, and reason.

As we watch Louis's measured, reasoned world come apart, as we watch his capacity to love turn into crazy obsession, as we watch his sanity melt before our eyes, we pity this man we have come to love, and we fear for him and, more importantly, for ourselves. In some measure, Louis Creed, like other tragic figures, represents all of us, and, though we might try to detach ourselves from his circumstances and his actions, ultimately we cannot do that completely. How safe are our own reasoned lives? Are we, too, not susceptible to the madness of grief, to the cruelty of death? We are, and in that realization lies the tragic horror of *Pet Sematary*.

REFERENCES

Aristotle. *Poetics.* Trans. S. H. Butcher. New York: Hill and Wang, 1961.

Barker, Clive. "Surviving the Ride." In *Kingdom of Fear: The World of Stephen King,* edited by Tim Underwood and Chuck Miller, 59–69. New York: New American Library, 1986; Signet, 1987.

Bosky, Bernadette Lynn. "The Mind's a Monkey: Character and Psychology in Stephen King's Recent Fiction." In *Kingdom of Fear: The World of Stephen King,* edited by Tim Underwood and Chuck Miller, 241–76. New York: New American Library, 1986; New York: Signet, 1987.

Frye, Northrop, Sheridan Baker, and George Perkins. "Tragedy." In *The Harper Handbook to Literature,* 465–67. New York: Harper & Row, 1985.

Hyles, Vernon. "Freaks: The Grotesque as Metaphor in the Works of Stephen King." In *The Gothic World of Stephen King: Landscape of Nightmares,* edited by Gary Hoppenstand and Ray B. Browne, 56–63. Bowling Green, Ohio: Bowling Green State University, Popular Press, 1987.

King, Stephen. *Danse Macabre*. New York: Everest House, 1981; Berkley, 1983.
———. *Pet Sematary*. Garden City, N.Y.: Doubleday, 1983; New York: Signet,
    1984.
Magistrale, Tony. *Landscape of Fear: Stephen King's American Gothic.*Bowling
    Green, Ohio: Bowling Green State University, Popular Press, 1988.
Notkin, Deborah. "Stephen King: Horror and Humanity for Our Time." In *Fear
    Itself: The Horror Fiction of Stephen King*, edited by Tim Underwood and
    Chuck Miller. San Francisco: Underwood-Miller, 1982; New York: Signet,
    1985.
Podhoretz, John. "The Magnificent Revels of Stephen King." *The Wall Street Jour-
    nal*, September 4, 1980, 26.
Schroeder, Natalie. " 'Oz the Gweat and Tewwible' and 'The Other Side': The
    Theme of Death in *Pet Sematary* and *Jitterbug Perfume*." In *The Gothic World
    of Stephen King: Landscape of Nightmares*, edited by Gary Hoppenstand and
    Ray B. Browne, 135–41. Bowling Green, Ohio: Bowling Green State Uni-
    versity, Popular Press, 1987.
Underwood, Tim. "The Skull Beneath the Skin." In *Kingdom of Fear: The World of
    Stephen King*, edited by Tim Underwood and Chuck Miller, 295–311. New
    York: New American Library, 1986; New York: Signet, 1987.
Winter, Douglas E. *Stephen King: The Art of Darkness*. New York: New American
    Library, 1984; rev. ed. 1986.

8

The Mythic Journey in "The Body"

ARTHUR W. BIDDLE

There's a high ritual to all fundamental events, the rites of passage,
the magic corridor where the change happens. (King, 399)

"The magic corridor where the change happens" is the special territory of
Stephen King. This zone of extraordinary power takes many shapes. In *It*
Ben Hanscom maintains a connection to his own adolescent past by returning again and again in memory to the glassed-in corridor that connects the children's wing to the adult section of his hometown library.
Finally, at the end of the novel, this conduit is fully realized when Ben
and the Losers' Club merge past and present in their return to Derry. In
The Talisman the Oatley Tunnel is the symbolic passageway for Jack Sawyer from the protected world of his mother to the depraved town of Oatley. In "The Body" the "magic corridor" for Gordie Lachance and his
friends is the railroad tracks they follow in their search for the dead Ray
Brower.[1]

The fundamental event in "The Body" is the coming into identity of the
young hero, Gordon Lachance. From Friday afternoon until Sunday
morning at the end of August 1960, Gordie undergoes a series of trials
that bring him to selfhood, to identity both as a young man and as a
writer. The narrative pattern that King employs is the archetypal rite of
passage that marks the transition from one life stage to another.[2]

In a recent interview, Stephen King acknowledged the influence on his
work of mythologist Joseph Campbell: "I was particularly taken by the
book *The Hero with a Thousand Faces*" (Magistrale, *Stephen King*, ms. 5).
That influence shapes the structure and major themes of King's tale of the

journey of four boys on the brink of adolescence. Their adventure, especially that of the central hero Gordie, recapitulates the timeless rites of
passage that order human experience. In his *The Hero with a Thousand
Faces,* Campbell summarizes the pattern:

The standard path of the mythological adventure of the hero is a magnification of
the formula represented in the rites of passage: *separation—initiation—return:*
which might be named the nuclear monomyth. A hero ventures forth from the
world of common day into a region of supernatural wonder: fabulous forces are
there encountered and a decisive victory is won: the hero comes back from this
mysterious adventure with the power to bestow boons on his fellow man. (30)

The modern reader has become accustomed to viewing the journeys of
Jason or Ulysses (both Homer's and Joyce's versions) or even Jesus in
these terms. But it may seem a bit pretentious to apply the mythic pattern to the experiences of four twelve-year-olds in the Maine of 1960.
Critic Northrop Frye recognizes the modern author's difficulty in incorporating "a mythical structure into realistic fiction" (136). The solution is
what Frye calls "displacement," essentially deemphasizing and disguising
the mythic elements in order to achieve plausibility (136–138). King accomplishes this displacement with great skill: the story of "The Body"
works for the contemporary reader as a nice bit of adventure that seldom
strains credulity. Yet, the underlying structure is clearly that of Campbell's monomyth: "a separation from the world, a penetration to some
source of power, and a life-enhancing return" (Campbell, 36).

THE KINGDOM OF CASTLE ROCK

The "kingdom" of Castle Rock is a drought-stricken, heat-beaten wasteland. The soil is barren; no garden has produced a crop in this the driest
and hottest summer since 1907. The metaphoric ruler of this land—King
of Castle Rock—is Gordie's father, a figure of abject futility as he stands
amidst the dust of his ruined garden, "making useless rainbows in the air"
with his watering hose (King, 324). He looks "sad and tired and used. He
was sixty-three years old, old enough to be my grandfather," Gordie observes (305). His powers have deserted him, and as a result his entire
realm suffers a corresponding loss of vitality. The older Lachance is a
modern version of an ancient figure—the Fisher King. Jessie L. Weston
remarks, "the intimate relation at one time was held to exist between the
ruler and his land; a relation mainly dependent upon the identification of
the [Fisher] King with the Divine principle of Life and Fertility" (*From Ritual to Romance,* 114). Mr. Lachance and Castle Rock are in death's grip.
    Reinforcing this theme of sterility in the Kingdom is Gordie's mother,
who has suffered alternating periods of fertility and barrenness. After

three miscarriages she was told she would never have a child; five years later she became pregnant with Dennis. Ten years after that at age forty-two she conceived Gordie, whose birth is unusual: "the doctor had to use forceps to yank me out" (306). His parents have told him this story many times: "They wanted me to think I was a special delivery from God" (305).

Special delivery from God or not, Gordie was always ignored in favor of his older, more talented brother Dennis. When Denny was alive, Gordie felt like Ralph Ellison's Invisible Man: "Nobody ever notices him at all unless he fucks up. People look right through him" (306). With Denny's death in a jeep accident, his parents behave as if they have nothing to live for. The senior Lachance is a king without an heir: "He'd lost a son in April and a garden in August." When his father notices Gordie at all, it is only to attack his friends as "a thief and two feebs," and by implication to put Gordie into the category of social misfit (305). Gordie accounts for his mother's distracted behavior by flatly pointing out that "her only kid was dead" (304). He sees himself as the true target of the ultimate putdown, "Did your mother ever have any kids that lived?" (398).

One result of this treatment at the hands of his parents is his fear of his brother's ghost, which he is sure lurks in Denny's closet. In his dreams Denny's battered and bloody corpse emerges from his closet and confronts him: "It should have been you, Gordon. It should have been you" (309). These dreams are the product of the guilt Gordie feels for being alive. Subconsciously he feels that his survival somehow makes him responsible for Denny's death as well as for his parents' grief. Gordie dreads that "it" might yet become him, accounting in part for the power that Vern's tale of the discovery of Ray Brower's body exerts over him. These fears move out of his dreams and into his writing – "Stud City," "The Revenge of Lard Ass Hogan," and the Le Dio stories – a literature of guilt and death.

Joseph Campbell provides some insight into the role Gordie is to play in the ensuing adventure. The hero of the monomyth "and/or the world in which he finds himself suffers from a symbolical deficiency" (Campbell, 37). In "The Body" that deficiency is two-fold: both personal and societal. Gordie experiences a grave crisis of identity, not so much an uncertainty about who he is, but that he is. If no one acknowledges your presence, do you really exist? Gordie's very being is called into question. Thus as soon as Vern tells about his brother's discovery of the body, Gordie empathizes with the dead boy: "I felt a little sick, imagining that kid so far away from home, scared to death" (300). His ego is so undeveloped that he needs to view the body of young Ray Brower to be sure it is not he himself who has died. He also needs to acknowledge the existence of death in life, something he was unable to do at Denny's funeral. Ray Brower's body offers a concretization of Gordie's many fears. Only through this quest can Gordie begin to deal with the shadow that hangs over all our lives.

The second symbolical deficiency inheres in the world in which he lives, a parched and infertile wasteland, like the land of the Fisher King. On the surface, the sterility of Castle Rock is a result of the prolonged drought and extraordinary heat of the summer of 1960. But at a deeper level, it is the aridity of a community that cannot love. Castle Rock is a place where parents maim their children by burning their ears, bruising their faces, or destroying their spirits. Where teachers steal and shift the blame to their students by lying. Where shopkeepers cheat their innocent customers. And where public employees train their dogs to attack children. The destructive machine appetites of Castle Rock are shown throughout the book—from Milo's junkyard of American waste to the pollution of the Castle River to the life-threatening train itself bearing down on the boys from the direction of the town. The true purpose of Gordie's journey, then, is to remedy these two deficiencies of self-identity and sterility of the kingdom, although he is aware of only the first and that but inchoately.

Twelve-year-old Gordon Lachance is, admittedly, an unlikely candidate for hero. But that shouldn't be a total surprise. The archetypal hero of the monomyth always fulfills a pattern according to the nature and the requirements of the particular narrative. Campbell describes two variations on the type of the hero and the fruit of his adventure:

Typically the hero of the fairy tale achieves a domestic, microcosmic triumph, and the hero of myth a world-historical, macrocosmic triumph. Whereas the former—the youngest or despised child who becomes the master of extraordinary powers—prevails over his personal oppressors, the latter brings back from his adventure the means for the regeneration of his society as a whole. (37–38)

Like the hero of the fairy tale, Gordie is the youngest and the despised child who confronts a variety of personal oppressors: his parents, the storekeeper, the dumpkeeper and his dog, the older boys. Only by mastering these trials will Gordie be able to achieve identity. But as the son of the King, he is also called upon to redeem the realm; through his tests he will develop the extraordinary powers required to regenerate his society. By tracing the course of his quest, we may come to understand the achievement of these prizes.

THE CALL TO ADVENTURE

"You guys want to go see a dead body?" Vern Tessio sounds the call to adventure by bringing news of the discovery of the body of a boy missing for three days. By announcing the challenge to find the dead Ray Brower, twelve-year-old Vern acts as herald who calls the hero to the adventure. Chris Chambers supports the call and embellishes it: "We can find the

body and report it! We'll be on the news!" (301). Gordie's three friends —
Chris Chambers, Vern Tessio, and Teddy Duchamp — have also been
scarred by the adult world and denied its love. The boys see this as an
opportunity to achieve attention and perhaps even affection.

Campbell explains that the call "signifies that destiny has summoned
the hero and transferred his spiritual center of gravity from within the
pale of his society to a zone unknown" (58). As we shall see, Gordie is
challenged to an adventure which promises a spiritual transformation
through a dying and a re-birth. Jungian analyst Erich Neumann supports
the psychological import of this type of archetypal experience: "The
dragon fight of the first period [onset of puberty] begins with the encounter with the unconscious and ends with the heroic birth of the ego" (415).
In accepting the call, Gordie (accompanied by Chris, Vern, and Teddy)
enters on a quest that, unlike their existence in Castle Rock, is life-confirming and morally unambiguous. "We knew exactly who we were and
exactly where we were going" (335).

Although their preparations are scant (mainly concocting stories to
cover their absence), they sense intuitively the significance of the journey
ahead. It is high noon when they set off. The older Gordie, sitting at his
computer twenty years later, reflects: "I'll never forget that moment, no
matter how old I get" (328).

CROSSING THE FIRST THRESHOLD

Leaving behind the security of home, the boys walk through the afternoon heat until they come to the dump, that repository of "all the American things that get empty, wear out, or just don't work any more" (332).
Situated on the edge of town and populated by a vaguely demonic assort-
ment of rats, woodchucks, seagulls, and stray dogs, it marks the limits of
their known world. The dump functions as what Campbell calls the
threshold, representing "regions of the unknown" that are "free fields for
the projection of unconscious content" (82). Poised on the brink of puberty, the boys have outgrown their old haunts and pastimes. To develop,
they must move forward. But first they must penetrate the threshold to
the source of power.[3]

Barring the way are the threshold guardians, Milo Pressman, the
dumpkeeper, and his dog, Chopper. Campbell points out that the watch-
man functions as the guardian of established bounds of consciousness:
"And yet — it is only by advancing beyond those bounds, provoking the destructive other aspects of the same power, that the individual passes,
either alive or in death, into a new zone of experience" (82). Reminiscent
of Cerberus, the three-headed watchdog of the underworld encountered
by Aeneas, Chopper is "the most feared and least seen dog in Castle Rock"
(333). Legends abound. Chopper, it was said, had been trained not only to

attack, but to attack specific parts of the body on command from Milo. The command every boy dreaded to hear was "Chopper! Sic! Balls!" (333).

As in the subsequent episode with the leeches, the boys' paramount fear is emasculation. The pubescent boy, unconfirmed in his sexuality, is sensitive to every threat, real or imagined. Their town and families have symbolically emasculated them. And the boys' frequent teasing about being a "pussy" or being "queer" and the boasting of penile size impress the centrality of this concern to all of them. Gordie doesn't even see Chopper as he races for the fence and safety, but he feels him gaining. Like Cerberus, that other threshold guardian, Chopper is perceived as a hound from Hell: "shaking the earth, blurting fire out of one distended nostril and ice out of the other, dripping sulphur from his jaws" (342). It is only when Gordie has scaled the fence and looks back through its mesh from a place of safety that he actually sees that Chopper is a rather ordinary mongrel of medium size: "My first lesson in the vast difference between myth and reality" (342). Paradoxically, though, King's narrative (as well as Jung's and Campbell's world views) shows that myth and reality are not poles apart. Indeed reality recapitulates myth. So that even though Chopper may not be truly a hound of Hell, he fulfills the function of threshold guardian perfectly well. And as both the reader and Gordie will soon discover, the journey to see the body emphasizes the similarities, rather than the differences, "between myth and reality."

Gordie's experience at the dump allows him passage beyond the realm of ordinary existence in Castle Rock, through trial, to new possibilities. With his friends he leaves the dump/threshold much as Ulysses departed from the Cyclops, hurling imprecations. The threshold gained, the adventurers move into unfamiliar territory and new tests of their will.

"THE MAGIC CORRIDOR"

Gordie and his friends have now completed the first phase of the rite of passage: separation from the known world. As they seek to penetrate to a source of power thus far denied them, they, and especially Gordie, will have to pass even more severe tests. Although Gordie is accompanied by three friends, they play distinctly supporting roles as far as the mythic quest is concerned. They are reminiscent of J.R.R. Tolkien's merry band of Hobbits who support Frodo on his adventures in Middle Earth. Chris Chambers, of course, does stand out as Gordie's special friend and guide, more like Tolkien's Sam or Dante's Virgil than Don Quixote's Sancho Panza. (Their relationship and the special kind of love they share is too rich a theme to explore here.) But though Chris and the others participate in the communal tests, only Gordie is tested alone. He is the singular hero challenged to relieve the symbolical deficiencies of self and society through an act of initiation.

The mature narrator characterizes the rites of passage as "the magic corridor where change happens." "Our corridor," he continues, "was those twin rails, and we walked between them, just hopping along toward whatever this was supposed to mean" (399). Those twin rails pose a more-than-symbolic threat, though, when the boys must cross a railroad trestle over the Castle River. Its height—fifty feet above the river—is dizzying. Its length—well over a hundred yards—is terrifying because the time of the next train remains unknown. The will to face the danger is perceived as a test of masculinity: "Any pussies here?" Chris asks (353). Gordie accepts the dare "and as I said it some guy pole-vaulted in my stomach. He dug his pole all the way into my balls, it felt like, and ended up sitting astride my heart" (354). To Gordie, the fear of death is perceived largely as a sexual threat. Chris and Teddy lead the way, followed by Vern and then Gordie far behind.

Gordie is halfway across when he has to stop to calm his jitters and overcome his dizziness: "that was when I had my first and last psychic flash" (355). He realizes that the train is coming and that he will surely be killed if he is caught on the trestle. Fear grips him, he urinates involuntarily, time stops. Transcendent terror causes mind and body to disconnect. He is unable to move. "An image of Ray Brower, dreadfully mangled and thrown into a ditch somewhere like a ripped-open laundry bag, reeled before my eyes" (356). The gut-wrenching fear that Gordie felt when he first heard of the boy's death was premonitory. In his mind's eye he is reliving Ray Brower's fate, he is *becoming* Ray Brower. That thought breaks the spell, freeing Gordie to rise from the railbed like "a boy in underwater slow motion" (356).

Gordie never saw the train, just as he never saw Chopper during his pursuit. The train, Chopper, the mills of Castle Rock, the fate that took Dennis away—all seem larger than life, like Ace and his gang of bigger boys. One purpose of Gordie's journey is to humanize these mythic enemies by obtaining control over them.

When the four find a cool, shady spot where they can rest and recover, Gordie admits his fear,"I was fuckin *petrified*." But in facing that fear Gordie gains a new-found strength. "My body felt warm, exercised, at peace with itself. Nothing in it was working crossgrain to anything else. I was alive and glad to be" (359). Through his brush with death he has discovered a new sense of wholeness and well-being. Twice he has been pursued, once by a creature of nature, Chopper, and once by a creature of technology, the train. Twice he has confronted the worst fears of his subconscious and the threat to his emerging ego and survived. In the next test he is actually touched by death.

THE DARK NIGHT OF THE SOUL

The group walk only a mile beyond the trestle before making camp for the night. After an improvised supper and a manly cigaret, they lie in

their bedrolls talking about things twelve-year-olds talk about: cars, baseball, teachers. Gordie thinks about how different nightfall is in the woods
with no lights and "no mothers' voices" calling their children to the safety
of home. Teddy tells about witnessing a near-drowning at White's Beach.
What they don't talk about is Ray Brower, but Gordie thinks about him,
"so alone and defenseless. . . . If something wanted to eat on him, it
would. His mother wasn't there to stop that from happening" (383). A necessity of every boy's journey to adulthood is leaving forever the comfort-
ing bosom of the mother. Gordie feels the pain of that separation and the
danger to which it exposes him; he does not yet understand the potential
gains of the break: freedom and power.

When Gordie finally falls asleep, he has the first of two swimming
dreams: he and Denny are bodysurfing at Harrison State Park. The
dream is interrupted as he awakens, confused and disoriented, unsure of
where he is or what woke him. Then he hears a drawn-out unearthly
scream. Everyone is awake now and speculating on the source: a bird? a
wildcat? Ray's ghost?

Again Gordie dreams of swimming, this time with Chris at White's
Beach, the scene of the near-drowning Teddy had told of earlier in the
evening. As the boys swim out over their heads, one of their teachers
floats over on an inflatable raft and orders Chris to give Robert Frost's
"Mending Wall" by rote. In despair he begins to recite, then his head goes
under water. He rises again, pleads with Gordie to help him, and sinks
beneath the surface once more.

Looking into the clear water I could see two bloated, naked corpses holding his
ankles. One was Vern and the other was Teddy, and their open eyes were as blank
and pupilless as the eyes of Greek statues. Their small pre-pubescent penises
floated limply up from their distended bellies like albino strands of kelp. Chris's
head broke water again. He held one hand up limply to me and voiced a screaming, womanish cry that rose and rose, ululating in the hot summer air. I looked
wildly toward the beach but nobody had heard. The lifeguard . . . just went on
smiling down at a girl in a red bathing suit (388–89).

As Chris is dragged under a last time, his eyes and hands implore Gordie's help. "But instead of diving down and trying to save him, I stroked
madly for the shore" (388). Before he can reach safety, though, he feels
the grip of "a soft, rotted, implacable hand" pulling him down (388). The
dream ends when he is shaken into wakefulness by Teddy's grip on his
leg.

Every element of this dream either derives from Gordie's recent experiences and present fears or presages events yet to come. The dream again
links Gordie with Ray Brower, the child as helpless victim cornered by
forces larger than himself. The corpses of Vern and Teddy grow from

Chris's earlier observation that "your friends drag you down. . . . They're like drowning guys that are holding onto your legs. You can't save them. You can only drown with them" (380). Their small limp penises reflect both their physical immaturity and Gordie's fears about his sexual adequacy. Their corpses also foreshadow their deaths at an early age, although Gordie couldn't have foreseen that. And Chris will be murdered when he is only twenty-four years old. His imploring figure reflects his reliance on Gordie, as an understanding friend in the present and as a mentor in the college prep courses in high school. His thin womanish scream is the unexplained cry they heard earlier in the night. Fearful for his own life, Gordie does not dive down to save Chris. Instead, he looks to the adult world on the beach for help. In the person of the lifeguard charged with protecting swimmers, that world ignores Gordie's pleas, just as the adult world of Castle Rock has failed to heed the cries of its children. As Gordie himself is being dragged under water by "a soft, rotted, implacable hand," he is awakened by Teddy; it is time to stand his tour of guard duty.

This dream represents the first stage of Gordie's night sea journey, an archetypal pattern symbolic of rebirth. Briefly, the archetype as employed by Virgil, Dante, and the author of the Book of Jonah among others, sees the hero making a perilous journey, usually by night, into the depths of the sea or a dark cavern. He may be swallowed by a sea monster. Joseph Campbell characterizes the hero's perilous journey as a descent "into the crooked lanes of his own spiritual labyrinth" (101). Entering a cavern, the belly of a whale, or the depths of the sea, the hero leaves behind the upper world of light and life to confront his own death. Jungian analyst Erich Neumann explains that puberty is a time

of rebirth, and its symbolism is that of the hero who regenerates himself through fighting the dragon. All the rites characteristic of this period have the purpose of renewing the personality through a night sea journey, when the spiritual or conscious principle conquers the mother dragon, and the tie to the mother and to childhood, and also to the unconscious, is severed. (408)

The second part of the archetypal pattern, the dragon fight, will take place the next day.

During the rest of the night Gordie passes in and out of consciousness. Finally, he awakens from a light sleep to discover that dawn has broken. He is savoring his solitude when he notices a deer standing less than thirty feet away, looking at him. The impact of the sight nearly overwhelms him: "My heart went up into my throat. . . . I couldn't have moved if I had wanted to" (389). When he perceives the deer to be looking at him "serenely," Gordie projects into her being, "seeing a kid with his hair in a sleep-scarecrow of whirls and many-tined cowlicks" (389). It is as if "he" (some part of him) has moved out of his body and looks at that twelve-year-old standing there. The doe emphasizes her trust of Gordie by confidently crossing the tracks and beginning to feed. "She didn't look back at me and didn't need to" (389). They coexist in a state of perfect trust and harmony. The deer remains until an approaching train frightens her off.

"What I was looking at was some sort of gift, something given with a carelessness that was appalling" (389). For the psychic meaning of this remarkable gift, we look to the symbolic values of the deer. The opening lines of the Jerusalem Bible version of Psalm 42 equate the deer with the human spirit: "As a doe longs for running streams, so longs my soul for you, my God." Cirlot's *A Dictionary of Symbols* doesn't treat *doe*, but identifies an analogous animal, the gazelle, as "an emblem of the soul" and of "the persecution of the passions and the aggressive, self-destructive aspect of the unconscious" (110). Another related animal, the stag, is said to represent "the way of solitude and purity" (294). Interestingly, the same source notes that the stag is "the secular enemy of the serpent," a variation on which will figure prominently a little later in the adventure. What this gift seems to signify is the awakening of Gordie's spiritual nature. The deer is his soul, which he had not known before. Although the boy doesn't understand all this, he does intuit the deer's import: "for me it was the best part of the trip, the cleanest part, and it was the moment I found myself returning to, almost helplessly, when there was trouble in my life" (390). We realize that this state of grace is not carelessly given at all, but earned by Gordie's inner readiness. An awakened soul is essential for the tests that are yet to come. When Gordie returns to the camp and the other boys, he doesn't tell them about the deer. This is his secret.

THE DRAGON FIGHT

A final obstacle stands between the boys and the object of their quest, between Gordie and the development of his ego. That obstacle is the dragon who guards the treasure, denying access to all comers. In his discussion of the child archetype, Carl Jung asserts that "the threat to one's inmost self from dragons and serpents points to the danger of the newly acquired consciousness being swallowed up again by the instinctive psyche, the unconscious" (*Archetypes*, 166). Gordie's recent experiences of individuation—crossing the threshold, escaping the train, seeing the deer—have strengthened and developed his conscious ego and his spiritual dimension. But he is not yet secure. As Neumann pointed out earlier, the dragon must be slain in order to sever the tie "to the mother and to childhood, and also to the unconscious" (408). As dragons are scarce in Maine, the leeches infesting the beaver pond must function as a displaced dragon, just as the pond itself is a continuation of Gordie's sea journey into the unconscious.

Gordie's dreams have anticipated this swim and warned of the threat that the unconscious poses to the developing consciousness. When the four boys emerge from the pond after their swim, they discover their bodies covered with bloodsuckers. Gordie and Chris take turns plucking the repulsive creatures off the other's body. Then Gordie sees "the grand-daddy of all of them clinging to my testicles, its body swelled to four times its normal size" (393).

Jung relates a patient's dream that is remarkably like Gordie's situation. In the dream "a snake shot out of a cave and bit him [Jung's patient] in the genital region. This dream occurred at the moment when the patient was convinced of the truth of analysis and was beginning to free himself from the bonds of his mother-complex" (Campbell, 11). The snake-dragon-leech, by threatening Gordie's sexuality, is attempting to prevent matura-tion and the subsequent ego independence it represents.

Terror-stricken, Gordie can't bring himself to touch the leech and ap-peals to Chris to remove it. But Chris cannot help. Gordie must confront the dragon himself. "I reached down again and picked it off and it burst between my fingers. My own blood ran across my palm and inner wrist in a warm flood. I began to cry" (394). Although Gordie has killed the leech, he himself is wounded. The leech, the chthonic symbol of the sub-terranean world of the unconscious, appears to have achieved mastery even in the moment of its own death. Gordie faints, that is, he loses his consciousness, and falls to the ground as if dead. Symbolically the wound is fatal. This is as it must be: Gordie has to die in order to be reborn. The sacrificial blood that he sheds is in the cause of his own growth and of the redemption of his society. Neumann explains that "the transformation of the hero through the dragon fight is a transfiguration, a glorification, in-deed an apotheosis, the central feature of which is the birth of a higher mode of personality" (149).

That transfiguration marks for Gordie a significant step in his passage from childhood to maturity, establishing an ego consciousness indepen-dent of his parents. This development is both a fruit of his quest and a precondition for the successful completion of his journey which he re-sumes when he regains consciousness.

THE DISCOVERY OF THE BODY

As the four boys approach their destination, the weather begins to change. The arrival of storm clouds signals the end of three months of bright clear skies. The boys' shadows grow "fuzzy and ill-defined" (400). Then the sun is blotted out: "I looked down and saw that my shadow had disappeared entirely" (401). To Jung the shadow is the primitive, instinc-tive part of the psyche. Gordie stands poised on the brink of discovery. Elemental forces are gathering to punctuate the climax of the adventure.

A cosmic blue-white fireball races along the track, passes the boys, and then disappears without a trace.

When Vern, the herald who called the adventure, spots Ray Brower's pale white hand sticking out of the underbrush, the skies open, loosing a downpour. "It was as if we were being rebuked for our discovery, and it was frightening" (404). Rebuked perhaps, but the rain marks the end of the drought that has oppressed the land for months. The consequences for the life of the community of Gordie's long journey have already begun.

In death Brower is defenseless against the chthonic forces: black ants crawl over his hand and face, a beetle creeps out of his mouth and stalks across his cheek. Gordie is sickened, but what makes a stronger impression still is that Ray's feet are bare. His sneakers are caught in some brambles several feet away. The realization hits Gordie hard: "The train had knocked him out of his Keds just as it had knocked the life out of his body" (404). The Keds are a powerful symbol for Gordie – of youth, of life, of the physical journey itself. He reflects on what death means for a twelve year old, what he wouldn't get to do, ordinary things like pulling a girl's braid in homeroom or wearing out the eraser on his pencil. Through the agency of a pair of filthy tennis shoes, Gordie finally is able to transmute death from an abstraction to a concretion and to understand it as a denial of life.

When Ace Merrill, Eyeball Chambers, and their gang arrive to claim the body as their prize, Chris and Gordie warn them off. Gordie senses the unfairness of it: "as if their easy way was the right way, the only way. They had come in cars" (407). The older boys are disqualified from victory, from achieving the goal, not only because they took the easy way but also because they have broken the law in stealing the car. They represent negative forces that would usurp the treasure.

Ace Merrill orders Gordie to be sensible and relinquish the treasure and credit to his gang. Gordie's scorn is as great as his courage: "Suck my fat one, you cheap dime-store hood" (409). His assertion of masculine dominance enrages Ace, who starts toward him intending to break both his arms. Only through Chris's introduction of a weapon, his father's pistol, is Gordie spared an immediate beating. Firing the gun first into the air and then at Ace's feet, Chris drives off the usurpers. That Chris, not Gordie, uses the gun is striking, but is in accord with Chris's status as the leader of the gang, war chief of the tribe. Gordie's role has always been that of the shaman, the story-telling medicine man in touch with the spirit world.

The big boys driven off, Chris and Gordie discuss what to do with the body. The strength of Chris's desire to carry it out of the woods suggests the depth of his need for approval and acceptance by his parents and the entire adult world. Finally, he is persuaded by his friend not to risk potential trouble if the big boys somehow implicated them in Brower's death.

As they leave, Gordie reflects on Ray Brower and mortality: "He was a boy our age, he was dead, and I rejected the idea that anything about it could be natural" (417). Why? Probably because he felt he could guard against extra-natural causes; it was the natural ones that sneak up on you. The berry pail haunts him, though. Throughout his adventure Gordie has projected onto the missing boy. His own sense of self was so fragile that he had to see the body to be sure it wasn't himself. This confusion is evident in the mature writer's reflection: "That boy was *me*, I think. And the thought which follows, chilling me like a dash of cold water, is: *Which boy do you mean?*" (419). The matter is still not entirely settled. We see the twenty-two-year-old Gordie exploring similar themes in "Stud City." Even the thirty-four-year-old writer is troubled from time to time. He remembers the berry pail and thinks about finding it: "it's mostly just the idea of holding that pail in my two hands, I guess—as much a symbol of my living as his dying, proof that I really do know which boy it was—which boy of the five of us" (419).

THE RETURN

Unlike the journey to the body, the return is uneventful. Retracing their steps, the boys cross the trestle and pass through the dump without incident. The town is still asleep when they arrive at five o'clock on Sunday morning, a propitious time for a return or a rebirth. Chris needs confirmation of their adventure: "We did it, didn't we? It was worth it, wasn't it?" "Sure it was," Gordie assures him (421). The parting from Vern and Teddy is routine, but between Chris and Gordie there is an undercurrent of things left unsaid: "I wanted to say something more to Chris but didn't know how to. . . . Speech destroys the functions of love, I think" (422–423).

After the two boys part, there remains for Gordie one final act to conclude the adventure: the ritual cleansing and dressing of wounds. Standing at the kitchen sink, he scrubs his body all over with especial attention to his crotch. The mark left by the leech is fading, but a tiny scar will always serve as a reminder of his struggle.

What has Gordie's *agon* accomplished? At the onset of the journey two kinds of deficiencies required remedy. The first was Gordie's own psychic need to defeat his personal oppressors and to grow beyond the bounds of childhood. As he recapitulated the archetypal rites of passage, he prevailed over Milo and Chopper, the leeches, and the older boys. He achieved his goal of discovering the body and helped prevent the negative forces represented by the older boys from claiming it. He confronted the loss of his brother and his own worst fears of death and emasculation.

He forged bonds of affection and mutual support with Chris. He moved beyond childhood and mother in the discovery of his spirit and the development of his own ego.

The second deficiency that Gordie was called upon to remedy was the sterility and lack of love in the kingdom of Castle Rock. Here, the fruit of his journey would appear less than "a world-historical, macrocosmic triumph" (Campbell, 38). His actions have not created a revolution of fertility and love. Yet Gordie's initiation does have results that impact on the larger community. When Gordie and his companions arrive at Ray Brower's body, the skies open and rain pours down for the first time in three months, ending the devastating drought that has plagued the land. When Gordie and Chris stand up to Ace Merrill's gang, they reestablish a rule of justice that had been lost in Castle Rock. And Gordie's actions testify to a truth forgotten by the adult world—the truth of love and caring. His concern for the lost body of Ray Brower initiates his quest. His love for Chris closes it and enables the one-time loser to succeed in a college prep course in high school and go on to college and graduate school.

But it is as writer that Gordie can have the greatest influence on his world.[4] In a 1989 interview Tony Magistrale asked about the use of writers as protagonists in several of King's recent books.

Magistrale: But it also seems to me that in the many books which feature writers and writing you have endowed these characters with certain powers. . . .

King: Well, we do have powers. The guy in *The Dark Half* says that writers, actors, and actresses are the only recognized mediums of our society. (Magistrale, *Stephen King,* ms. 16–17)

The storyteller is shaman, then, the one in touch with the world of spirit. His function is to reveal that world to his people.

The early stories ("Stud City" and "The Revenge of Lard Ass Hogan") show the suffering and the guilt and the need for retribution experienced by the young Gordon Lachance. The final story, told by the mature narrator, of four twelve-year-olds venturing along the railroad tracks to see a dead body—that story demonstrates the power of honesty, courage, and love. The great boon that Gordie Lachance brings back from his quest are those values that offer redemption for his society.

NOTES

1. A number of people assisted in the development of this chapter. Shellie Levine, Ph.D., Burlington psychotherapist; Brother Chrysostom, O.C.S.O., Abbey of Gethsemani; and my editor Tony Magistrale shared information and responded to drafts. Bill Paden, of the religion department at the University of Vermont, launched my study of Carl Jung, although he shouldn't be blamed for

any errors of understanding or application. Through lively and penetrating discussion, students in several American literature classes at the University of Vermont helped me develop my understanding of "The Body."

2. Leonard G. Heldreth discusses the journey motif and rites of passage. See his "Viewing 'The Body': King's Portrait of the Artist as Survivor," in *The Gothic World of Stephen King* (Bowling Green, Ohio: Bowling Green State University, 1987). The journey motif is also treated by Douglas E. Winter in *Stephen King: The Art of Darkness* (New York: New American Library, 1984).

3. King's literary ancestor Nathaniel Hawthorne also understood the power of the threshold; for him it was the forest where Hester and Dimmesdale could meet and where Young Goodman Brown would confront his shadow. For a fuller discussion, see Tony Magistrale, "Hawthorne's Woods Revisited: Stephen King's *Pet Sematary*," *Nathaniel Hawthorne Review* 14 (1988): 9–13.

4. For an exploration of the relationship between writing and sexuality that the narrator establishes in the novella, as well as the role that writing plays in Gordie's search for identity, see Leonard G. Heldreth's "Viewing 'The Body': King's Portrait of the Artist as Survivor."

REFERENCES

Campbell, Joseph. *The Hero with a Thousand Faces.* Bollingen Series XVII. Princeton, N.J.: Princeton University Press, 1949.

Cirlot, J. E. *A Dictionary of Symbols.* New York: Philosophical Library, 1962.

Frye, Northrop. *Anatomy of Criticism.* Princeton, N.J.: Princeton University Press, 1957.

Heldreth, Leonard G. "Viewing 'The Body': King's Portrait of the Artist as Survivor." In *The Gothic World of Stephen King,* edited by Gary Hoppenstand and Ray B. Browne. Bowling Green, Ohio: Bowling Green State University Popular Press, 1987.

Jung, C. G. *The Structure and Dynamics of the Psyche.* Bollingen Series XX. New York: Pantheon, 1960.

———. *The Archetypes and the Collective Unconscious,* 2nd ed. Bollingen Series XX. Princeton, N.J.: Princeton University Press, 1969.

King, Stephen. "The Body." In *Different Seasons.* New York: New American Library, 1982.

Magistrale, Tony. "Hawthorne's Woods Revisited: Stephen King's *Pet Sematary.*" *Nathaniel Hawthorne Review* 14 (1988): 9–13.

———. *Stephen King, The Second Decade:* Danse Macabre *to* The Dark Half. New York: Macmillan, forthcoming, 1992.

Neumann, Erich. *The Origins and History of Consciousness.* Bollingen Series XLII. Princeton, N.J.: Princeton University Press, 1970.

Weston, Jessie L. *From Ritual to Romance.* Garden City, N.Y.: Doubleday/Anchor, 1957.

Winter, Douglas E. *Stephen King: The Art of Darkness.* New York: New American Library, 1984.

9

"Everybody Pays . . . Even for Things They Didn't Do": Stephen King's Pay-out in the Bachman Novels

JAMES F. SMITH

> Thinking about writing under a pseudonym was like thinking about being invisible. . . . The more I played with the idea, the more I felt that I would be . . . well . . . reinventing myself.
>
> — Thad Beaumont

In an Author's Note to *The Dark Half,* Stephen King acknowledges his debt to Richard Bachman without whom the novel could not have been written. Neither King nor Thad Beaumont was the first writer to publish under a pseudonym, but in many other ways his doing so has challenged and changed the conventions of authorship. With total sales, name recognition, and popularity rivalling the success of McDonald's hamburgers, King has become a household word. And just as the American public has a seemingly insatiable hunger for fast food, readers eagerly await the next Stephen King novel to devour as they propel it to the top of best-seller lists. There is no question that he has found a nearly invincible formula to spark the interest of the public. At the risk of oversimplification, let us say that King presents immediately recognizable people with whom the audience can identify and places them in extraordinary and terrifying circumstances. His themes tap the motherlode of the American psyche and mine it to the limit, usually through the juxtaposition of the Apollonian rationality of modern life with the Dionysian chaos and dread of natural or supernatural evil.

But like Thad Beaumont, King, too, has a "dark half"; and in many ways Richard Bachman, like George Stark, is "not a very nice guy." Readers who suspected all along that Bachman was King had good reason: recurring settings, oblique and obvious references to King's characters and incidents, recognizable language patterns, black humor. But most of all, the Bachman novels offer the most stark (no pun intended) versions of a standard Stephen King motif—the pay-out. No one exits a Stephen King narrative unscathed; this is especially true of the characters who populate the world according to Richard Bachman.

In *A Farewell to Arms* Ernest Hemingway asserts, "The world breaks everyone and afterward many are strong at the broken places. But those that will not break it kills. It kills the very good and the very gentle and the very brave impartially" (249). This naturalistic vision is at the heart of the Bachman cosmos in *Rage* (1977), *The Long Walk* (1979), *Roadwork* (1981), *The Running Man* (1982), *Thinner* (1984), and even *Misery* (1987), a book intended to be a Bachman before the cover was blown (discussed elsewhere in this collection). *If* a victory over evil or over circumstance is won, and in the Bachman books victory is always questionable, it comes at a great price. In fact, because Bachman's world tends to be naturalistic and the source of evil, both internal and external, tends to be within the realm of natural causes and circumstances, the cost may be seen as greater, and ultimately more wrenching, than that exacted in any other King novel with the possible exceptions of *The Stand* and *Cujo*.

Rage was written when King was still in high school, and it reflects his understanding of adolescent *angst* that would mark his first published novel, *Carrie*. Charlie Decker, scarred by his inability to feel part of his peer group and by his stormy relationship with his father, loses control: "My brain had checked to the power, so to speak; the little guy wearing the Napoleon hat inside was showing aces and betting them" (Bachman, 25). When he returns to his algebra class, he contemplates a distinctly naturalistic logic "of napalm, paranoia, suitcase bombs carried by happy Arabs, random carcinoma. This logic eats itself. It says life is a monkey on a stick. It says life spins as hysterically and erratically as the penny you flick to see who buys lunch" (27). Decker shoots his teacher, Mrs. Underwood, in the head and holds his class hostage in Room 16 behind closed door and drawn shades while the school is evacuated and police squads mass outside. However, the students, directed in the process of "getting it on" by Charlie, experience an "encounter session" where they come to share their innermost secrets, dreams, and disappointments—all shrouded in the immutable logic of everyday life in Placerville, Maine. The focus of Decker's rage, and ultimately that of the entire class, is Ted Jones, the embodiment of the all-American high school hero, everything that Charlie is not. Ted's problem may be nothing more than always being on the right side, at the right place, at the right time. He is the one to whom the authorities speak over the intercom as they try to assess the situation, and ultimately he is seen as the representative of the establishment status quo in the classroom. Because Charlie's rage has triggered the acknowledgement of similar emotions by the members of his class, Ted becomes their target as well.

They were smiling at Ted, who hardly looked human at all anymore. In that brief
flick of time, they looked like gods, young, wise, and golden. Ted did not look like
a god. Ink ran down his cheeks in blue-black teardrops. The bridge of his nose
was bleeding, and one eye glared disjointedly toward no place. Paper protruded
through his teeth. He breathed in great white snuffles of air.
    I had time to think: *We have got it on. Now we have got it all the way on.*
    They fell on him. (124)

With Ted reduced to a drooling idiot by the physical and verbal abuse of
his classmates, Charlie seems to have won his vengeance for all the injustice, misunderstanding, and loneliness he has endured, but the fury of
his classmates frightens even its instigator. As the novel closes, neither he
nor Ted, each institutionalized, has come to terms with the events that
transpired in Mrs. Underwood's class that day. Charlie and, to a greater
extent, Ted both pay for things they did not do.
    Chuck Barris, the emcee of television's "The Gong Show" is quoted as
saying "The ultimate game show would be one where the losing contestant was killed" (178). Appropriately enough, King uses quotations from
various TV game-show hosts as epigraphs to chapters of *The Long Walk*.
This annual May Day ritual is a competition (with extensive TV coverage,
throngs of onlookers, and millions of dollars in wagers on the result) in
which ninety-nine losing contestants are killed while the winner's prize is
anything he desires. Charlie Decker's logic rules in this fractured vision of
a military state where "the squads" protect the status quo and the long
walk becomes an ultimate rite of passage for the adolescent boys "lucky"
enough to be chosen as walkers. In a caricature of American success
myth, there is no finish line in this race; the object is simply to walk
everyone else to death. Since there can be only one survivor/winner, the
game is a perfect model of selfish competition.
    Ray Garraty, "Maine's own," is an unlikely hero. Not even sure why he
is involved in the contest, he contrasts sharply with others like Scramm,
the odds-on favorite, who seem to possess confidence, dedication, stam-
ina, and goals that Garraty lacks. Ray finds a semblance of community
among some of the walkers, and even bonds with a group of "Musketeers"
who, in fact, violate long-walk protocol, and competitive common sense,
by helping each other continue. Yet as the walk unfolds, he comes to recognize the absurdity of it all even as he reaches into himself for the will to
continue walking. Fear of getting his "ticket" becomes the desire to outwalk obvious cutthroats such as Barkovitch, to make it to Freeport to see
his mother and girlfriend, to stay in the company of his new friends, and
finally to keep on keeping on.

It seemed that he had once been loved, once he himself had loved. But now it was
just jazz and the rising drumbeat in his head and his mother had only been
stuffed straw in a fur coat, Jan nothing but a department store dummy. It was

over. Even if he won, if he managed to outlast McVries and Stebbins and Baker, it was over. He was never going home again. (317)

He does manage to outwalk these last three contestants, but the walk is not over. Even as the Major waits to award the victor his prize, Garraty keeps going, trying to reach a "dark figure . . . [who] beckoned in the rain, beckoned for him to come and walk, to come and play the game" (321).

Both Charlie Decker and Ray Garraty have lost whatever dreams and possibilities they might have had as young adults with their future ahead of them. Both have had their spirits crushed by circumstances beyond their control. Charlie never seems as innocent as Ray, but in the few days of the long walk, Garraty endures a puberty rite that robs him not only of his youth but also of his illusions and his sense of connection with loved ones and with life itself. Certainly this is a high price to pay for something he did not do.

In *Roadwork* King draws on two dark themes — the meaningless loss of a child, and the malevolent impersonality of government bureaucracy — each of which he has used in other works.[1] Barton George Dawes confronts two of Bachman-King's deepest fears and responds accordingly: "He kept doing things without letting himself think about them. Safer that way. It was like having a circuit breaker in his head, and it thumped into place every time part of him tried to ask: But *why are you doing this?*" (333). There is no doubt that he fears the answer to his own questions, and perhaps the answer to the larger question of whether there is any meaning to his suffering. A contented suburbanite, firmly middle-class and happily married, Dawes sees his world come apart with the death of his only child and the eminent-domain destruction, in the name of progress, of both his house on Crestallen Street and the laundry that he manages. Charlie's inoperable brain tumor confounds rational explanations:

You see if that collection of bad cells, no bigger than a walnut, had decided to grow on the outside of Charlie's brain, minor surgery would have vacuumed it right up. . . . But instead, it had grown down deep inside and was growing larger every day. If they tried the knife, or laser, or cryosurgery, they would be left with a nice, healthy, breathing piece of meat. If they didn't try any of those things, they would be building a coffin for their son. (464)

Bart's relationship with his son was so close that the loss was unbearable and set him up for the proverbial last straw, the construction of the I-784 extension through both the Blue Ribbon Laundry and his Crestallen Street neighborhood during the time of the first gasoline crisis.

His frustration and grief turn him inward, contemplating nothing, as he dulls his pain with massive doses of television washed down with Southern Comfort. He neglects his job, allowing a relocation deal to fall through, and he sabotages highway construction equipment with gasoline bombs. Losing both his job and his wife, who can no longer endure his irrational self-destructive behavior (after all, *she* healed from the trauma of Charlie's death), Dawes obtains explosives and decides to make his stand. But like Charlie Decker's, Bart's stand is doomed from the start, and Bart will sacrifice his life to make his point. But if his son's tumor "could destroy . . . things that are so personal [he] hardly dared admit their existence . . . what did that leave? How could [he] ever trust life again? How could he see it as anything more meaningful than a Saturday night demolition derby?. . . wouldn't one be justified in stepping out of his car? But what after that? Life seemed only a preparation for hell" (466).

Dawes' Last Stand receives TV news coverage, and a reporter wins a Pulitzer prize for his work. But there are other issues, other crusades, and the highway is completed ahead of schedule. Nothing gained, but much is lost.

The fourth Bachman work, *The Running Man,* distills the notion of righteous indignation, the portrait of a futuristic military state, and the context of competitive greed into a narrative that King admits is "nothing but story" and one of his favorites.[2] The world of this novel is the gloomy portrayal of the manipulative establishment that Charlie Decker, Ray Garraty, and Bart Dawes define in their extended interior monologues. In the year 2025, the government and the Network hold the masses in check with legalized drugs, police with electric move-alongs and guns, and their ultimate weapon: the Free-Vee and its procession of game shows. Ben Richards does not muse about his condition or the state of affairs; just as the narrative is pure plot, Richards is a man of action. Out of work, he joins a mile-long line of others from the wasteland south of the Canal who turn to the Network for salvation. But in spite of the throngs of "maggots" surrounding him and the watchful eyes of the authorities measuring this "dinosaur" from another time, Richards, too, is alone. Though he becomes a contestant to save his daughter from the flu and his wife from turning two-dollar tricks, they become victims of this Orwellian dystopia even as he qualifies for the biggest game of all. The billion-dollar prize for a successful running man has never been awarded, thanks to the perseverance and skill of the Hunters and the treachery of greedy and deluded citizens. The runner is truly left to his own devices to survive. Richards manages to secure help from Stacey, Bradley, and their mother, the black family who help him link with an "underground." But they, like Elton Parrakis, are victims of the Network's lust for ratings and revenge. They are just as powerless against the establishment as his hostage, Amelia Williams, is against his desperate will to survive. Ironically, it is McCone, the Hunter, and Killian, the host of "The Running Man" and director of The Games who have the most in common with Ben Richards—each is capable of doing anything in order to accomplish his goal. In fact, when Killian offers Richards the defeated McCone's position of chief hunter, Ben believes that he is telling the truth. But the rage Ben feels against Killian, the Network, and the society they control climaxes in an explosion lighting up the sky "like the wrath of God," but not before

[t]he entire window [of Killian's office in the Games Building] was filled with an oncoming Lockheed TriStar jet. Its running lights blinked on and off, and for just a moment, an insane moment of total surprise and horror and disbelief, he could see Richards staring out at him, his face smeared with blood, his black eyes burning like the eyes of a demon.
    Richards was grinning.
    And giving him the finger. (691)

The last novel published under Richard Bachman's name, *Thinner*, is the most satisfying. In fact, King had hoped that this book would make Bachman a best-selling author. Of all the Bachman protagonists, one with whom most readers can identify is Billy Halleck. Billy seems to have everything that characters like Charlie Decker (in the internal torment of his "sanity"), Garraty Davis (in the innocence of his youth), Barton Dawes (in the depth of his sense of loss), Ben Richards (in the futuristic dystopia of his desperation), and Paul Sheldon (in the isolation of his captivity and artistic solitude) lack. Unlike the others, Halleck is *connected*— to his family, to his community, to his social world and professional position. Yet in *Thinner* he comes to repudiate each of these connections as he is caught in the snare of vengeance; and in so doing, Billy becomes as separate from his world as Charlie, Ray, Bart, and Ben are from theirs.
    Ironically, Halleck's most reliable "connection" proves to be someone at odds with the world that Billy represents. Richie Ginelli, a client with an unsavory reputation, warns Billy Halleck that he had better not come around so often now that the "legal problems" are over, even though the two men had become friends. Admitting that the world considers him a gangster, Ginelli continues:

"Young lawyers who associate with gangsters do not get ahead, William, and that's what it's really all about—keeping your nose clean and getting ahead."
    "That's what it's all about, huh?"
    Ginelli had smiled strangely, "Well . . . there *are* a few other things."
    "Such as?"
    "William, I hope you never have to find out." (*Thinner,* 14)

Thinner illustrates several of these "other things" that Billy Halleck is forced to find out. The world Halleck enters is a far cry from the safety of suburbia; it is the world of the "pay-out" as the notion of legal justice is surrendered to vengeance.

The novel's preoccupation with justice and vengeance constitutes a major theme. We see justice take many forms: the view of the solid citizens of Fairview and that of the legal system, Halleck's sense of personal responsibility, and finally the more primitive attitude of Taduz Lemke, shared, ironically, by Richie Ginelli. King balances the rational conventions of law against the visceral desire for revenge, and his conclusions are unsettling. For as others before him, Mario Puzo in *The Godfather* is an appropriate example,[3] King finds the legal system of justice wanting and the primitive notion of vengeance compelling and ultimately more satisfying. The adage of "An eye for an eye, a tooth for a tooth" is alive and well in late-twentieth-century America.

The world of William Halleck represents a modern American version of the good life, material rewards for keeping his nose clean and getting ahead, and a far more appealing world than that of the earlier Bachman novels. He is a partner in his law firm, and has just settled the most financially rewarding case of his career. Halleck, his wife Heidi, and his teenaged daughter Linda live on Lantern Drive bordering the country club in a prosperous suburb. Houses, comfortably set back from the street, run to the "indoor-pool-and-sauna" price range. Halleck's golf and poker buddies include Judge Cary Rossington and Dr. Michael Houston. Too much good food and too little physical activity have left on his large frame 249 pounds to haul around, rapidly pushing him toward "heart attack country." But habits, and the fact that he stopped smoking as a New Year's resolution, have prevented him from losing his large belly—at least until the accident and the curse. As concern over his condition and the brooding guilt cause Billy to be more introspective than he has ever been in his life, he gives us a self-portrait that is both familiar and ludicrous: "Here was a man of almost thirty-seven with Bally shoes on his feet and Bausch & Lomb soft contact lenses on his eyes, a man in a three-piece suit that had cost six hundred dollars. A thirty-six-year-old overweight American male. Caucasian, sitting at the wheel of [an] . . . Oldsmobile Ninety-Eight, scarfing a huge hamburger" (14).

Fairview, Connecticut is an idyllic New England suburb, complete with quaint shops downtown, surrounding a common where townsfolk like Billy Halleck and his family enjoy picnics and band concerts. Into this comfortable world comes a caravan of Gypsies on the day of the first band concert of the season, looking "bright, alive, [and] somehow dangerous" (40). Fairview's Apollonian predictability is confronted by Dionysian spontaneity: a young Gypsy man juggles bowling pins, and a beautiful Gypsy girl with a slingshot flawlessly shoots ball bearings at a target, attracting a crowd of young Fairviewites. Predictably, the chief of police, Duncan Hopley, appears on the scene with other officers and proceeds to

run the Gypsies out of town. Their exotic vitality and dangerous stereotype make them outsiders and unwelcome. As Halleck later reflects to
himself, trying to explain the situation to his daughter,

Not in Fairview. Not where you see the common from Lantern Drive and the
country club, not when that view is part of what you paid for, along with the private schools which teach computer programming . . . and the relatively clean air,
and the quiet at night. The Shrine Circus is okay. The Easter-egg hunt is even better. But Gypsies? Here's your hat, what's your hurry. We know dirt when we see
it. Not that we touch it, Christ, no! We have maids and housekeepers to get rid of
dirt in our houses. When it shows up on the town common, we've got Hopley.
(47)

Two days later, Susannah Lemke, an old Gypsy woman, steps out between two parked cars into the path of Halleck's Oldsmobile. Because his
attention has been distracted by his wife's unprecedented sexual behavior—a spontaneous daylight "hand-job," the first in sixteen years of marriage—Halleck strikes and kills the old woman. The police investigation
is perfunctory, and when a preliminary hearing is held, Cary Rossington
not only fails to disqualify himself as judge, but he dismisses any charges
against Halleck. As Duncan Hopley ruefully reminds Halleck later, this is
only normal behavior in towns like Fairview: "[The Gypsies] weren't the
first bunch of drifters I ever busted out of town, and I've done other little
cosmetic jobs when some hot-shit townie got involved in a mess. Of
course I couldn't do anything if the townie in question made the mess
outside the Fairview town limits . . . but you'd be surprised how many of
our leading lights never learned that you don't shit where you eat" (105).
By the time of this conversation with Hopley, however, Billy Halleck is
not surprised. Nagged by his memory of the accident and plagued by
nightmares as his bathroom scale records his plummeting weight, he
comes to an acceptance of his guilt and an understanding of Lemke's pain
and need of satisfaction. As he is about to embark on his chase of the
Gypsy caravan, he reveals a sense of disconnection similar to Ray Garraty's as he writes in a letter to Heidi:

I want to tell [Lemke] that there was no evil intent. . . . But what I want to do
more than anything else . . . is to apologize. For me . . . for you . . . for all of Fairview. I know a lot more about Gypsies than I used to, . . . I guess you could say
that my eyes have been opened. . . . [I]f I find I have a future to look forward to
after all—I will not spend that future in Fairview. I find I've had a bellyful of
Andy's Pub, Lantern Drive, the country club, the whole dirty hypocritical
town. (141)

When he finally confronts Taduz Lemke, he acknowledges his own guilt
and that of his community but reminds the ancient Gypsy that there was

guilt on both sides. And just as he himself is partner in the curse ("I helped do it to myself."), the Gypsies must assume responsibility for the accident:

If she had crossed at the corner she would be alive now. There was fault on both sides, but she's dead and I can never go back to what my life was before. It balances. Not the best balance in the history of the world, maybe, but it balances. They've got a way of saying it in Las Vegas – they call it a push. This is a push, old man. Let it end here. (179)

But Taduz Lemke does not let it end here: " 'No poosh!' he cried at Billy, and shook his fist. 'No poosh, not never!' " Lemke's position is clear as are the reasons for it. Duncan Hopley the cop knows the Gypsy well and predicts failure for Billy's quest:

All his life he's been on the move, busted out of a place as soon as the "good folks" have got all the maryjane or hashish they want, as soon as they've lost all the dimes they want on the wheel of chance. All his life he's heard a bad deal called a dirty gyp. . . . [H]e's seen canvas tents burned for a joke back in the thirties and forties, and maybe there were babies and old people that burned up in some of those tents. He's seen his daughter or his friends' daughters attacked, maybe raped, because all those "good folks" know that gypsies fuck like rabbits and a little more won't matter. . . . [T]he final crack of the whip comes. This hotshot lawyer with three chins and bulldog jowls runs your [daughter] down in the street, . . . and you hang around thinking maybe this once, *just this once,* there's going to be a little justice . . . an instant of justice to make up for a lifetime of crap. (169–170)

But we know that in the thousands of Fairviews of America, justice is not always blind, nor does it always satisfy the injured party, so Lemke takes matters into his own hands: "I known who done what, I taken care of it. Mostly we turn and we drive out of town. Mostly, yeah, we do dat. But sometimes we get our justice. . . . *Rom justice, skummade ignemom* [ignorant scum. . .]. Justice ain't bringing the dead back, white man. Justice is justice" (178–179).

Vengeance as justice is nothing new; it has been recognized throughout human history and across cultural lines. It is a kind of justice that Richie "the Hammer" Ginelli knows well as *vendetta,* personal responsibility for avenging a wrong. Halleck sees Ginelli as a supremely practical and realistic man who believes only in guns and money. It is Ginelli of whom Halleck thinks repeatedly after the accident, for Richie, like Duncan Hopley, is used to taking care of "little messes" that folks are likely to encounter. But Billy does not call upon Ginelli until after he confronts Lemke and lays upon him the "curse of the white man from town."

Whatever reluctance Halleck may have had about involving Ginelli is soon erased, for this practical man immediately believes Billy's story. Unlike Heidi and Mike Houston who believe Halleck is crazy (they have signed a *res gestae* order for his commitment), Ginelli, after all, believes in more than guns and money: "Well, there's one more thing I believe in, William. I believe in what I see. That's why I'm a relatively rich man. That's also why I'm a *living* man. Most people, they don't believe what they see" (195). Instead of the irrationality of rationalizations, a flaw in the old Billy Halleck (as in his weighing rituals denying his true physical state), Ginelli and the new Billy confront the situation head-on in order to find a way to take off the curse.

While Billy, who is now down to less than 120 pounds and suffering cardiac arrhythmia due to his emaciated state, lies in a Bar Harbor motel, Richie "the Hammer" becomes the curse of the white man from town. Having ruled out a "hit" on Lemke as inefficient, Ginelli executes a carefully planned terrorist raid on the Gypsy encampment. Though he harms no one, he is able to negotiate a final confrontation between Halleck and Lemke at which Lemke is to remove the curse.

On a park bench in Bangor, Billy meets the old man and learns more about the nature of a curse. Lemke sees his curse not as a *thing*, something that can be taken off. Instead, he explains it as a "[c]hild of the night-flowers," something that *lives*: "[Y]ou bring it into the world like a baby. Only it grows strong faster than a baby, and you can't kill it because you can't see it—only you can see what it *does*" (255). The Gypsy curse, like the hate of the white men from town, lives and grows strong over time. There may no longer be a rational explanation for its existence (the curse will not resurrect Susannah; the Gypsies were not doing anything wrong), but it lives nevertheless. The curse will not disappear; it must be passed to someone else. Lemke offers a Gypsy pie, a warm, pulsating—live—strawberry concoction. In a ritual blood-letting and healing, Lemke tells Billy that the curse is now contained in the pie. If Halleck wishes to be rid of it and to recover completely, he is to feed the pie to someone else. If he fails to do this, he will die "weak" and "thin." However, Lemke, dying himself from rapidly spreading cancer, offers this parting advice: "I feel a little sorry for you. . . . Not much, but a little. Once you might have been *pokol*—strong. Now your shoulders are broken. Nothing is your fault . . . there are reasons . . . you have friends. . . . Why not eat your own pie, white man from town? You die, but you die strong" (257). Lemke leaves, looking utterly weary, but he reminds Billy, "No poosh, white man from town. . . . Not *never*" (258).

Halleck returns to the car where Ginelli was to meet him. A kind of cold peace and certainty has absorbed him, and so he is not hysterical when he finds only Richie's severed hand clutching a fistful of ball bearings on the car seat. With his mind set on the final disposition of the curse, Halleck sees Ginelli's murder as part of a logical A + B = C equation. But this realization cannot keep him from thinking along the lines of the old Gypsy and his gangland friend:

I think if I could lay my hands on her [Gina, Lemke's great-granddaughter and probably Ginelli's murderer], I'd hurt her myself . . . hurt her plenty, for what she did to Richard. Her hand? I'd leave that old man her *head* . . . I'd stuff her mouth full of ball bearings and leave him her head . . . because no one knows exactly how things like this get started; they argue about that and finally they lose the truth altogether if it's inconvenient, but everybody knows how they keep on keeping on; they take one, we take one, then they take two, and we take three. . . . Because that's what it's *really* all about, isn't it? Blood in the gutters. (267)

No one escapes unscathed; everyone pays, even for something he did not do. This theme is clearly seen in the case of Billy Halleck and in the case of Lemke and his Gypsies. In his nightmares, Billy sees the whole town of Fairview "paying" as hideous, spectral shadows of townspeople move about the familiar idyllic setting to Taduz Lemke's curse of "Thinner." But the nightmares of sleep are almost finished as the nightmare of reality reaches a crescendo. The curse must be passed on before the story's end, and Halleck knows who the recipient will be, even before he accepts the pie: His wife, Heidi, just *loves* strawberry pie.

The relationship between Billy and Heidi Halleck appears to be fairly typical, if not desirable. They not only live a storybook lifestyle in a storybook town with the proverbial "all-American" teenage daughter, a *cheerleader* on the verge of lovely young womanhood, no less, but they seem to care for one another very much. Surely there are the predictable annoyances of contemporary living, but their relationship seems healthy. The most significant cause of friction is Heidi's continued smoking after Billy goes cold-turkey: "January and February had been tense – too many 'discussions' that were only disguised arguments, too many nights they had finished sleeping back to back. But they had reached a *modus vivendi:* she had stopped dunning him about his weight and he had stopped yapping at her about her pack-and-a-half-a-day butt habit. It had made for a decent enough spring" (3). The "decency" of the spring is attested to by the fact that Heidi embarks on some spontaneous sex-play on Fairview's main street; unfortunately, it is this ill-timed fondling that contributes to Susannah Lemke's death.

After the accident, Billy has an obviously difficult time putting the whole incident behind him in spite of Heidi's encouragement. As his weight drops, his depression deepens, and he begins to suspect that Heidi is having an easier time forgetting the event because she has not assumed her own share of the guilt. Although they pass an idyllic interlude at Mohonk, the site of their honeymoon, to celebrate Billy's settlement of the

Duganfield case and to forget the recent accident, a fissure begins to open in the rock of their marriage. Heidi notices Billy's weight loss in spite of no change in his eating habits, and she fears he is ill, possibly with cancer. Mixed with his own fear of "the big C" and his brooding over the Gypsy "Thinner"-touch, Billy also comes to a biting realization that Heidi is conscious of her own failure to quit smoking. She must rationalize his loss of weight to an illness, not to his own efforts to lose it.

When illness is ruled out by Michael Houston's tests and Halleck's visit to a special clinic, Heidi cannot/will not accept Billy's interpretation of a curse. Is this because she is too *rational* to accept a superstition as reality, or is it because she is unwilling to accept it because to do so would mean assuming at least part of the responsibility for the Gypsy's death and for Billy's plight. As Billy comes to the conclusion that he alone is cursed, he hates Heidi for not sharing the guilt and the curse: "[H]e felt shame for his bright hate . . . but in the days which followed . . . the hate recurred more and more often, in spite of all he could do to stop it or hold it back" (70). Like a "flower of the Night Children," Billy's hate has a life of its own that cannot be denied.

In his farewell letter to Heidi, Billy confronts her with the proposition that she *does* believe in the curse and "to believe in the curse is to believe that only one of us is being punished for something in which we both played a part. I'm talking about guilt avoidance on your part . . . [and] in the craven and cowardly part of my soul, I feel that if I'm going through this hellish decline, you should be going through one also" (140).

Thus when Halleck accepts the Gypsy pie from Lemke, he knows who will eat it. In much the same way that Richie became the curse of the white man from town – Billy realizes that once started Richie cannot be stopped (he seems to enjoy carrying out his plan) – Halleck is rolling down the steep grade of vengeance with no brakes. He returns home to offer Heidi the pie. But instead of celebrating their "reconciliation," the exhausted Halleck retires to the bedroom, leaving Heidi to enjoy the pie alone. She does enjoy the pie, but when Halleck awakens from yet another nightmare in which his daughter's nose falls off, recalling Lemke's rotted face, he finds two strawberry stained plates in the kitchen – one for Heidi, one for Linda. "No blame you say. . . . But there is no poosh, white man from town. Everybody pays, even for things they didn't do. No poosh" (281), Billy recalls as he cuts a slice of Gypsy pie for himself. Like the gypsy curse itself, the thirst for vengeance has a life of its own, and once the vendetta is started everybody loses. This is a man-made distortion of the random and impartial pain that the world can inflict.

Everybody pays, *that's* what it's all about. Even the well-fed citizens of all the Fairviews in America cannot escape the pay-out. William Halleck's profession makes him part of the judicial machinery. His standing in the community makes him invulnerable to the little messes of everyday life.

But neither these facts nor his rational mind can protect him from the curse of guilt laid upon him or from the hate that grows inside. The power of darkness can be seen in the most prosaic lives. This realization is part of every Stephen King novel, and in his exploration of justice versus vengeance, the author gives *Thinner* a compelling and universal theme.

As he introduces his most recent published work, *Four Past Midnight,* Stephen King tells his audience:

I still believe in the resilience of the human heart and the essential validity of love; I still believe that connections between people can be made and that the spirits which inhabit us sometimes touch. I still believe that the cost of those connections is horribly, outrageously high . . . and I still believe that the value derived far outweighs the price which must be paid. I still believe, I suppose, in the coming of The White and finding a place to make a stand . . . and defending that place to the death. (xv)

This credo is at the center of nearly everything of substance that King has written. The "pay-off" of at least a temporary victory over the forces of darkness by the righteous stand of his heroes can give some comfort despite the magnitude of the "pay out" they must endure. But in the bleak world according to Bachman—in *Rage, Roadwork,* and *Misery*—the connections among people are dysfunctional or they are frustrated and ultimately severed by the turn of events—in *The Long Walk, The Running Man,* and *Thinner.* The resolutions of these novels are disquieting in that nothing lasting seems to be gained by the sacrifice: no pay-off for the pay out. Perhaps here lies the greatest horror of all.

NOTES

1. The untimely death of a child and its effects on the family appear most prominently in *Pet Sematary* but are significant in *It, Cujo,* and "The Body." Bureaucratic madness is at the heart of *Firestarter* and *The Stand,* and is a subtext of *The Dead Zone, Tommyknockers,* and all four of the early Bachman books.

2. Noted in Douglas E. Winter, *Stephen King: The Art of Darkness* (New York: New American Library, 1986), 183–184. The novel is said to have been written in only 72 hours.

3. In this enormously popular novel, the Sicilian understanding of *vendetta* is explored in numerous ways. The justice system is found lacking in the case of Amerigo Bonasera, the undertaker, who comes to Vito Corleone "for justice." Corleone instructs him in Sicilian courtesy before granting his request for vengeance. One of the appeals of the Godfather's subculture versus America's mainstream culture is that the Sicilians take care of business personally. There is an immediacy and satisfaction, a responsibility and allegiance, too often lacking in modern civilization.

REFERENCES

Bachman, Richard [Stephen King]. *The Bachman Books: Four Early Novels by Stephen King.* New York: New American Library, 1985. [Contains *Rage, The Long Walk, Roadwork,* and *The Running Man*].

———. *Thinner.* New York: New American Library, 1984.

Hemingway, Ernest. *A Farewell to Arms.* New York: Scribners, 1929.

King, Stephen. *The Dark Half.* New York: Viking, 1989.

———. *Four Past Midnight.* New York: Viking, 1990.

Winter, Douglas E. *Stephen King: The Art of Darkness.* New York: New American Library, 1986.

10

Science, Politics, and the Epic Imagination: *The Talisman*

TONY MAGISTRALE

> It was clear that if I had an ideal reader anywhere in the world, it was probably Stephen King; and it was also clear to me that the reason for this was that his aims and ambitions were very close to my own. . . . [The] experience of first reading King was like that of suddenly discovering a long-lost family member – of finding a brother, really – and that is no exaggeration. (Straub, 9)

Peter Straub's reflections on Stephen King, the latter perceived in the dual roles of reader and writer, would be interesting and noteworthy even if the two men had never decided to coauthor a novel. That *The Talisman* (1984), a work so centered on family (both nuclear and extended) and fraternal relationships, should emerge from their joint effort gives added significance to Straub's simile. For a good portion of *The Talisman* concerns family: the quest to aid a dying mother/queen in her fight against cancer, uncovering the sobering truth about the deaths of a father and an uncle, and the existence of a twin brother who died in infancy somewhere in a parallel universe. In addition, Jack Sawyer, the twelve-year-old boy who is at the center of these concerns, goes on to discover "long-lost family members" in the unexpected fraternal relationships he forms with several of the men and beasts he encounters across America and in the mythological Territories – Speedy Parker, Wolf, and Richard Sloat. None of these individuals is related by blood to Sawyer, yet they are clearly meant to serve as family surrogates for Jack's lost father (Speedy) and the absence of siblings (Wolf and Richard).

According to Douglas Winter, the collaboration of these two distinct and successful writers had been planned since 1977, the year when King and Straub first met in London and commenced their friendship. The story line for *The Talisman* was not established until Straub returned to the United States in 1980, but from that point on the book apparently unfolded quickly. Both men took turns writing alternate sections and experimenting freely with each other's established style and voice (Winter, 1986 ed., 158–159). As Straub recounts, "the book is full of little tricks between us where we're trying to fool the reader into thinking the other guy wrote it" (Underwood & Miller, 172).

Surely part of the artistic success represented by *The Talisman* is the measure of its quality as a collaborative work of fiction. Anyone who has ever attempted to coauthor an important memo, much less an article or a book, understands the inherent difficulties of collaborative writing projects. However, not only have King and Straub managed to overcome such obstacles, they appear to have also discovered the great joy that attends successful collaborations: the assistance of another perspective to aid in problem-solving, of gathering excitement and momentum from a shared goal and the labors of a fellow writer. Although the last hundred pages of the novel are anticlimactic, labored, and in need of severe condensing, the remainder of the book is remarkably well plotted and fluidly paced. The world of the Territories – a parallel medieval-like universe through which Jack travels – is not rendered as a vague abstraction, but a concrete reality. And it is one of the great achievements of this novel that King and Straub are able to translate their sense of that world's real existence into images that enable the reader to visualize it.

Straub and King's joint writing voice in this book is seamless; I don't think it is possible to distinguish, at least from style alone, which of the two writers contributed a given chapter or section. And this is no small accomplishment, especially since the author of *Ghost Story*, with its Jamesian diction and symmetry, constructs strikingly formal prose compared to King's loose and colloquial style of narration. I suspect Straub and King nourished one another's writing in this enterprise; surely a book the size of *The Talisman* would not have been written in so short a period of time and with such a corresponding level of quality had the two writers not found major points of similarity along the way. Moreover, each learned something from the other. Straub felt that the collaboration made him more aware of narrative possibilities, "as if some rough spots were knocked off because of the closeness I had to the way Steve works." If Straub's narrative range was broadened through King's influence, the latter found himself paying greater attention to stylistic details: "I can't remember ever writing anything and being so conscious about what I was writing" (Underwood & Miller, 173).

The Talisman borrows heavily from epics as diverse as Dante's *Divine*

Comedy and Tolkien's *Lord of the Rings*. The concept of the hero was important to the coauthors, and in preparation for writing *The Talisman* they read several books about the epic hero, the meaning of the hero, stages of heroic development, the Christ figure, and apotheosis (Beahm, 286). King himself is deeply attracted to the epic design; *The Stand* (1979) prefigures *The Talisman* and is also about a westward journey across the United States, while *It,* which follows *The Talisman* by two years, is also epic in its dimensions, measuring a town's historical battle between good and evil. I will have more to say about the epic tradition and its connection to *The Talisman* at a later point in this chapter. The significance of this tradition notwithstanding, the singlemost important literary influence to shape King and Straub's collaborative vision is not a formal epic at all, but a colloquial narrative about a distinctly American adventure.

"WHERE THE WATER AND LAND COME TOGETHER": *ADVENTURES OF HUCKLEBERRY FINN* AND *THE TALISMAN*

From *The Talisman*'s epigraph to its concluding citation from *Tom Sawyer,* Mark Twain's inspiration pervades the entire breadth of the narrative King and Straub published exactly one hundred years after the release of *Huck Finn.* Although his name is Sawyer, *The Talisman*'s adolescent protagonist shares little in common with Twain's romantic idealist whose sense of adventure is always greater than the risk involved. Rather, Jack Sawyer's real kin is the orphan-child friend of Tom Sawyer, Huck Finn. Huck's experiences on the Mississippi would allow him to empathize with the trials and brutality Jack encounters on his own American adventure. While Tom Sawyer's terrors are primarily self-constructed, Huck and Jack need to work constantly at repressing their imaginations. For terror is no mere abstraction for either of these boys; the real world provides them both with more than enough stimulation. One suspects that had Huck Finn had access to *The Talisman*'s Territories, he would have migrated there frequently (the very word "Territories" is used in conscious homage to Twain, although Huck Finn's "territories" are always more psychological than geographical, more myth than reality). Compare, for example, these two quotations from *Huckleberry Finn* and *The Talisman.* Not only do they reveal sympathetic points about the similar journeys these children undertake and their reaction to what they encounter, but these are also sentiments Tom Sawyer would never have understood, much less been capable of articulating himself. The first, from *Huckleberry Finn:*

When I got there it was still and Sunday-like, and hot and sunshiny – the hands was gone to the fields; and there was them kind of faint dronings of bugs and flies in the air that makes it seem so lonesome and like everybody's dead and gone; and if a breeze fans along and quivers the leaves, it makes you feel mournful, because you feel like it's spirits that's been dead ever so many years – and you always think they're talking about *you*. As a general thing it makes a body wish *he* was dead, too, and done with it all. (Twain, 276)

And Jack Sawyer in *The Talisman:*

Loneliness raged through him; his realization of his outcast status was now complete. Jack began to cry. He did not weep hysterically or shriek as people do when they mask rage with tears; he cried in the steady sobs of one who has discovered just how alone he is, and is apt to remain for a long time yet. He cried because all safety and reason seemed to have departed from the world. Loneliness was here, a reality; but in this situation, insanity was also too much of a possibility. (King & Straub, 119)

Like his fictional prototype from the nineteenth century, Jack Sawyer begins *The Talisman* under someone else's control. Huck must ascribe to the civilized virtues of Miss Watson, while Jack has been transported, against his desires, from one end of the country to the other: "His mother was moving him through the world, twitching him from place to place; but what moved his mother?" (King & Straub, 3). As is the case in Twain's narrative, *The Talisman* is a novel that highlights, through the metaphor of a geographical journey, the struggle of a young boy and his effort to pursue goodness in the face of worldly evil; a quest to retain the spirit of hope in spite of the terrible events that he is made to experience; and, most important, the attempt on the part of this young man to maintain his identity and purpose against forces that would strip him of both.

Huck's journey takes him south through Twain's and America's past. There, Huck discovers a patriarchal world of violence and stupidity – a world amply characterized by Colonel Sherburn and his mock gentility, defining his manhood by killing an unarmed drunk under the barest of provocations, and by the Duke and King, who rely on their cultured hypocrisy to trick people out of their dollars and dignity. In *The Talisman*, Jack's journey is west instead of south, but the violent portrait of America he discovers in both the Territories and contemporary America is profoundly reminiscent of Huck's landscape. (Moreover, *The Talisman* should be seen as a continuation of the general social critique found throughout King's canon, and particularly in the Bachman novels.) The rural America Jack encounters bears much in common with the towns and villages Huck and Jim visit along the Mississippi: these are wide-angled portraits of humanity at its worst. Kindness and generosity are seldom found, while ignorance and greed are seemingly rewarded.

Smokey Updike and the Oatley Tap epitomize Jack's experiences on the road. The boy finds himself in a bondage (he keeps referring to the metaphor of the pitcher-plant) that neatly parallels Huck's servitude at the hands of the Duke and King. Huck and Jack are trapped by virtue of their innocence and vulnerability, manipulated by men without scruples who are interested only in obtaining power and lining their pockets:

> "Digger and me go back," Smokey said. "And if you was to just walk out of here now, Jack, I couldn't guarantee that you wouldn't have some trouble with Digger. Might end up getting sent home. Might end up picking apples on the town's land—Oatley Township's got . . . oh, I guess forty acres of good trees. Might end up getting beat up. Or . . . I've heard that ole Digger's got a taste for kids on the road. Boys, mostly."
>
> Jack thought of that clublike penis. He felt both sick and cold. (King & Straub, 148)

In the societies delineated by Twain and King and Straub, Morgan Sloat/Orris embodies the dominant value system. This explains why Jack feels Morgan is always somehow capable of monitoring his progress westward: the entire geography Jack traverses, like the shore world in *The Adventures of Huckleberry Finn,* is littered with individuals who wish to place Jack into some form of economic or psychological bondage. As Jack quickly discovers, both the Territories and America itself are governed by some version of the Morgan business ethic. The American capitalist has been setting the tone for society since the start of this country, and in exporting the doctrine of oppressed labor to the Territories, Morgan Sloat represents the most contemporary illustration of capitalist imperialism: "Uncle Morgan lived for business, for deal-making and hustling; and he was so ambitious that he challenged every even faintly dubious call in a tennis match, so ambitious in fact that he cheated in the penny-ante card games his son had now and then coaxed him into joining" (King & Straub, 25).

In light of this pessimistic portrait, it is not surprising that both *Huckleberry Finn* and *The Talisman* should also highlight the unholy alliance between religion and money. In *Huck Finn* the word of God is employed to justify even the most inhuman of acts—slavery—while in *The Talisman* a warped religious vision rationalizes the psychosexual exploitation of children in Sunlight Gardener's home.

In contrast to the bleak social backdrops for both *Huck Finn* and *The Talisman,* the spirits of Huck and Jack are continually renewed by contact with black father-figures. Nigger Jim and Speedy Parker exist outside the forces of alienation and violence that characterize the larger white culture in each book. Speedy is a blues musician, while Jim is a primitive mythologist, the music and folklore that give a rich center to these men is located apart from the sterility of Morgan Sloat and the society whose values he has both internalized and further warped. As a consequence,

they are immune to the dying spirit of the white world; in its place, however, they present an alternative vision rooted in nature and folk tradition. Speedy and Jim are uncorrupted by the mood of capitalist America,
and they have none of the anguish that besets the men and women of the
waste land—the inhabitants of Twain's shore world or the Oatley Tap.
From conversation and interaction with Jim and Speedy, Huck and Jack
gain strength against the despair that pervades their respective worlds.
The climactic scene of *Huck Finn* occurs when Huck elects to forsake the
moral posturing of his society and "go to hell" rather than return Jim to
slavery: "It was awful thoughts, and awful words, but they was said. And
I let them stay said; and never thought no more about reforming. I
shoved the whole thing out of my head; and said I would take up wicked-
ness again, which was in my line, being brung up to it, and the other
warn't" (Twain, 271).

There are several scenes in *The Talisman* that parallel this moment, as
Jack is forced to accept responsibility not only for Speedy (when the latter is injured on the California beach, chapter 40), but for Wolf and Richard Sloat as well. Significantly, Jack must assume the role of the
"shepherd" when Wolf is pulled from the Territories to modern America
and, conversely, when Richard Sloat is travelling with Jack through the
Blasted Lands in the Territories. Although these duties severely incon-
venience Jack in his quest for the Talisman, they signal another level of
maturity and ethical development in his personality. As Huck selects human compassion over social and religious dogma, Jack risks his life and
his quest by refusing to abandon either Wolf or Richard. The journeys
across America and down the Mississippi parallel one another insofar as
they are really about the moral education of Huck and Jack. The quest
for Jim's freedom and the Talisman are finally inextricably related to
these ends—before Jim can truly be free, Huck must understand the real
value of freedom; before the Talisman can work its healing magic, Jack
must possess a set of moral principles that makes him worthy of its
powers: "Uncle Tommy had been fond of quoting a Chinese proverb that
went: *The man whose life you save is your responsibility for the rest of your
life.* Never mind the ducking, never mind the fancy footwork; Wolf was
his responsibility" (King & Straub, 248).

There are undoubtably other points of comparison that link *The Talisman* to *Huck Finn,* but the final one that should be raised here is the emphasis placed upon historical transitions in both novels. During the
1880's the tension between the belief in change and the awareness of the
destructiveness of change was unavoidable. Twain was interested in
drawing a preindustrial portrait of nineteenth-century America, even as
he was forced to acknowledge the inevitable violation of an agrarian
ideal. *Huck Finn* is set at that moment in which the artistic hope for a balance between industry and nature, progress and conservation, was lost.
Unlike Jack Sawyer's voyage through America, Huck and Jim are often

provided with moments of pastoral tranquility on the river (Jack Sawyer finds such occasions only in the Territories). Yet these periods of harmony within nature are always ephemeral, threatened by other men, social institutions, and especially in the intrusion of progress itself in the form of the steamboat that literally breaks up their floating home (Twain, chapter 16). In this last illustration of an uneasy historical shift, Twain places his voyagers in the most precarious of situations: abruptly set adrift in the middle of the night. The scene is shocking, terrifying, but most of all filled with implication, suggesting that all the extravagant possibilities for independence and romantic joy projected upon the American landscape since the age of discovery might be as easily and inexorably snapped as a raft in the path of a steamboat. It was as if Twain, as Leo Marx argues, with little conscious awareness of the convention, somehow discovered the tragic thread that runs through the fabric of complex pastoralism (Marx, 339).

Beneath the surface of Twain's adventure story is a subtext concerning America's transition to a new age of industrial capitalism; the novel initiates Twain's skepticism about industrial civilization and his faith in the kind of world that humans create. Straub and King have likewise projected upon the literal landscape of *The Talisman* a commentary on three unique historical epochs: contemporary America in the mid-1980s (Jack travelling westward along the interstates), the distant American past (the eastern Territories and Outposts), and a sobering projection of an America to come (the Blasted Lands). In a manner even more explicit than in the *Adventures of Huckleberry Finn, The Talisman* is a discourse on the destruction of the pastoral ideal and its technological aftermath. In America's cities and suburbs, Jack and Wolf can not dream of honesty and wholeness; only in the Territories is some measure of psychic unity still available. And as this was the case for Twain's pastoral America, there exists the awareness that the Territories are an endangered landscape; that the Blasted Lands, like the very progress of civilization itself, are expanding outward. Inherent in this perception is a sense of tragic inevitability that somehow is never fully counterbalanced by Jack's personal survival or the Talisman's magical properties. It is, however, this aspect of *The Talisman* that effectively links the novel to *Huck Finn, Walden, Moby-Dick,* the stories of Hemingway and Faulkner, and the poems of Robert Frost: all are unflinching, characteristically American examinations into the implacable advance of history.

A DEREGULATED JOURNEY THROUGH "REAGAN'S AMERICA"

In discussing the political subtext of *The Talisman*, Peter Straub has observed that its grim picture of American society and values is a "description of 'Reagan's America' . . . The book does seem to be about the death of the land, the terrible poisoning of the land" (Winter, "Quest for *The Talisman,"* 68). If this is indeed a novel, on both literal and semiotic levels of meaning, that is critical of, and inspired by, "Reagan's America," it is no coincidence that the dark evils of both Morgan Sloat and Morgan Orris emerge from the west coast and head east, roughly paralleling Ronald Reagan's political ascendancy in California and eventual consolidation of power in Washington, D.C. There can be little doubt that the authors shaped Morgan in Ronald Reagan's image—at least in terms of how these men realigned the political and environmental agendas of their respective worlds—while Sunlight Gardener is modelled after the television evangelists of the religious right.

King's popular acceptance as a writer of the macabre and supernatural often precludes or devalues his importance as a social critic of American life. Although simple equations between cultural products and generalized consciousness can only be maintained within a plethora of qualifications, the reading of works of popular fiction as reflectors and affirmations of social and cultural realities remains valid and profitable (Grixti, 5). In a 1980 interview with *Rolling Stone* King made a self-assessment that emphasized a cultural context necessary for properly understanding his work: "I maintain that my novels, taken together, form an allegory for a nation that feels it's in a crunch and things are out of control. We're in that situation now . . . How do we cope? What do we do?" (Underwood & Miller, 94). Supernatural phenomena in *The Talisman* (and, for that matter, throughout King's canon) are hardly terrifying when held in comparison to the realistic portrait of a "nation that [is] out of control."

As a specific indictment of the Reagan legacy, *The Talisman,* perhaps again elaborating upon a central metaphor found in the Bachman books, employs cancer as a means for highlighting a deteriorating social and physical environment. The novel dramatizes the following statistics that certainly reflect Reagan's general philosophy of governmental deregulation and callous indifference towards the environment (James Watt, the bureaucrat who once justified the selling of vast tracts of National Park forestland to private developers, was, after all, Reagan's initial appointment as secretary of the interior):

A recent report by the Hudson River Sloop *Clearwater* shows that there are more than 500 factories and sewage treatment plants that together dump hundreds of pounds of suspected carcinogens like formaldehyde and trichloroethylene into the river each year. And while most of the dumping is performed under permit from the state, there are dozens of spills each year that exceed permit levels. (Kolbert, 33)

Jack's mother, Lily Cavanaugh, is dying from an illness that is reflective of her time and place. Her cancer is both the physical manifestation of

the polluted landscape Jack trudges across as well as the symbol of a morally polluted society. As events that take place in the Territories echo occurrences in modern America (and vice versa), Queen DeLoessian, who
is also sick, is likewise the visible symbol of her world's slow collapse because of Morgan's growing influence. King and Straub have merely altered the sex of the Fisher King legend: the King's illness, as Weston
notes, like Lily's and Queen DeLoessian's, is symptomatic of a cultural
wasteland. Jack, in his role as Jason, the Territories' word for "Jesus," is
given the allegorical task of renewing these dying worlds and restoring
their spiritual health.

The pristine beauty of the eastern Territories is meant to contrast
sharply with what modern technology has created in merely a century of
transforming the American landscape. The Blasted Lands, on the other
hand, are the only occasion where the Territories may well be both a reflection of the nuclear tests conducted by the army in Arizona and Ne-
vada, as well as a dark prognosis for America's larger future. King and
Straub indict the highly rational minds, which produced nuclear weap-
onry, for the highly irrational consequences in animal and vegetable mu-
tations. Perhaps this is the reason the Blasted Lands are depicted so
vividly in *The Talisman:* the authors required little imagination, given the
examples of Hiroshima and Nagasaki, to envision the results of radiation
poisoning, the after effects of a nuclear nightmare that King at least feels
will be technological man's legacy to the earth:

As the train pulled past the animals, Jack saw that the testicles of the male had
swollen to the size of pillows and sagged onto the ground. What had made such
monstrosities? Nuclear damage, Jack supposed, since scarcely anything else had
such power to deform nature. The creatures, themselves poisoned from birth,
snuffled up the equally poisoned water and snarled at the little train as it passed.
Our world could look like this someday, Jack thought. (King & Straub, 470)

Morgan Sloat would transform the Territories into another version of
the American wasteland, and Wolf's highly developed sense of smell is a
constant reminder that corporate executives such as Sloat are bringing
America ever closer to the realization of Jack's future fear. Tied to the
earth by virtue of his vulpine genes, Wolf is unable to adjust to industrial
America; as such, his yearning to leave the wasteland fuels and parallels
Jack's evolving appreciation for the Territories. It is significant in itself
that Jack's closest friend in his journey is half man and half beast, implying that Jack's sensibilities have enlarged beyond the human (and rational) sphere to the point where he has come to respect *all* living beings.
Jack's trek across America, the lush Territories, and the Blasted Lands
helps to transform his consciousness. Before he can restore the wasteland, he must first learn to appreciate what has been sacrificed in its
place. Wolf's aesthetics are instructive to this end, so that by the conclu-

sion of the novel Jack is as radical a twelve-year-old environmentalist as America has seen since Huck Finn pronounced that there "warn't no home like a raft" (Twain, 155).

Jack's love of the Territories' air and delicious foods, his willingness even to accept the magic inherent in Migration, indicate that he, unlike his friend Richard Sloat, is no rationalist. Because of Jack's willingness to accept the possible, he is in a position to grapple effectively with the various terrors he encounters – both human and supernatural. When evil does manifest itself in the various archetypes portrayed in King's writing, only those characters with imaginations to transcend the "ossified shield of rationality" – to recognize and accept evil for what it is – stand a chance in fighting it (Grixti, 52–53). Thus, while Richard cowers in shocked disbelief when confronted with the supernatural horrors of the Blasted Lands, Jack trusts in their reality and in his perception of it and is thereby empowered to overcome his own fears and rational urge toward denial. This ability proves especially important in the chapter "Jack and Richard Go to War," where Jack must battle in close contact with Morgan's grotesque legions.

Jack's understanding of the world is not grounded by Sloat's incessant need to explain the inexplicable. In fact, King and Straub are so critical of Richard Sloat's practical rationality, that it serves to mirror the distorted emphasis on control and structure used to characterize Sunlight Gardener and Richard's father, Morgan. Richard adheres to a belief that there must be a logical arrangement to the world, that science imposes laws and maintains a certain basis for order. His is the voice of the eighteenth-century man further refined and bolstered by the phenomenal advances of the modern age. Unfortunately, such logic is also responsible for the Blasted Lands and a severely polluted American landscape. Jack's sensibilities, however, are essentially medieval; he is a child of poetry and magic. As Jack's contact with greater levels of social corruption grow, his connection to the mystery and magic of the primitive world, represented from Speedy to Wolf at the extreme, expands accordingly. And *The Talisman* goes on to posit that if the waste land is to be renewed, it will take the world-view of a poet or fantasist to do so. Indeed, this perspective might not be so impractical after all, King and Straub appear to argue; the very survival of the earth may well depend upon just how seriously we are willing to pursue such aesthetics.

THE TALISMAN AND THE EPIC TRADITION

Unlike the devastation of the landscape associated with Sloat and his influence, Jack Sawyer is affiliated with the world of nature and the primal energies that reside in the Territories:

And he would have been astounded if told he had wept several times as he stood watching those great ripples [of grasses] chase each other toward the horizon, drinking in a sight that only a very few American children of his time had ever seen – huge empty tracts of land under a blue sky of dizzying width and breadth and, yes, even depth. It was a sky unmarked by either jet contrails across its dome or smutty bands of smog at any of its lower edges. (King & Straub, 189)

Jack/Jason is not only the prince of this land, fighting, like a medieval representative of Arthur's court, to reclaim the order of the crown, he also comes to embody the life spirit that animates the earth itself. Sloat seeks to disrupt the regal line of succession in the Territories, and in a novel that hinges upon as many medieval conceits as *The Talisman* does, it is appropriate that all of nature should turn against such men. Thus, the ocean fish protect Jack in his quest toward the Talisman (chapter 40) because they recognize him as the legitimate heir to the Territories' throne.

Early in *The Talisman*, as Jack makes his way across Ohio, he comes face-to-face with the recognition that he is no longer a "typical" American adolescent. In a suburban mall parking lot, Jack is confronted by three teenage girls and their football hero boyfriend:

They were leggy in their tight jeans, these confident little princesses of the tenth grade, and when they laughed they put their hands over their mouths in a fashion which suggested that laughter itself was laughable. Jack slowed his walk into a kind of sleepwalker's stroll. One of the princesses glanced at him and muttered to the brownhaired girl beside her.

I'm different now, Jack thought: *I'm not like them anymore.* The recognition pierced him with loneliness. (King & Straub, 204)

Jack's immediate understanding of the distance separating these young women from himself is more than just hair and perfume. By the time he meets these "little princesses of the tenth grade," Jack is poignantly aware that they belong to a world he has been forced to abandon. Yet even as he is made to feel his loss, he also senses that his "difference" has made him somehow stronger, investing him with qualities that are greater than those of the boy he would have been had he remained in New Hampshire with Lily. At this moment of isolation and humiliation, Jack is already in possession of an inner strength that could never be communicated to the three princesses or their jock boyfriend: "Something in Jack Sawyer's face was both strong and forbidding – something that had not been there almost two months ago, when a much younger boy had set the small seafront town of Arcadia Beach to his back and had begun walking west" (King & Straub, 310).

The roadways of America and the Territories have abused Jack, but they have also taught him how to survive. In the tradition of epic heroes throughout Western culture—from Homer's Achilles and Odysseus to Tolkien's Frodo—Jack learns not to be afraid of conflict, that human vultures must be personally confronted if evil is to be held in check. Thus, by the end of the novel Jack has reached the opposite extreme of the victim boy-child the reader remembers from the Oatley Tunnel: standing in the dark, afraid of shadows, clutching his toothbrush. Throughout *The Talisman* Jack is warned of the obvious dangers awaiting a young boy alone on the road. But no one mentions that such direct experience also toughens the individual who is able to survive it. When Jack meets Osmond early in the book, his "fear and loneliness combined in the sharpest, most disheartening wave of unhappiness he had ever known. *Speedy, I can't do this! Don't you know that? I'm just a kid"* (King & Straub, 110). One of the most persuasive elements in *The Talisman* is the degree to which this early attitude toward the world is transformed as Jack's journey brings to him an evolving sense of self-confidence and mental hardiness. Speedy dispatches Jack on this cross-country errand without money (he later gives Sawyer a guitar case full of it [King & Straub, 630]), without the aid of an automobile (Speedy has access to both cars and drivers [King & Straub, 628]), and on his own (even as Speedy follows him westward) because the black man knows that an epic quest requires an epic hero. Just as the four representatives from the Free Zone, following Mother Abagail's instruction, must cross the mountains into Las Vegas on their own without food and modern conveniences in mental preparation for battle against Randall Flagg in *The Stand,* Speedy likewise seeks to strengthen young Sawyer. Like Homer's Odysseus, Jack learns to lie and disguise himself (King & Straub, 122–123) not out of evil's intention to defraud, but because he must learn how to survive in a hostile environment. The powers of the Talisman pale in comparison to the transformation that occurs to Jack while on the road; in fact, the Talisman remains useless until its owner can prove himself worthy of its use.

Like characters in many of the epic narratives that shaped the writing of *The Talisman*—Dante's *Divine Comedy,* Virgil's *Aeneid,* Milton's *Paradise Lost,* Ovid's *Metamorphosis,* and Tolkien's *Lord of the Rings*—Jack Sawyer must pass through hell on his journey to selfhood and the salvation of the two queens. Sunlight Gardener's Home for Wayward Boys is *The Talisman*'s equivalent to Dante's inferno. Rudolph, the home's dishwasher, insists that Gardener himself is a "devil from hell" (King & Straub, 336), and when Jack and Wolf flip into the Territories from the home's lavatory, hell is exactly what they find. Gardener is the essence of the evangelical evil that haunts King's religious fanatics—from Margaret White in *Carrie* to the children in "Children of the Corn." But Sunlight's evil is slightly more refined than the religious prototypes that precede him. His particular madness carries a political agenda: he wishes to serve Sloat in transforming the Territories into a sterile reflection of his own American reformatory. The devil-creatures in charge of the infernal Territories' work-force mirror the forced labor camp that Sonny Singer and Heck Blast supervise in Sunlight's Far Fields. Again, the medieval flavor of this description makes it a verbal appropriation from the "hell" section in Bosch's "Garden of Earthly Delights."

The guards toiled beside them, and Jack saw with numb dismay that they were not human; in no sense at all could they be called human. They were twisted and humped, their hands were claws, their ears pointed like Mr. Spock's. . . . *Did somebody see them here? Somebody from the Middle Ages who flipped over, saw this place, and thought he'd had a vision of hell?* (King & Straub, 343)

As Dante had to descend literally through the levels of hell as an integral part of his journey to paradise, Jack must endure the physical and psychological torment he undergoes while a prisoner in Sunlight's home. The section dealing with Jack and Wolf's incarceration at Gardener's is located literally at the center of the novel. This is appropriate as it signals a clear break distinguishing Jack Sawyer, who began this quest against his will and full of trepidation, from Jack/Jason DeLoessian, whose spirit Jack really comes to embody while a prisoner at Gardener's home. Not only is the Jack we see there willing to fight to protect himself and Wolf, he likewise possesses a mental toughness that refuses, even under the duress of torture, to provide Sunlight with answers to his information requests. That Jack endures the violent loss of Wolf, a homophobic trauma that would destroy the stability of most American adolescents, and still continues his journey only highlights Sawyer's attributes as an epic hero: he emerges from the hell of Gardener's captivity a stronger individual resolute in his commitment to the task that awaits him.

The underlying theme of Dante's *Divine Comedy* is that love is the force that holds the universe together and links the individual fragments of creation to its God. Love is the motivating force behind Dante's spiritual pilgrimage. But for Dante, the concept of love is no mere abstract principle; it is a focused psychic experience on one specific object. In Dante's life, it is his deep commitment to Beatrice that starts him on the road to salvation; his love for her guides him through the darkness of his own soul and toward "the love that moves the sun and other stars."

Dante's journey is reflected in what Jack learns in the course of *The Talisman*. It is likewise love that motivates Jack's quest for the object. But the personal commitment to his mother that serves as this initial stimulus enlarges in the course of his journey westward to include other people, even other worlds. The movement of the novel, again corresponding to the epic tradition, is from the personal toward the universal. At the moment in which Jack finally bonds with the Talisman, he is no longer Jack but some sort of mystical axis, like the Talisman itself, bringing together

the individual elements of the universe into a unified whole. In contact
with the Talisman, he gains insight into the meaning of the spiritual principles that underscore not only human life, but the life of the universe:

Here was enough transcendentalism to drive even a cave-dwelling Tibetan holy
man insane. Jack Sawyer was everywhere; Jack Sawyer was everything. A blade
of grass on a world fifty thousand worlds down the chain from earth died of thirst
on an inconsequential plain somewhere in the center of a continent which
roughly corresponded in position to Africa; Jack died with that blade of grass. . . .
He was God. God, or something so close as to make no difference. (King and Straub,
591–592)

The quest for the Talisman, however, is always more than the journey to
a specific place to secure a single object; it is, rather, the fulfillment of
fundamental Christian principles: that life can only be measured in terms
of the love it inspires. As a Christian epic, *The Talisman* takes as its subject the soul's, and by extension, society's, pilgrimage from despair to salvation. As Dante must learn humility and selflessness (the sin of pride is
the one that proves the most difficult to exculpate in purgatory) if he is to
progress in his moral evolution, Jack Sawyer must come to the point at
which he is able to give up what he has come so far to secure:

Jack felt a sudden twist of Scrooge-miserliness. He snatched the Talisman close to
himself for a moment. *No! You might break it! Besides, it's mine! I crossed the country for it! . . .* The weight of the Talisman suddenly seemed immense, the weight
of dead bodies. Yet somehow Jack lifted it, and put it in Richard's hands. . . . Jack
realized that sensation of weight had been only his imagination, his own twisted
and sickly wanting. As the Talisman flashed into glorious white light again, Jack
felt his own interior darkness pass from him. It occurred to him dimly that you
could only express your ownership of a thing in terms of how freely you could
give it up . . . and then that thought passed. (King & Straub, 598–599)

   Jack is successful in his quest because through the course of his journey he has been internalizing the "healing message" of the Talisman. His
unions with Speedy, Wolf, and Richard teach him the value of love and
friendship. In contrast to Morgan Sloat and his egocentrism, Jack does
not seek power for himself: *"I don't want to be God,* I ONLY WANT TO
SAVE MY MOTHER'S LIFE!" (King & Straub, 592). The quest for the Talisman, like the search for the Grail, or Beatrice's love, or the Seventh ring is
as religious in its nature as it is mythic. Concluding back in New Hampshire on the night of the winter solstice, *The Talisman*'s cosmological message signals the advent of hope. Jack's mother is reborn on the day that
signifies the annual rebirth of creation: "a wondrous odor spilled out with
the gray-golden cloud, an odor sweet and unsweet, of flowers and earth,
wholly good, yeasty; a smell of birth, Jack thought, though he had never

attended an actual birth" (King & Straub, 642). An appropriate ending for a narrative that locates itself firmly in the tradition of the Christian epic – within the reassurance that the universe is not haphazardly arranged, that life can be lived constructively and with purpose, and that evil operates within the purview of our control.

REFERENCES

Beahm, George, ed. *The Stephen King Companion.* Kansas City, Mo.: Andrews & McMeel, 1989.

Grixti, Joseph. *Terrors of Uncertainty: The Cultural Contexts of Horror Fiction.* London: Routledge, 1990.

King, Stephen, and Peter Straub. *The Talisman.* New York: Viking, 1984.

Kolbert, Elizabeth. "The Drink of Millions." *New York Times Magazine,* March 4, 1990.

Marx, Leo. *The Machine in the Garden: Technology and the Pastoral Ideal.* New York: Oxford University Press, 1964.

Straub, Peter. "Meeting Stevie." In *Fear Itself: The Horror Fiction of Stephen King,* edited by Tim Underwood and Chuck Miller. San Francisco, Calif.: Underwood-Miller, 1982.

Twain, Mark. *The Adventures of Huckleberry Finn.* Berkeley, Calif.: University of California Press, [1884] 1985.

Underwood, Tim, and Chuck Miller, eds. *Bare Bones: Conversations on Terror with Stephen King.* New York: McGraw-Hill, 1988.

Winter, Douglas. *Stephen King: The Art of Darkness.* New York: New American Library, 1984; rev. ed. 1986.

———. "Stephen King, Peter Straub, and the Quest for *The Talisman.*" *Twilight Zone Magazine* (January/February, 1985).

11

A Clockwork Evil: Guilt and Coincidence in "The Monkey"

GENE DOTY

In "The Monkey," Stephen King has used an extremely unlikely object to arouse terror in his readers, a toy that is "nothing but cogs and clockwork" (King, 177). This chapter will explore the means by which King makes the monkey's association with the deaths in the story convincing and answer William F. Nolan's charge that, while powerfully written, "The Monkey" "lacks interior logic" (116).

Douglas Winter, who calls "The Monkey" "one of King's best short stories" (263), sees the monkey as representing a random, or fated, evil, "without apparent logic or motivation" (80). Tony Magistrale takes an opposite view when he says that the monkey represents Hal's "dark recollections" of "childhood . . . guilt and anxiety" (74–75). The tension between these two possible understandings of the monkey creates much of the effect of the story.

The question of the story's "interior logic" centers on the relationship between Hal and the monkey. There is an alternative to Winter's view that the monkey is an external, irrational evil, and Magistrale's view that the monkey is an objective correlative for Hal's guilt. In explaining this third possibility, I will also show the interior logic, which Nolan says the story lacks.

In the story, Hal Shelburn returns to his boyhood home after his aunt's death, bringing with him his sons, Dennis (aged 12) and Petey (aged 10), and his wife, Terry. His sons discover the monkey in the attic, and its discovery brings back the fear and guilt that Hal felt after discovering the monkey as a young child. After perceiving its association with several deaths, including his mother's, Hal attempts to destroy it by throwing it down a dry well. The story narrates the "present" when Hal as an adult has to deal with the monkey again, but the narration is interwoven with extensive flashbacks to Hal's childhood experiences with the monkey.

Hal first finds the monkey in his mother's attic when he is four years old. The monkey holds two cymbals, which it is supposed to clash together when wound up. Hal quickly discovers, to his disappointment, that the monkey does not work when he winds it up, but it does sometimes spontaneously clash its cymbals together. The horrible thing is that when it does so, someone dies. Its first victim is a child who falls from a tree. Other victims include Hal's and his brother's babysitter, a dog, yet another child, and the boys' mother.

The deaths associated with the monkey are not narrated in chronological order, but in an order of increasing emotional intensity. The effect of the interweaving of Hal's childhood and adult experiences is to identify Hal the adult with Hal the child, and also to create a strong link between Hal and Petey, his younger son. The interweaving also establishes a strong but ambiguous link between Hal and the monkey.

King describes the monkey both as a mindless mechanism and as taking malicious pleasure in the deaths it causes. Being a mere mechanism, it lacks conscious purpose; nor does it act directly to cause the deaths with which it is associated. Hal, as the viewpoint character, connects the monkey with the deaths. No one but Hal, and at the end Petey, perceives the connection between the monkey and the deaths. Through Hal, the reader is convinced of the connection between the monkey's cymbals and the deaths.

On one level the monkey embodies our dread of the accident that can befall any of us at any time. As much as we would like to pretend otherwise, none of our lives are secure. Heart embolisms, enraged lovers, drunken drivers, bizarre accidents: all of these and more are possible every moment of our lives, and all of them bring death in "The Monkey." Hal's life seems to have a large share of such dreadful accidents, beginning with the disappearance of his father, who may have been a victim of the monkey also, although neither Hal nor the reader is ever sure of this.

In connecting the monkey with the deaths, Hal has found a cause for these irrational accidents. Tragically, the monkey is beyond Hal's control and understanding. William F. Nolan asks the obvious question; why doesn't Hal "simply *destroy* the monkey?" (116). Part of the answer is that the monkey exerts a will of its own, returning from the junk dealer whose truck Hal has thrown it on, reappearing in the same carton he originally found it in, and even appearing again twenty years after Hal had thrown it into a dry well. Terrified of the monkey, the child Hal is powerless to destroy it, disable it, or throw it away. Hal's inability to rid himself of the monkey suggests that the connection between them is complex.

When Hal takes the monkey to the well to dispose of it, he almost falls through the rotten boards covering the well, and becomes badly scratched by the thorns growing around it (165). This scene clearly suggests that the monkey has the power to destroy Hal, that Hal endangers himself when he threatens the monkey. In an earlier incident, when he is seven, after kicking the monkey violently, Hal "hears" the monkey telling him that Hal can kick as much as he wants, the monkey is "not real, just a funny clockwork monkey," implying that Hal really cannot injure or deter it (177); the monkey is both intimately linked to Hal and independent of his conscious control.

On this occasion, which results in the death of another child, Hal attacks the monkey, determined "to stomp it, smash it, jump on it"; but as Hal rushes the monkey, it sounds its cymbals again, quietly, "and a sliver of ice seem[s] to whisper its way through the walls of [Hal's] heart, impaling it, stilling his fury and leaving him sick with terror again" (177). The monkey has the power to act on its own, even though it is "merely" a toy. Furthermore, the terror that the monkey instills in Hal keeps him from being able to destroy it.

On the day his mother dies, Hal comes home from school to find the monkey on a shelf in his room, after he thought he had hidden it in the attic where he originally found it. So far in the story, Hal's father has disappeared, Beulah the babysitter has been shot, and Bill's friend, Charlie Silverman, has been run over by a drunk. Hal connects the monkey's sounding its cymbals to the deaths and suspects that the monkey is connected to his father's disappearance. Now, home from school, Hal approaches the monkey "as if from outside himself — as if his own body had been turned into a windup toy at the sight of the monkey" (179). Hal watches himself take down the monkey and turn the key, and he hears its mechanism begin to work. The nightmarish quality of this experience is due to Hal's awareness of the significance of what he is doing, and his inability to stop himself from winding up the monkey.

When his mother dies (of a brain embolism — there is always a natural cause for deaths associated with the monkey), Hal and the monkey exchange conditions. Hal becomes an automaton, doing the monkey's will, and the monkey becomes alive: "it *was* alive . . . and the vibration he felt through its balding brown fur was not that of turning cogs but the beating of its heart" (180). In addition to the loss of his mother, Hal feels "guilt: the certain deadly knowledge that he had killed his mother by winding up the monkey on that sunny after-school afternoon" (180–181). Neither Hal nor the monkey is the physical cause of his mother's death, but Hal feels guilty because he associates the monkey's action with her death — and he wound up the monkey.

Hal's relationship to the monkey is complex. When Hal first finds the monkey, it startles him because he thinks it is alive. Then, realizing it is a toy, he is delighted: "Its funny grin pleased him" (172). Remembering the incident as an adult, Hal wonders if there was not another element in his initial response to the monkey: "Hadn't there been something else? An almost instinctive feeling of disgust?" (172). As this passage shows, when Hal remembers his initial, childhood response to the monkey, he is unsure of exactly what that response was. But what King records in the narrative of Hal's discovery is delight. This delight expresses an immediate bond between Hal and the monkey, a bond that leads to his obsession with it. Because of this bond, Hal believes that the monkey has somehow caused the deaths of several people, a dog, and even a fly.

Hal is not simply the witness and indirect victim of the monkey's malevolence. Instead, several details indicate a close relationship between Hal and the monkey. When Hal returns to his childhood home at the beginning of the story, he looks into the well where he had thrown the monkey twenty years before. At the bottom of the well, Hal sees a reflected face, which he at first thinks is the monkey's. However, as Hal quickly realizes, the reflected face is his own (164). Throughout the story, Hal "hears" the monkey's voice speaking to him personally and directly. The monkey also influences Hal's consciousness and his actions; for instance, the monkey tries to get Hal to wind it up (192). After Hal has tried to get rid of the monkey by putting it on a rag-man's truck, it returns, and "speaks" to him: "Thought you got rid of me, didn't you? But I'm not that easy to get rid of, Hal. I *like* you. We were made for each other, just a boy and his pet monkey, a couple of good old buddies" (188, King's emphasis).

The story is not really about a spooky toy monkey; it is about Hal, his fears and shames, and his desperate efforts to deal with them. Hal, like any normal child, must experience resentments toward the other people in his life, and, consequently, must also fantasize about their deaths. Abandoned by his father, orphaned by his mother's death, Hal has more than the usual reasons for resentment and fantasies of what his life might have been. Such resentments and fantasies create guilt in the normal person, and in Hal's case, they bind him to the deadly monkey. This guilt, violence, and anxiety link Hal and the monkey at a deep level but also make them antagonists. Hal struggles with the monkey, seeking to resist the attraction it exerts on him, and to cleanse himself of the negative qualities it expresses.

Hal's childhood guilt and rage have carried over into his adulthood. The monkey expresses a destructive urge in Hal as a father and husband. Hal feels an "uncontrollable hostility toward Dennis [his older son] more and more often" (168). In this scene, Hal slams Dennis against the door several times; the monkey grins, "as if in approbation" (168). The monkey's malevolent grin expresses a facet of Hal himself. As a man and a father, Hal is unpredictable and violent. He fears the growing disaffection of his older son, Dennis, and is inwardly terrified that something awful will happen to his younger son, Petey. He feels alienated from his wife, who is taking "a lot of Valium" (162). These anxieties and frustrations lead Hal to unintended violence against his son. They also repeat the fears of his childhood, providing the emotional context for the monkey's return; Hal is bonded to the monkey by his fear and guilt.

Petey, the favored son, shares Hal's sensitivity to the monkey. Having touched the monkey, he tells Hal that he both hates and likes the way the monkey feels. Then he informs Hal, "Daddy, I don't like that monkey" and also recognizes that the monkey is "bad" (182). Like Hal, Petey has heard the monkey's voice, urging him to wind it up: "Wind me up, Petey, we'll play, your father isn't going to wake up, he's never going to wake up at all" (182). The monkey has displaced Hal's father, and now seeks to displace Hal as Petey's father. The monkey's power of initiative and malevolent will are shown clearly as it seeks Hal's death.

When Hal rows out on the lake to sink the monkey, it appears to him that Petey regresses from nine years old to four (193). Significantly, Hal was four when he first found the monkey. Even though Petey does not go out in the boat with Hal, he definitely plays a part in sending the monkey to the bottom of the lake. From his position on the shore, Petey encourages and exhorts Hal, and warns him of the cloud that blows up with the storm. The love between father and son makes it possible for Petey to help Hal reexperience his original contact with the monkey, and rid his life of its maliciousness by banishing the fear and guilt rooted in his own childhood.

Even though it appears to be an ordinary toy, there are several indications that the monkey is unnatural. These include the monkey's apparent delight in the deaths it causes, as well as the anxieties it produces in Hal. King's repeated descriptions of the monkey's teeth and grin imply that the monkey consciously relishes its role in bringing death and suffering to human beings. In these descriptions, King clearly suggests that the monkey is more than a toy, but the descriptions do not in themselves suffice to make the monkey an objective agent of evil.

The reader is partly convinced of the monkey's malice by the credibility of Hal's experience. Hal is believable largely because, like many of King's characters, he is one of us. One might see him in line at Radio Shack or at a PTA meeting. He experiences the same family difficulties that many middle-class fathers face. The reader can easily recognize and identify with these experiences and emotions.

Thus, the reader is prepared to accept Hal's memories of his childhood, as well as the new terrors he experiences after returning to his childhood home and rediscovering the instrument of his earlier terrors. Many readers will find their own childhood fears and anxieties intensified in the unusual ones that Hal experiences.

The story has a subtler dimension that gives the monkey its air of dread: even though nothing shows it directly causing the deaths, it is clearly connected with them. In fact, all of the deaths are "accidental," with natural causes to explain them. The closest thing to an act directly caused by the monkey is the death of the fly toward the end of the story. Petey drops the bag with the monkey in it; the monkey's cymbal strikes a rock and clangs. At that moment, a fly drops dead (184–185). But the only connection between the sounding of the cymbal and the death of the fly is that they happen in immediate succession. No direct causal link between the two is apparent.

There is a suggestion in the story that the monkey is more than a clockwork toy. When Hal rows out onto the lake to sink the monkey into the deepest part, a monkey-shaped cloud appears in the sky, associated with a storm that arises suddenly: "The sun was behind the cloud, turning it into a hunched, working shape with two gold-edged crescents held apart" (194). King makes the nature of the monkey more complex by giving the earthly monkey a "celestial" counterpart, a cloud-spirit that manifests when the monkey is in great danger, almost bringing about Hal's death through the storm.

Just before Hal drops the monkey in the lake at the end of the story, he talks to Petey about its origins. Hal recognizes that while the monkey must have originally been one of many identical toys, subsequently "something bad" had happened to it. Hal then speculates that perhaps "most bad things" are not conscious of their badness, "that most evil might be very much like a monkey full of clockwork" (185). The monkey combines the horror of a mindless evil with that of a deliberately malicious evil, as it seems both a (broken) mechanical toy and a living force that Hal cannot throw away or destroy. And, as stated before, the only connection between the monkey and the deaths is Hal's consciousness of the coincidence of its clanging its cymbals as each death occurs.

Throughout the story, the pattern of simple coincidence is the same: the monkey sounds its cymbals, and then someone dies. The question remains, What is the link between the cymbals and the deaths? Or, in William F. Nolan's phrase, What is the "interior logic" of the story (116)? The monkey's role in the deaths is established through Hal's interpretation of events. Just because one event precedes or accompanies another does not mean it causes the other event. However, from an emotional and symbolic perspective, Hal's connecting the cymbals with the deaths is quite convincing.

The sound of the cymbals often initiates Hal's hearing the monkey's voice. In terms of sound-associations and resonances, when Hal (at seven years old) throws the monkey down the well, he hears the cymbals' *jang-jang* after it has hit the bottom, and flees, "his ears still *jangling*" (167, my emphasis). In several sentences that climax this section, King uses notable alliteration, establishing a cluster of sounds associated with the monkey's deadly action:

If the monkey wanted to *clap* its he*ll*ish *c*ymba*l*s now, *l*et it. It *c*ould *c*lap and *c*rash them for the *c*raw*l*ing *b*ugs and *b*eetles, the *d*ark things that *m*ade their home in the we*ll*'s *s*tone gu*ll*et. It would *r*ot *d*own there. Its *l*oathsome *c*ogs and wheels and *s*prings would *r*ust *d*own there. It would *d*ie *d*own there. In the *m*ud and *d*arkness. *S*piders would *s*pin it a *s*hroud. (167, emphases mine)

The sounds in these sentences are woven together so closely and subtly that there are more repetitions and partial alliterations than I have emphasized. The syntactical repetitions also contribute to the effect of this passage, which is an emotional and imagistic climax, effectively expressing the dreadfulness of the monkey.

Closely associated with the sound of the cymbals is the clicking sound the key makes when it is turned. In the scene narrating Hal's original discovery of the monkey (at age four), King describes the sleet "ticking" off the windows "sporadically," and off the roof "hypnotically" (171, 172). Both adverbs are significant: the monkey only works "sporadically," and it affects Hal "hypnotically." Further, the resemblance between the "ticking" of the sleet and the various "clicks" that the monkey's key makes is an example of the way sounds cluster around meaning, and, in the process, become expressive of the irrational qualities of experience. And, of course, the wintry chill of the sleet is congruent with the tone of the whole story.

The coincidence between the monkey and the deaths has an overwhelming and dreadful meaning for Hal because of his guilt over his part in its action, his fear of the monkey's apparent independence, and the emotional impact of the deaths themselves. The reader, in so far as he or she identifies with Hal's experiences, shares in the uncanny dread aroused by the monkey's association with the deaths and the apparent impossibility of getting rid of it.

"The Monkey" presents a world in which evil constantly threatens human beings, who do not even have the comfort of being afflicted by a personal evil, which they might at least be able to understand. The clockwork monkey's maliciousness embodies the accidental, irrational evil and suffering that constantly threaten all of us. In a world in which parents are absent (Hal's father), violent (Hal himself), or drugged (Hal's wife), the child must survive by his own resources. The return of the monkey puts Hal back in a child's state of terror and powerlessness. Paradoxically, by returning to a child-like state, Hal is able to relive his link with the monkey, and to untie the bonds of guilt and fear that connect him to it. His love for Petey gives him additional access to the innocence and directness of childhood. Through their shared love and courage, Hal and Petey are able to defeat the evil represented by the monkey, an evil that lies both outside them and inside them. Working together, Hal and Petey integrate the child and the adult.

Douglas Winter and Tony Magistrale posit two opposite interpretations of Hal's relationship to the monkey, Winter suggesting that the monkey is an objective evil, external to Hal, and Magistrale suggesting that it is a subjective evil, expressive only of Hal's personal fears and guilts. I have shown that the monkey's relationship to Hal is both objective and subjective — that the monkey is an evil beyond Hal's understanding and control, while at the same time, it is an evil intimate to Hal, a vehicle of his fears and guilts. One could say that the monkey embodies a more universal Evil, while Hal simply embodies a more personal evil.

The open-ended conclusion of "The Monkey" shows the subtle relationship between Hal and the evil toy. After Hal has sunk the monkey in the lake, he imagines a boy, fishing with his father, hooking the stuffed animal and reeling it in, "weeds draggling from its cymbals, grinning its terrible, welcoming grin" (197). Then the story ends with a newspaper column describing "hundreds of dead fish" found in the lake. King suggests that, while Hal may finally have rid his life of the monkey, it is not finished and is biding its time.

REFERENCES

King, Stephen. "The Monkey." In *Skeleton Crew,* pp. 160–198. New York: Signet, 1986.

Magistrale, Tony. *Landscape of Fear: Stephen King's American Gothic.* Bowling Green, Ohio: Bowling Green State University Popular Press, 1988.

Nolan, William F. "The Good Fabric: Of Night Shifts and Skeleton Crews." In *Kingdom of Fear: The World of Stephen King,* edited by Tim Underwood and Chuck Miller, pp. 111–120. New York: Signet, 1987.

Winter, Douglas E. *Stephen King: The Art of Darkness.* New York: Signet, 1986.

12

Playing the Heavy:
Weight, Appetite, and Embodiment
in Three Novels by Stephen King

BERNADETTE LYNN BOSKY

MONSTROUS APPETITE

> Take fat. How fat does a person have to be before he or she passes over the line and into a perversion of the human form severe enough to be called monstrosity? (King, *Danse*, 47)

> A poll was conducted among students asking them to assign adjectives to a picture of a thin child and one of a fat child. . . . About the fat child, they said: "dirty, liar, mean, lazy, tends to get into fights, ugly, stupid. . . ." (Kelly, 16)

"It's obvious," states Don Herron, "that King's fiction is a direct product of our times" (71). This is true of both "text and subtext," terms King uses to title a chapter of *Danse Macabre*. Bernard Gallagher has shown that King's approach in that chapter, used to analyze horror movies, can productively be used on fiction, including King's own, calling the method "allegorical," "a bimodal or dualistic vision" (37). Actually, despite his own mention of two levels (*Danse*, 15–16), King's critical method, and his books, more neatly break into three levels: the surface level of physical horror, and two kinds of "subtext." As King states in *Danse Macabre*, the subtext sometimes conveys pure primal fear – "something beyond art, something that predates art" (18) – and sometimes represents specific themes, which Gallagher identifies as "the political, social, and economic anxieties of the contemporary individual" (38).

It is to one, perhaps surprising, complex of such anxieties, values, and opinions, as expressed in King's fiction, that this chapter asks the reader to turn: body-weight and eating. Body-size may just be a shorthand way for King to distinguish characters, especially minor ones; yet other easy descriptors, such as height or coloration, are significantly less common. It seems this emphasis on body-size is not accidental, that the references are somehow relevant to the purpose and construction of King's fiction. Indeed, body-weight is highly charged with significance, both to King and to our culture in general.

On the psycho-social level, high or low weight often signifies a certain kind of character. King occasionally questions cultural assumptions; more often he reinforces them or uses them uncritically to help convey character or advance plot or theme. Thinness may be positive, associated with energy, youth, and normality; as a negative trait, it represents a mean, ungenerous temperament or lack of assertiveness, the latter especially in a thin male. Fat is always a sign of failure: social failure, psychological failure, and even moral failure.

Especially, men described as "fat" (rather than as "big") tend to be cruel and abusive or lazy, weak, and self-indulgent. This is true of almost all of the men in *It*, and of characters such as John Leandro in *The Tommyknockers* or Harry Wisconsky in "Graveyard Shift." Adult women are usually either slender, likable helpmates or oppressively dominating mother-figures—usually "fat" or "big"—who are pitied or feared, or both. This particularly characterizes *It* (Pharr), but examples abound: Wendy Torrance in *The Shining* versus Henrietta Dodd in *The Dead Zone*, *Pet Sematary*'s Rachel Creed versus Stella Randolph in *Cycle of the Werewolf*. Large adolescents, male or female, are tragic monsters, contributing to their fate but always put-upon, especially by their families: Carrie White in *Carrie*, Lardass Hogan in "The Body," Irma Bates in *Rage*, Elton Parrakis in *The Running Man*. King's male adolescents are more often "fat" and the females are more apt to be "heavy"; the reverse of his terms is common for adults.

On the archetypal level, eating and weight are material manifestations of appetite and the body, often connected with sex, both as appetite and as gender. Throughout King's fiction, fat represents a kind of dangerous, florid life, oppressive in its passions and demands. Body-size is also used in two contradictory ways, both of which suggest the ultimate triumph of mortality. Thinness often suggests wasting away and is associated with skeletal imagery, as in *Thinner*, "Apt Pupil," *The Tommyknockers*, "The Woman in the Room," and "Jerusalem's Lot." Fatness can also represent death, associated with corpulence and rot, as in "Gramma," "Graveyard Shift," and "Gray Matter." There is only one major work by King in which death is thematically central, yet body-size is not important: in *Pet Sematary*, age is iconic of death, used by King as he, elsewhere, uses body-size.

Obviously, this general topic can be approached in many ways. It is central to King, perhaps in his personal history and certainly in his fiction. Here we will confine ourself to three novels, examining both text and subtext: *It, The Stand,* and *Misery.*

UGLY DUCKLINGS AND UGLY DUCKS

> You look at the guy with three eyes, or you look at the fat lady, or you look at the skeleton man or Mr. Electrical. . . . And when you come out, well, you say, "Hey, I'm not so bad. . . ." It has that effect of reconfirming values, of reconfirming self-image and our good feelings about ourselves. (King, *Bare Bones,* 9)

> Five hundred people are asked by the pollsters what they fear most in the world and one hundred and ninety of them answer that their greatest fear is "getting fat." (Chernin, 36–37)

In *It,* the seven young/old protagonists are sympathetic monsters, rejected by the world around them but likable and even, ultimately, heroic. Each is marked by an outstanding trait that just barely (or almost) avoids simple cliche. (Regarding cliche characterization in King's fiction, see Warren.) They were, as an adult-Mike writes in *It,* "six boys and one girl, none of them happy, none of them accepted by their peers" (150). This is a common theme in King's fiction, in *Carrie* (as Yarbro discusses) and elsewhere. In *It,* the horrors are often explicitly those of fairy tales; similarly, the development of the Losers' Club into winners is an implicit fairy tale, the basic narrative of wish-fulfillment of which "Cinderella" and "The Ugly Duckling" are examples.

The trait that makes Ben a member of the Losers' Club is fat; in fact, he may be the only one who is not slender. Throughout *It,* the Losers are described in derogatory terms, often by Henry Bowers or other bullies in the novel—from Beverly's husband Tom to Eddie's mother—which simply gives the reader more sympathy for these objects of derision. The Losers may think of themselves with condemnation, or occasionally refer to each others' problems in bravado and camaraderie. However, only Ben is consistently described in a tone of revulsion, not only as a form of aggression from others, but routinely by himself and perhaps even as an implied objective estimation. In *The Obsession,* Kim Chernin discusses the "nightmarish, hallucinatory quality" of the description of fat by our culture, and compares its "immense exaggeration" to the similar fascinated horror seen in descriptions by Christian church fathers of sexual temptation and degradation (42–44). Exactly that kind of exceptional emphasis is brought to descriptions in *It* of Ben.

In the novel, the motion of Ben's body is described in terms both ludicrous and repulsive: "Ben shook his head again, his jowls quivering" (171); or mention of "the plopping sound his butt made" as Ben sat down (273). Special attention is paid to Ben's abdomen, which is described as almost having a horrible life of its own (169, 252). Perhaps significantly, the two times Ben is injured, it is on his belly, first by Henry Bowers and then by It as the Werewolf; and one trip to 29 Neibolt St. not only frightens but embarrasses Ben, as his "gut" gets stuck and he worries about "his extremely large ass practically in his beloved's face" (858). Most of all, the reader is privy to Ben's self-hatred over his fatness, only slightly modified by the delights of TV, including a role-model in the overweight Broderick Crawford of *Highway Patrol* (174–176). This horror Ben's fat holds, for others and himself, may make him the ugliest of the seven ducklings, though not the most unfortunate.

Descriptions of Harold Lauder in *The Stand* are far from flattering, but lack the full degree of attentive detail and disgust used to depict Ben Hanscom. However, Harold is more often regarded as emotionally and morally revolting, while Ben evokes more sympathy. In *The Stand,* when Fran Goldsmith first sees Harold, she feels "an instant surge of distaste" at the "fat sixteen-year-old"; she remembers being told that he "whacks off in his pants" (248). Although Fran thinks that she doesn't care "how much weight he carried," she does critically note his shape, especially as revealed by his clothes (249, 326). Still, she dislikes Harold primarily because, "looking at him, she always felt uncomfortable and a little disgusted, as if she sensed by a low-grade telepathy that almost every thought Harold had was lightly coated with slime." The worst aspects of Harold's appearance are due in part to lack of hygiene – his hair is "greasy" – or his choice of tight clothes. His "large buttocks joggling inside his tight pants" are unseemly, even sexual (249). Harold's choice in clothes contrasts sharply to Ben's self-effacing sweatshirts.

Like Ben, Harold is an ugly duckling. Tragically, however, even after his fat body is successfully transformed, he does not make the moral and emotional choice to embrace the new life (Bosky 227–230). Harold's physical changes are gradual and realistic, produced by the strenuous activity and radically different habits necessary since the superflu. Harold thinks of himself as "fat" and "pimply"; then he realizes that "he couldn't even properly be called stout," and "his pimples had vanished over the last seven weeks" (796). However, only as he is dying, betrayed by the Dark Man, can Harold accept the glories and responsibilities of being a swan – or a Hawk (971–978).

Ben's metamorphosis is almost the opposite: mythic rather than realistic, the change is necessary so that his exterior can reveal his interior. There are hints of possible self-acceptance for Ben. In one lyrical moment, reminiscent of Ray Bradbury's *Dandelion Wine*, Ben glimpses a grandeur incompatible with his shame: "He felt as tall as the standpipe and as wide as the whole town" (172). The novel also offers some acceptance by others, especially Beverly, that could ease Ben's self-hatred (168, 1083). When Beverly thanks him for the haiku, she makes clear that, unlike Ben himself (168), she does not think his love is ludicrous because he is fat (935–38).

However, hope of self-acceptance surfaces only in those few hauntingly warm moments, almost despite itself. Finally, Ben wins his love only after transforming himself physically, so that not only is he not fat, he is described as "lean" (809) and even "lanky" (163) and "thin" (487).

This is far from surprising. As Susie Orbach, Nancy Roberts, Susan Kano, and others point out, weight-loss is one of the strongest contemporary Cinderella myths, perhaps now surpassing even Horatio Algeresque dreams of economic success. "Slimming . . . has to do with fantasies," as Hillel Schwartz writes, "extrapolating into the best and lightest of futures. As slow miracle or instant metamorphosis, diets deal in possibilities" (v). Roberts describes the contemporary believer of this myth, "dreaming of the day when she will be thin enough to care about her looks and her life" (7) because, as Mary S. Stuart and Lynnzy Orr put it, in our society, "Thin is smarter and richer and better paid. Thin is easier to look at. . . . We've believed it, we've built our lives around it" (37). Like the original Cinderella story, this myth is primarily about and for women, but men also feel that being fat is incompatible with self-esteem, as Marvin Grosswirth shows. Thus, in Ben's physical change, King depicts the desires and beliefs of many of his readers.

However, like the story of Stan Uris's economic success or Bill Denbrough's early writing career, Ben's transformation is too good to be true. When King attributes this to the influence of a fateful force for good, the plot may be justified, but the situation remains emotionally unsatisfying, unlike, for instance, Donna Trenton's heroism in *Cujo* or Larry Underwood's maturation in *The Stand* (especially the longer edition). Bill imagines Ben at a bulldozer, "his shirt off, showing a stomach which protruded less and less over the waistband of his pants" (487–488), hinting at the total change in activity and situation that lent credibility to Harold Lauder's similar physical transformation in *The Stand.* But this approach is not followed up. Instead, Ben relates a Cinderella story that delivers rebellion against authority figures (the coach and his mother) and desirable slimness in one decisive, albeit not easy, step.

In a locker-room scene reminiscent of that in *Carrie,* Ben is derided and persecuted by his classmates. However, while Carrie is brought out of her shell primarily because of the sympathy she receives as a result, Ben is further reviled by his coach, who tells him, "You disgust them and you disgust me as well." Ben's weight-loss is motivated primarily by personal shame and by anger at the coach (492–497). This contrasts with more credible changes in *It,* all of which come about through self-acceptance, as when Bill stops blaming himself for his brother's death, or Beverly finally sees that she does not deserve abuse.

King does present specific motives for Ben's overeating, and for his weight loss; unfortunately, they are contradictory. First, Ben had already been shamed by his Aunt Jean, and this had only caused him to gain more weight (492–493). Second, Ben says that he had overeaten only to appease his frightened mother, who felt more secure when she saw him eat: "So the biggest fight wasn't in my head; it was with her" (496–497). However, elsewhere the causes of Ben's childhood overeating are very much shown to be in his own head. King depicts Ben using food as a palliative for fear (215), loneliness (175–176, 188), and perhaps, in a vicious cycle common to more severe eating disorders, such as bulimia, even his own self-hatred, including weight-related shame (176, 185).

One possible tool for change is both believable and directly relevant to the main subject of the novel: Ben's last, fading memory of the fight against It, with pride in his accomplishment and in "how *good*" he and his six friends had been "together" (495). Unfortunately, this is not developed further. In fact, *It* never shows Ben directly confronting (and healing) these aspects of himself, as a child or as an adult. The change in Ben, as depicted, is particularly unbelievable for this reason: although shame over fat and problems with food were supposedly a major part of Ben's childhood, they have no real effect on the adult Ben. King repeatedly stresses that in order to defeat It, the present-day Losers must recapture the joyous desires and face the puzzles, obstacles, and horrors of their cultural and personal pasts. Thus, concerns by the adult Ben about eating and weight are conspicuous by their absence.

There are only two mentions of Ben's relationship to food as an adult. The first may hint at a return of his old habits (492). However, the second, shortly thereafter, is untroubled, even jovial (528), and that is the last we hear of Ben's eating habits. Similarly, there is precisely one mention of any shame over body-size. As the five adults prepare to enter Its lair, "Ben felt his heart begin to pick up speed. There was a sour taste in his mouth and his head had begun to ache. He felt slow and frightened. He felt fat" (1046). Even compared to Mike Hanlon's thoughts and feelings about racism, which could also benefit from further development, this seems perfunctory, especially after the insistent concentration on the horrors of young Ben's obesity.

In a book with the scope of *It* (and edited down as *It* apparently was), one may expect some skimping occasionally. However, there is a riddle implied by the contrast of this extreme skimping on the one hand, and the extreme descriptions of young Ben's fat body on the other. Study of that riddle yields important insight into major pervasive themes in King's writing. Also, some clues will be provided by other characters described as being fat, or having extra body-fat. Harold is a failed swan, given a new chance by the superflu but unable or unwilling to take advantage of it. Ben is an ugly duckling, a good soul trapped in a corpulent body. Many older characters have personalities as unpleasant as their fat bodies; these are hopeless and even threatening, not ugly ducklings but ugly ducks.

FEEDING THE MONSTER

> We love and need the concept of monstrosity because it is a reaffirmation of the order we all crave as human beings. . . . it is not the physical or mental aberration in itself which horrifies us, but rather the lack of order which such aberrations seem to imply. (King, *Danse*, 50)

> Our bodies, we learn, are unruly animals. They must be tamed. Their urges are inappropriate. Their hungers are fed or denied according to someone else's will. (Dickenson, 37)

Behind Its many masks, the monster in Derry has five basic faces: eating, excreting, sex (including procreation), fighting or killing, and dying. These are, in other words, all of the universal activities of the animal body, except for sleeping and being born. In a sense, It *is* the body, a devilish body which tempts us with its appetites and betrays us into death. "Consciousness of the physical body – its sensations, vulnerability, and ultimate termination – is the focus of horror literature," Leonard G. Heldreth writes (64). Actually, it is not the only focus; there are also, for instance, fears of madness and isolation, which King uses well. However, this body-consciousness is important in King's fiction. It is finely rendered in "The Body," as Heldreth's article demonstrates, and is the driving force in many works by King.

"King," Douglas Winter writes, "tends to identify [human evil] with moral weakness" (211). One appeal of King's fiction is that few of his characters are actively malevolent; but in his stories, selfish choices or lack of self-control have much the same effect. Tony Magistrale has traced this theme throughout King's works, finding corollaries in and even influences from the moral allegories of the American Gothic tradition. King, Magistrale states, presents two remedies for the human capacity for evil, both of which depend on overriding those impulses inherent in humanity: "self-discipline" to "overcome the beast within," and the "selflessness" of love (*Landscape*, 53–72). In *It*, Ben's fat sometimes represents the twin sins of animality and self-indulgence; and in this context, his weight-loss represents self-discipline and self-control. In *The Stand*, Harold's fat corresponds to his moral looseness, especially his obsession with uncontrolled, adolescent sexuality; but his weight-loss contrasts ironically with his progressive descent into evil.

Leslie Fiedler, in his study of the symbolism of sideshow freaks, shows that fat has long represented both animal appetite – "without guilt or limit or satiety" – and selfish sloth (26–27, 136). Studies of contemporary American attitudes towards fat and dieting demonstrate this same symbolic point. Kim Chernin, for example, compares modern statements about fat or the need to diet and nineteenth-century writings about the perils of masturbation or the benefits of sexual abstinence (9, 38–44). In each case, what was said to be purely a health consideration was also influenced by a general societal distrust of the flesh and its appetites. Even one student of these attitudes said, when it came to self-image, "I can't help feeling it is immoral to be fat" (Dickenson, 38).

Slenderness, on the other hand, is often seen as iconic of self-control. The statements of those with anorexia nervosa are shockingly clear: "This is about control," one writes. "When nothing else in the world can be controlled I can control my body" (Giannino, 58). Yet in this, anorexia nervosa is merely the pathological extreme of outlooks like that of a normal "woman on a reducing diet" who said, "I feel good when I feel hungry. Each pang of hunger reminds me that I'm in control, so I feel proud and successful" (Mayer, 3).

Can all this be found in King's depiction of his characters, fat and thin? The match is striking. In *It,* this may be one source of Ben's self-disgust at being fat, which reaches a degree of shame felt by no other Loser – not even Beverly, though she is equally convinced that her problems could be avoided if she were good enough. Most of all, it is specifically a source of the coach's explicitly stated disgust. "It's a lot of self-indulgence," he says of Ben's uncontrolled fat, "and it makes me want to puke" (493–494).

Most of the secondary characters in *It* who are described as "fat" (rather than "big") are out of control, hurtful to themselves or others, though sometimes with the best intentions: Beverly's abusive husband Tom, Eddie's mother and wife, Henry Bowers both then and now (691, 620, 919), Henry's father Butch (947), and Henry's fellow-bullies Moose Sadler (680) and Patrick Hockstetter (781). Some of the minor characters described in terms of fat are also seen as violent, pompous, lazy, or selfish, all of which can be seen as forms of self-indulgence. These include the man next to Bill on the SST (218–219), the fat fellow-student in Bill's college creative writing class (124–128), the abusive guard Fogarty at Henry's institution for the criminally insane (612–613), and Butch Bowers's girlfriend Rena (817). There is a fat politician lampooned in a drawing owned by Mike, whose "show of mingles buffoonery and intemperance" is greeted by some distant "bonneted women" with "disgust" (727).

It links fat with self-indulgence or even immorality that borders on evil (and invites Its influence). There are two seeming exceptions to this, both of which actually support the symbolism. Beverly's father, the abusive precursor of her husband Tom, is "scrawny" (908). This reversal of King's iconography is deliberate: Mr. Marsh *seems* virtuous, but this is ironic.

"He did not drink, he did not smoke, he did not chase after women"–outward facts that allow him to say, "I have no vices" (395, 397), although he beats his daughter and covertly lusts for her. Significantly, his aggression and sexual desire are described in metaphors of eating (905, 908; 572–573). Bill Denbrough's small pot belly is less representative of appetite and more representative of age, as is the fact that he is balding (128, 478, 1129; see also 553). It does seem to show the possibility of uncontrolled appetite, especially linked to the risk of drinking too much alcohol, which Bill does not let get out of hand.

Thus, we see one reason why Ben's fat flesh is described in lurid detail, although there is no equivalent discussion of Mike's dark skin and negroid features, or any elements of Jewishness in Stan's appearance, though that may be displaced onto his wife's revery in her own Jewishness (45), which does have some of the same sad, loathsome power as the descriptions of Ben. These features certainly are the object of as much hatred (by the bullies) and self-consciousness (in the minds of the young friends). However, Ben's fat takes on a subtextual importance that Mike's blackness or Stan's Jewishness do not, a moral (or immoral) significance that is now considered improper to apply to race. It represents appetite gone wild and flesh without boundaries, like "his buttocks spilling over either side of the sagging seat" of his bicycle (854).

Both Ben and Harold represent self-indulgence and fear of the body's appetites, but Harold more specifically evokes the dangers of sexuality. As Collings points out, "sexuality appears as a threat" in *The Stand* as it does in other fiction by King; specifically, Harold's "perverted sexuality" causes and reflects his allegiance with Flagg's darkness (*Facets,* 113). One passage in *The Stand* defines Harold's problem, combining selfishness, gluttony, and sexual desire. Harold "glared sullenly" at Stu, "the eyes those of a piggy little boy who wants the whole cookie jar to himself. Ain't he going to be surprised, Stu thought, when he finds out a girl isn't a jar of cookies" (390). Thus, we see one reason why Harold rejects the potentials of his new, thin self: his flesh rules him more powerfully through lust than through gluttony. Harold indulges his appetites, though they cause ever greater harm to himself and others.

The horrors of appetite alone, however, are more the concern of *It.* In keeping with the more social and political thrust of *The Stand,* Harold's greatest sins are that he refuses to take advantage of possibilities offered by the new frontier cleared by the superflu, and that he is too proud and angry to share in the community being built around him. Like Carrie and other fellow-outcasts, Harold is separated from others by his weight and complexion; but when those stigmas disappear, he finds other excuses. Tony Magistrale discusses Harold's increasing, self-chosen isolation and his narcissism, seen also in his masturbatory sexuality. These contribute to his "vulnerability" to Nadine's carnal appeal, which Larry

Underwood resists through self-discipline and his sense of responsibility to Lucy (*Landscape*, 63–64).

In *It* and *The Stand*, King contrasts the immoral indulgence of bodily appetite, represented by body-fat, with virtuous self-control. Perhaps an even deeper level of symbolism, however, can be found in *It:* why would one have to control one's bodily appetites so rigorously, if the body itself were good? According to Chernin, Western dualism between the mind (or spirit) and the body, and emphasis that the former must overcome the latter, is one reason for contemporary obsession with slimming (49–61). In *It,* Ben is described in explicitly dualistic terms: his "mind" is "every bit as lean and quick as his body was obese" (171). (Similarly, young Bill Denbrough's "brains" did not stutter [240].) In terms of the novel's subtext, Ben's lively, effective, admirable mind must triumph over his torpid, self-sabotaging, suspect body. Thus, it is not enough for Ben to overcome his feelings of shame and loneliness, which some passages in *It* suggest might have happened without any weight loss. The fat must go, taming the body so that it reveals and serves the mind.

Until Ben's mind triumphs, his body is monstrous. The descriptions of fat in *It* go beyond moral suspicion to pure disgust, in which the belly itself becomes a horror. Beverly calls Tom a "tub of guts," an insult Victor Criss also hurls at Ben (118, 172). A bad enough image in its own right if taken literally, it also evokes our deepest fears and shames concerning the most central work of the body: eating, excreting, and possibly even sexual arousal, which we call "appetite." We have already seen one source of the repulsion engendered by the descriptions of Ben as a youth: his flesh, and especially his abdomen, moves on its own, as though it had usurped control and achieved a kind of independent life. Ben's fattened body is also described in terms of meat: his "huge hams" (238), his "meaty shoulder" (294). Overall, Ben is an icon of the flesh triumphant; since *It* is meant to provoke our fear, that is not a pretty sight. This basic body-shame is also shown in two minor characters, the union boss on Audra's film (633) and the man next to Bill on the SST (218–219), both of whom not only are fat but also stink of body odor.

One major reason for suspicion of the body, which Chernin says helps inform our culture's attitudes towards fat, is "the fact that our body dies and takes us with it" (61). Something which is partially real can also carry a symbolic charge beyond its realistic justification: Chernin argues that in our culture there is "an immense exaggeration" of "the dangers and terrors of overweight" that reveal the "deeper, less rational worry, having to do with fear and dislike for the body" (43). By a kind of synechdoche, conditions associated with some unavoidable physical risk, like obesity or age, can become charged with the full "fear of death and dying," as Marjorie Nelson puts it (231–232). Chernin quotes one writer who declares to fat, would-be dieters, "You are sentenced to death now in a prison of your own adipose tissue" (43). But of course, we are all sentenced to death in and by our flesh, no matter how much adipose tissue we have, or how little.

Modern horror literature, including King's own fiction, is indebted to the fear of mortality, as King repeatedly states in *Danse Macabre;* and the identification between fat and death is certainly evident in King's work, most obviously in *Thinner* but also in works from *The Cycle of the Werewolf* to "Gramma." In *It,* a sympathetic librarian thinks of young Ben Hanscom "digging a grave with a knife and fork" (188). Fat as an icon of fleshiness and hence death is also apparent in the treatment of the only other likable fat character in *It,* Tony Tracker (552–557), and in the morbid interest that pharmacist Norb Keene shows in fat and heart attacks (645, 768–769).

It is not surprising that Ben's fat could imply both death and the appetites or processes of physical life, because in *It* the two are treated as almost synonymous: death is consistently described in terms of eating, of being eaten, and of being trapped (swallowed) inside a body. Mike, in his journal, describes cancer as "eating" both his father (448) and his friend and informant, Carson (156). He also writes that Derry is haunted, and the definition of "haunt" that scares him most is "a feeding place for animals" (146). The central refrain of the novel comes from Ben's reverie on "The Three Billy Goats Gruff": "would the monster be bested . . . or would it feed?" (178, 540, 864, 1031).

"It, which only ate" (1054) is a dramatic and horrifying conflation of all things with appetites that we fear: time, which "all things devours," as Gollum's riddle puts it in *The Hobbit;* death, the ultimate unknown, which is, like It, "eternal . . . the Eater of Worlds" (1052); and the body, which in our culture often is seen as a trap for our mind, subjecting the true "us" to its unreasonable and uncontrollable passions, and ultimately delivering us up to those two other appetites that we fear even more. Ben can fight against It and win partly because of pure love – his love for Beverly and his other friends – but also because, on this thematic level, he has beaten appetite by subduing his own unruly flesh. In this, Ben is opposed to It, which is as out of control as the town of Derry, which It influences and reflects.

(S)MOTHER LOVE

> You know, King has this thing for fat women. Annie Wilkes. Gramma. And I don't mean fat; I mean *monstrous*. (Wornom, 158)

> These fearful she-monsters not only destroy men: they eat, they swallow, they suck. They are voracious. The idea of women as destructive seems inextricably involved with the idea of eating. (Chernin, 131–132)

In our culture, body-shape, and especially fat, is seen as a particularly female problem in many, often contradictory, ways. Biologically, women have a higher ratio of body fat to muscle, leading to a naturally curved appearance; symbolically, this roundness can stand for sexuality or sexlessness, childish self-indulgence or all-enfolding motherhood, strong bulk or feminine weakness, uncontrolled appetite or a softness that provides for others. Women are often seen as nurturers and feeders, because of both lifelong social roles and the physical ability to give birth and nurse the child.

All of these associations can be found in the fiction of Stephen King; since his fiction is horrific by design, the impact is often unpleasant. Michael Collings, for instance, refers to Mabel Wertz in 'Salem's Lot as "the archetypal monstrous woman common throughout King's works" (Facets, 75). The iconography of the large female body pervades King's fiction, from Rage, with ugly-duckling Irma and oppressive-mama Mrs. Dano, to The Dark Half, in which the meaty body of victim Dodie Eberhart is described as androgynous in its bulk, yet still charged with female eroticism. Different works by King emphasize different aspects of this iconography.

King has some sympathy for his female ugly ducklings, as he does for their male counterparts. However, their corpulence is stigma, isolating them socially. (Collings makes this point, also, about Stella Randolph in Cycle of the Werewolf [Facets of Stephen King, 81].) Adult females described as fat or overweight are often morally condemnable, as are fat men; but the women are even more threatening, encompassing both the general human problems seen in King's male characters and those particular to female sexuality and motherhood. Most of all, King frequently depicts domineering mother figures that are either fat or associated with providing food for others, or both. In extreme cases, their attempts to control others are especially dangerous because they cannot even regulate their own behavior. Issues of fat, feeding, and control (or chaos) are clear in The Stand and central to It and Misery.

In It, the identification between fat and femaleness is clear, and clearly horrible. The description of Eddie Kaspbrak's fat, overprotective mother could be that of a paleolithic goddess like the Venus of Willendorf, except for the condemning tone: "She had become something nearly monstrous . . . her body had seemed nothing more than boobs and butt and belly, all overtopped by her pasty, perpetually dismayed face" (90). Eddie's wife, Myra, wears "a white nightgown which swelled, comber-like, at bosom and hip" and complains that her chauffeur uniforms have become "too tight in the tits" (25–26). Even more significantly, young Ben Hanscom's fat is often described in female terms. His male, fat-produced "titties" are objects of derision and cause of his own shame (169, 494, 849); fellow students later nickname him "Jugs" (874). Victor Criss thinks of Ben's "ass wiggling like a girl's inside his new bluejeans," calling Ben "the pansy" (177). Thus, extra fat not only accentuates or mimics female roundness, but also reveals a basically feminine nature, just as Victorian physicians believed that certain hormonal disturbances created not only a "feminine distribution" of fat in men, but also "effeminacy in disposition" (Howard, 103). This association may be behind the worries of Harold Lauder's father, in *The Stand,* that his son could be "hommasexshul," a "queerboy" (329, 796, 971–973).

Kim Chernin reports that in *Pornography and Silence,* Susan Griffin "has shown that our culture . . . tend[s] consistently to associate both women and Blacks with the body, with instinct and with sensuality, and to fear both women and Black people because of this association" (128–129). (Chernin provides a striking example from William Faulkner's *Light in August.*) In King's fiction, this association is split: Blacks represent a positive tie to nature and a benevolent source of nurture. As Tony Magistrale shows, characters such as Dick Hallorann in *The Shining,* Mother Abagail in *The Stand,* and Speedy Parker in *The Talisman* combine natural virtues of prophetic insight and "an instinctive understanding of how the world operates" with a civilized "sense of moral integrity" (*Landscape,* 100). All three also provide the white protagonists with tools they need to survive and triumph, and all three are associated with food in a healthy, positive way. Fat women in King's fiction, on the other hand, represent a sinister corporeality and an oppressive, smothering nurture.

Study of Mother Abagail makes clear how deep this split is: for her to represent goodness her blackness must be asserted but her female flesh must be subdued. Douglas Winter writes, "Her image is that of an earth mother, spawned of the fertile cornfields" (195), and she does sustain and feed her flock from those fields (508–510). Yet she is an "earth mother" whose slender flesh is moderate and disciplined, whose Christian virtues control her appetite. Her final victory, as Collings states, is "to starve herself into submission, to destroy pride in herself, and to die in the clarity of vision that starvation brings" ("*The Stand,*" 88). Finally, spiritual victory erases her female shape entirely. When she returns from fasting in the wilderness, it states in *The Stand,* "She seemed without sex," and "her breasts were gone" (901).

In an interview, King identifies Beverly as "an earth mother," who "becomes a symbolic conduit between adulthood and childhood for the boys in the Losers' Club," bringing about "the symbolic advent of manhood through the act of sex" (Magistrale, *Stephen King,* ms. 9–10). Yet, Pharr shows, Beverly is oddly powerless for one so powerful, and all of her female force is expressed for and through the male Losers. She is symbolically opposed to the ravenous appetite of It, as Pharr points out, and to the Losers' parents, whom Beverly either substitutes for as she does with Eddie (1081), or supercedes by initiating their sons into maturity. Ultimately, Beverly seems intended by King to indicate not only the proper role for a woman, but the nature of Woman. She is passionately female, but the physicality that she represents is kept within proper bounds. Thus, her body is described in the novel as round, but only in the right places: "slim but abundantly stacked" (105). Beverly holds the only hope present in *It* for bringing body and spirit into a functional unity. Having sex with her young friends, Beverly at first feels only "a kind of mental ecstasy" herself, but this blossoms into "pleasure" and "passion" with Ben and Bill. The act, Beverly thinks, is an "essential human link between the world and the infinite, the only place where the bloodstream touches eternity" (1082–1086).

Other earth mothers in King's fiction, however, are monstrous females, often depicted as fat, who both nurture and devour. In *It,* the final face of the monster is a devouring, fleshy, procreating force in the shape of a huge she-spider. Not only "pregnant" with Its own spawn (1048–1049), It is used to express a general fear of the female body. Even worse than being killed by It is to be incorporated in it alive: as It says, "you'll go mad . . . but you'll live . . . and live . . . and live . . . inside [the deadlights] . . . inside me" (1055). This image presents a horror of corporeality, a duality of mind trapped inside flesh. In conjunction with Its pregnancy, the image also suggests a fear of the female body, which shelters yet engulfs, within the womb or through a hungry sexuality.

When Eddie injures It with his aspirator, he triumphs over the interiorized voice of his overprotective mother (1067). This culminates a constellation of associations linking It to both diseased sexuality and oppressive mothering. The monster appears to Eddie as the Leper, a creature of sexuality and disease, but Its final guise is, "the most terrible thing of all: his ma's face." Mrs. Kaspbrak, herself fat, has a love that devours Eddie. When he sees the "predatory" look in her "small eyes" buried in "pockets of flesh," he thinks, "she's not the leper . . . she's only eating me because she loves me" (789–790). Eddie's final attack on It is disturbingly sexual; then Its jaws rip Eddie's arm off at the shoulder, perhaps in symbolic castration. As he dies, Eddie experiences purity when the mind leaves the body, "washed clean" of the emotions and problems of the body to experience "that perfectly rational light" of discorporeality (1068). With the defeat of It, Eddie frees himself of disease, fear, sexuality, the flesh, and the devouring mother, all at once.

The monster's end combines resonances of body-hatred, mother-hatred, and rape. The smelly, "bloated body," with its "writhing wetness," terrifies and disgusts Its adversaries. Bill's attack suggests both sexual violation and a kind of reverse, forced birth, in which he penetrates Its "pulsing bag of guts and waters"; his cries of triumph are explicitly sexual. As many a child or husband has been accused of doing, Bill literally breaks Its heart. Finally, It is abandoned, reduced to a "huge bundle of steaming alien meat" (1092–1094).

Significantly, in *It,* King also sometimes expresses the devouring, sexualized love of Beverly Marsh's father in female terms. When Beverly's father chases her, a brief mention connects him to Its final, maternal form as a spider (905, 909). The monster appears directly to Beverly in a male form that resembles both her father and the hungry giants of fairy tales; first, however, It appears as the witch from Hansel and Gretel who "always scared" Beverly "because it ate the children" (569–574). Like many of King's females, the witch both feeds others and devours them. In this case the threat, while still tied to embodiment, nurture, and even sexuality (861) is more a matter of *thanatos* than of *eros,* as seen in the descriptions of the witch's appearance and animalistic eating (570–571). However, *eros* and *thanatos* are just different aspects of the unified threat of physicality.

Themes of appetite and embodiment are depicted explicitly in Its actions and appearances, but they also influence the ostensibly realistic description of oppressive mother-figures in *It* and the rest of King's writing. Even a minor character such as Butch Bowers' girlfriend Rena Davenport, "fat, forty, and usually filthy," combines sexuality, eating, and cooking in one unpleasant mess (817–818). The major characters in *It* make these associations even more clear.

In that novel, Eddie Kaspbrak repeatedly compares his wife and his mother; in fact, he believes that he married Myra because of the resemblance, an act of "psychological incest" (84–100). Myra seems far too dependent and childlike for the maternal role in which Eddie casts her, but his "domineering tank of a mother" (148) also ultimately proved weak and afraid. Though flustered and incompetent, Myra is still imposing by virtue of her fat, female body: as Chernin states, "large size, girth, immensity in a woman means always mother" (139; also Stuart & Jacobson, 61–62). Eddie Kaspbrak's reaction mixes the allure and revulsion of this identification, a combination he can overcome only by death.

While Myra controls Eddie through a kind of passive, hyperfeminine "sweetness" (91), his mother combines that approach with another, just as common in King's writing: the strong mother, almost always a single parent, who manages admirably in difficult circumstances but spoils her child, often by feeding him too much. Sometimes, the child is fat rather than the mother, but it is still seen as the mother's fault, and the fear evoked is still one of over-nurturing. Even the abusiveness of Beverly's husband Tom is rooted in the behavior of Tom's mother, a determined working single mother (113–115).

We have seen that Ben Hanscom's "freedom diet" in *It* (497–498) depended on his rebellion against his mother. Unfortunately, she is fearful enough to want reassurance, yet strong enough to demand and get it (183). She says that Ben is "big" rather than "fat" and continues to overfeed him, a dangerous euphemism for which she is culpable, despite her good intentions (185–186). Similarly, in *The Stand,* Harold Lauder was ignored by his mother; yet after his family is killed by the superflu, he misses his mother most (328–329). One of his final memories is of his mother talking on the phone, explaining away his weight as "just baby fat," although Harold suffers for this rationalization (971–972).

Eddie Kaspbrak's mother combines the weakness of Myra and the armored strength of Ben's mother, a blend far more threatening than either alone. Sometimes she is described, as we have seen, in terms of fat and a kind of hyperfemininity; yet elsewhere she is described, not as fat and weak, but as big and strong, "a huge woman" with "trunklike" legs (787). Such a woman insists on controlling her family, yet cannot control herself; her size symbolizes strength yet instability, a bad mix (see 766). These bullying, crazy women are among the most dangerous characters in King's fiction; and the most dangerous example of the type is Annie Wilkes, in *Misery*. The sexual imagery of "fleshiness," Susan Brownmiller writes, "is problematic": "while fat creates the celebrated dimorphic curves of womanhood, it is also the agent of massiveness and bulk, more readily associated with masculine solidity and power" (32). This paradox is expressed perfectly in the threatening bulk of Annie Wilkes, who is at once dangerously maternal and repugnantly androgynous.

In a kind of joking reference King often makes, *Misery* includes a mention of "Mrs. Kaspbrak," a friend of Annie's late mother (91). This is doubly appropriate. Hints in the novel indicate that Annie was shaped by her dominating mother, a "fleshy" woman whom Annie resembles (72, 88), even more fully than Eddie's mother dominated and shaped him. (Annie also shares Eddie's covertly incestuous desires [192–193].) More importantly, Annie wants to become a protective mother to Paul Sheldon, the severely injured writer whose "number one fan" she is. However, like Sonia Kaspbrak in *It* and presumably like her own mother, Annie has a distorted, manipulative idea of motherhood.

Most of King's overprotective mothers genuinely love their children, but that love is often contaminated by selfishness, fear, and ignorance of what their offspring really need. The most dangerous mother-figure of all, Annie Wilkes is incapable of real love, but that only makes her try harder in her role of mother to an unwilling surrogate child. The most frequent descriptions of Annie Wilkes in *Misery* refer to motherhood (19, 43, 254), but this is ultimately revealed as "bogus" (94): her "expression of maternal love and tenderness" is "disconcerting because of the total solid blackness underlying it" (159). For concern, Annie substitutes sentimentality; she must exert total dominion over Sheldon, not to fulfill her love for him, but because it is the closest to love that she can manage, or even imagine. This makes her the most monstrous of King's large women, yet also one of the most compellingly pathetic.

When Annie Wilkes is not described as maternal, she displays a harsh, unnatural androgyny. She first appears in the novel as a mouth, "unmistakably a woman's mouth in spite of its hard spitless lips," with "stinking breath" that "she had forced into him the way a man might force part of himself into an unwilling woman" (5–6). Her clothes are explicitly androgynous: "If she went to town in a dress, she carried a big, clunky purse," such as "maiden aunts tote to church jumble sales." On the other hand, "If she went in pants, she went with a wallet stuck in her hip pocket, like a man" (269). Neither masculine nor fully feminine, Annie can only be grotesque. "Other than the large but unwelcoming swell of her bosom," she "seemed to have no feminine curves at all." Her body is "big but not generous. There was a feeling about her of clots and roadblocks rather than welcoming orifices or even open spaces" (7–8).

Despite statements by critics like Wornom, Annie is never described as "fat"; the closest that *Misery* offers is one mention of her as a "crazy overweight ex-nurse" (112). (This same mistake is often made regarding Carrie, as in Warren [109–110].) Fat, as we have seen, tends to be seen as feminine, in King's writing as in the culture he reflects. Annie is described in terms of solidity and bulk; second only to maternity, the characteristic most frequently attributed to Annie is strength, sometimes explicitly connected to her size (10, 15, 64–65, 270). She is twice described as a "big woman," a goddess whose nature is stony rather than soft (7, 13). Perhaps Annie's true counterpart in *It* is the monster itself, blending fleshy excess and fatal threat in a sickening androgyny: "It was possessed of a stinger long enough to impale a man," from the tip of which a "poisonous clear fluid dripped"; but above that are the masticating jaws, and below that Its pregnant "belly bulged grotesquely" (1048).

"Stern yet maternal" (41), Annie both nurtures and punishes, giggling girlishly one day and violently assaulting her dependent captive the next. Within the microcosm of her house, she represents life and death to Paul. She is not, however, everything to him. Increasingly, her control of him weakens as he falls under the spell of a rival female: Misery Chastain. It is a spell he creates for himself, as Paul finally realizes (243–244).

Paul Sheldon not only battles Annie on the textual level of *Misery,* he thematically opposes her in every subtextual association. While Annie is described in terms of motherhood, Sheldon is often associated with childhood or infancy (4, 20, 43). His injury has rendered his sexless (18) in a tragic but innocent way that contrasts with Annie's sinister androgyny. Most of all, Annie is a creature of the body, at the mercy of her uncontrollable feelings and biochemical swings (168–170, 172–175), which are accompanied by messy orgies of compulsive eating (177–179). Paul, on the other hand, represents the power of self-control, planning, and intelligence. Annie may pretend to motherhood, but Paul is the true creator: "a man who could think of Misery Chastain, first think of her and then *breathe life* into her" (20), not as Annie resuscitated Paul but as God breathed life into Adam.

As *Misery* progresses, the balance of power in the Colorado farmhouse shifts. While Annie can keep a superficial hold on herself, she and Paul Sheldon maintain a tenuous stability. She controls him through his physical appetites: hunger, thirst, and above all addiction to the painkillers she dispenses. Conversely, as he writes *Misery's Return,* he controls her through her desire for fictional thrills, romance, and emotional gratification. The strong, fleshy nurse and the crippled, emaciated writer represent the body and mind in uneasy alliance; despite their dislike of each others' demands, they know that each needs the other. However, this situation changes. As is often the case in King's stories, self-discipline leads to more self-discipline and finally to triumph, while unbridled appetite ends in murder and death.

Like Andy Dufresne in "Rita Hayworth and the Shawshank Redemption," Paul's careful progress eventually secures his freedom. Like Harold Lauder and Randall Flagg in *The Stand,* or the ubiquitous devouring figures in *It,* Annie spirals downward into chaos. Seeking to control Paul, Annie fails disastrously because she cannot control herself; because he seeks only to control himself, Paul can dominate Annie. The violence and bodily invasions in *Misery* begin with Annie's oral "rape" of Paul (6), and end as Paul shoves burning manuscript-bond down Annie's throat, thinking, "I'm gonna rape you all right, Annie. . . . Suck my book. Suck on it until you fucking CHOKE" (317). Paul's true victory, however, is in the return to artistic creation with which the book closes.

In King's fiction, eating and body shape are iconic. In addition to presenting problems of self-esteem and lack of social acceptance on the textual level, fat and eating carry a heavy subtextual load concerning the moral and mortal problems that come from living in meat.

While the heart of *It* is its depiction of the struggles of childhood and of growing up, the novel runs on the energy generated by appetite, by a tension between wish and satisfaction. The two prime expressions of appetite in the novel are often opposed thematically, and sometimes compared: the death-appetite of It, a hungry force that consumes the children of Derry both literally and figuratively; and the sexual yet spiritual life-appetite of the human heroes, which King calls "desire," embodied in the attractive female form of Beverly Marsh Rogan. Secondarily, a concern with appetite overlaps the issue of embodiment, exploring the implications of being a mortal, physical human being in a mortal, physical human body.

Despite its profound moral dimension, *The Stand* has more realistic action and less allegorical action than *It;* accordingly, body-size and eating are somewhat less thematically charged. Still, in a book about virtue and choice, Harold Lauder's fat body represents his lack of self-control, especially in sexual matters. Even after his circumstances cause him to lose weight, his uncontrolled appetites lead to his downfall. Mother Abagail presents an opposing emblem of moderate life, in which the passions of the body are tempered by moral restraint. *Misery* combines the realistic and allegorical approaches most successfully: Annie Wilkes is, at the same time, a threatening goddess-figure and a lost, crazy woman.

In *It,* after the monster is finally put down and even Mike begins to forget everything that happened, he wonders, "Was Ben fat, or did he have something like a club foot?" (1126). But that just shows how much Mike has already forgotten: a club foot just would not have been the same at all.

NOTE

The author wishes to thank the following people for their invaluable help in developing this analysis and procuring helpful materials: Anni Ackner, Andrea Antonoff, John Fast, Ginnie Fleming, Nancy Lebovitz, and Tony Magistrale. Further thanks to Arthur Hlavaty, Kevin Maroney, and Kadmon.

REFERENCES

Bosky, Bernadette Lynn. "The Mind's a Monkey: Character and Psychology in Stephen King's Recent Fiction." In *Kingdom of Fear,* edited by Tim Underwood and Chuck Miller, pp. 209–238. New York: New American Library, 1986.

Brownmiller, Susan. *Femininity.* New York: Simon & Schuster, 1984.

Chernin, Kim. *The Obsession: Reflection on the Tyranny of Slenderness.* New York: Harper & Row, 1981.

Collings, Michael R. *The Many Facets of Stephen King.* Mercer Island, Wash.: Starmont House, 1985.

———. *"The Stand:* Science Fiction into Fantasy." In *Discovering Stephen King,* edited by Darrell Schweitzer, pp. 83–90. Mercer Island, Wash.: Starmont House, 1985.

Dickenson, Joan. "Some Thoughts on Fat." In *Shadow on a Tightrope: Writings by Women on Fat Oppression,* edited by Lisa Schoenfielder and Barb Wieser. Iowa City, Iowa: Aunt Lute, 1983.

Fiedler, Leslie. *Freaks: Myths and Images of the Secret Self.* New York: Simon & Schuster, 1978.

Gallagher, Bernard J. "Reading Between the Lines: Stephen King and Allegory." In *The Gothic World of Stephen King: Landscape of Nightmares,* edited by Gary Hoppenstand and Ray B. Browne, pp. 37–48. Bowling Green, Ohio: Bowling Green State University Popular Press, 1987.

Giannino, Joanne. "The Menu for Love," *Heresies* 21 (1987): 58–59.

Grosswirth, Marvin. *Fat Pride: A Survival Handbook.* New York: Harper & Row, 1971.

Heldreth, Leonard G. "Viewing 'The Body': King's Portrait of the Artist as Survivor." In *The Gothic World of Stephen King: Landscape of Nightmares,* edited by Gary Hoppenstand and Ray B. Browne, pp. 64–74. Bowling Green, Ohio: Bowling Green State University Popular Press, 1987.

Herron, Don. "Horror Springs in the Fiction of Stephen King." In *Fear Itself: The*

Horror Fiction of Stephen King, edited by Tim Underwood and Chuck Miller, pp. 57–82. San Francisco: Underwood-Miller, 1982.

Howard,Martin. *Victorian Grotesque.* London: Jupiter Books,1977.

Kano, Susan. *Making Peace with Food: Freeing Yourself from the Diet/Weight Obsession.* New York: Harper & Row, 1989.

Kelly, K. "The Goddess Is Fat." In *Shadow on a Tightrope: Writings by Women on Fat Oppression,* edited by Lisa Schoenfielder and Barb Wieser, pp. 15–21. Iowa City, Iowa: Aunt Lute, 1983.

King, Stephen. *Bare Bones: Conversations on Terror with Stephen King.* Edited by Tim Underwood and Chuck Miller. New York: McGraw-Hill, 1988.

———. *Danse Macabre.* New York: Berkley, 1982.

———. *It.* New York: Viking, 1986.

———. *Misery.* New York: New American Library, 1988.

———. *The Stand,* rev. ed. New York: Doubleday, 1990.

Magistrale, Tony. *Landscape of Fear: Stephen King's American Gothic.* Bowling Green, Ohio: Bowling Green State University Popular Press, 1988.

———. *Stephen King, The Second Decade:* Danse Macabre *to* The Dark Half. New York: Macmillan, forthcoming, 1992.

Mayer, Vivian. "The Fat Illusion." In *Shadow on a Tightrope: Writings by Women on Fat Oppression,* edited by Lisa Schoenfielder and Barb Wieser, pp. 3–14. Iowa City, Iowa: Aunt Lute, 1983.

Nelson, Marjory. "Fat and Old." In *Shadow on a Tightrope: Writings by Women on Fat Oppression,* edited by Lisa Schoenfielder and Barb Wieser, pp. 228–236. Iowa City, Iowa: Aunt Lute, 1983.

Orbach, Susie. *Fat Is a Feminist Issue.* New York: Berkley, 1978.

Pharr, Mary. " 'They Also Serve': Helpmates and Monsters in *It.*" Paper presented to the International Conference on the Fantastic in the Arts, Ft. Lauderdale, Florida, March, 1990.

Roberts, Nancy. *Breaking All the Rules.* New York: Penguin, 1987.

Schwartz, Hillel. *Never Satisfied: A Cultural History of Diets, Fantasies, and Fat.* New York: Free Press/Macmillan, 1986.

Stuart, Mary S., and Lynnzy Orr. *Otherwise Perfect: People and Their Problems with Weight.* Pompano Beach, Fla.: Health Communications, Inc., 1987.

Stuart, Richard B., and Barbara Jacobson. *Weight, Sex and Marriage.* New York: Simon & Schuster, 1989.

Warren, Bill."The Movies and Mr. King." In *Fear Itself: The Horror Fiction of Stephen King,* edited by Tim Underwood and Chuck Miller, pp. 105–128. San Francisco: Underwood-Miller, 1982.

Winter, Douglas E. "The Night Journeys of Stephen King." *Fear Itself: The Horror Fiction of Stephen King,* edited by Tim Underwood and Chuck Miller, pp. 183–229. San Francisco: Underwood-Miller, 1982.

Wornom, Howard. "Terror in Toontown." In *The Stephen King Companion,* edited by George Beahm, pp. 155–60. Kansas City: Andrews & McMeel, 1989.

Yarbro, Chelsea Quinn. "Cinderella's Revenge—Twists on Fairy Tale and Mythic Themes in the Work of Stephen King." In *Fear Itself: The Horror Fiction of Stephen King,* edited by Tim Underwood and Chuck Miller, pp. 45–55. San Francisco: Underwood-Miller, 1982.

13

Riddle Game: Stephen King's Metafictive Dialogue

JEANNE CAMPBELL REESMAN

. . . and the voice of the turtle
is heard throughout our land.

As with all horror fiction, Stephen King's work articulates fears that go
beyond the physical monsters his characters encounter. Following the
important American novelistic tradition of replacing an authoritative narrative voice with the voices of many characters, King, through his characters' dialogues, constructs a model of knowledge that asks for freedom
and community for readers as well as characters, a model which thus explores how the fictional imagination can help humankind endure and
prevail against evil. When evil appears for King, it always tries to make
its knowledge the only knowledge. It manipulates, restricts, and kills.
When evil is defeated in King's works, generally a community of people
must band together and democratically strive to maintain their freedom
while fighting the evil force. Their struggle involves communicating with
each other.

Accordingly, "dialogic" narrative structures have developed over the
span of King's career, from stories such as "The Boogeyman" to the longer
works, especially *The Shining, The Stand, The Dead Zone,* "The Body," *The
Talisman, Misery,* and *The Dark Half.* In its failures as well as successes,
protagonists' dialogue in all these works may be addressed as ways of
building community. A particularly instructive pairing of failed dialogue
with successful dialogue is to be found in the contrast between what is
arguably the most unusual and perhaps the best of King's short stories,

"Apt Pupil" (1982), and King's longest and most complex novel, *It* (1986). These two narratives may both be described as metadialogic, and therein lies their power. The Losers in *It* manage to substitute process for control, communality for singleness of view, polyphony for monology, and they do this through language as a metaphor for larger, communal action. In his uniquely successful position between low and high culture in America, King writes the language of the people, to be sure, but in such a way as to address social and moral issues beyond what is thought to be the usual realm of the popular novelist.

Conversation as a model for moral knowledge is an important theoretical and critical issue in current literary studies, particularly as regards the American literary tradition in which King's work occurs. Like Hawthorne, London, and Faulkner, King ultimately rejects reductive models for knowing the self and others in favor of communal ones. His work is heavy on dialogue, and it is more often through dialogue that his characters find a way to save themselves and their communities – or fail to.

Perhaps the most important current theoretical source for describing this type of polyphonic narrative is the work of the Russian critic Mikhail Bakhtin. Bakhtin's works, widely cited by critics of American literature, define his general theory of dialogicity in the novel in such a way as to involve narrative structures in making moral statements. Bakhtin believes that all language is *addressed,* uttered by one human being to another or others. Literary language thus occurs within a relationship and *as* language upholds community. Bakhtin is most suggestive for American novels such as King's when he connects the power of dialogues in the text not only to the "dialogue" between author and reader but also to the tradition of the grotesque. Particularly in his *Problems of Dostoevsky's Poetics* and *The Dialogic Imagination,* Bakhtin suggests how and why the interrelated elements of the grotesque, dialogue with "the other," and Gothic fiction's traditional attempt to shock its readers into addressing the unconscious or dark side of personality – as well as each other – make King's fiction so powerful.

"Apt Pupil," one of the four novellas of *Different Seasons,* accomplishes its exploration of evil through its failed dialogues. The story contains no supernatural references. This tale of mutual moral depravity combines its sunny California suburban present with the dark historical context of Nazi atrocities during World War II. Young Todd Bowden, an all-American teen, wants to hear the secrets of evil the old man possesses: "[Todd] stared at Dussander with an open and appealing frankness. 'Why . . . I want to hear about it. That's all. That's all I want. Really' " (King, "Apt Pupil," 127). In a dialogical context, the power struggle between past and present, good and evil, pupil and master, appearance and reality combines suspense with a numbing, almost mechanical certainty as to the development and outcome, as it also furthers role reversal for the characters and a growing sense of denial for the reader. As Todd's and Dussander's dialogues lead them deeper and deeper into a mutual hell, their minds exhibit on page after page their horrible "fit": Dussander thinks of their minds as "feeding off each other . . . eating each other. If his own belly was sometimes sour with the dark but rich food they partook of in his afternoon kitchen, what was the boy's like?" (147). Despite all the dialogue and information it offers, the many details of the story itself emphasize unanswered questions rather than solutions. Is Todd's malady the fault of his parents, with their strained hipness and hidden secrets? Is it the school's fault, especially as personified by "Rubber" Ed, the ineffective high school counselor? Is Todd perhaps a contemporary manifestation of the social evils that propelled Hitler's Germany? Or is the "answer" to such mind-bending global evil unavailable from personal as well as historical sources? Indeed, from where does evil such as that of the Holocaust come? The historical context presents itself as the most nagging question: as the Israeli Special Operative Weiskopf asks, "Have you ever thought that maybe this boy began with a simple interest in the camps? An interest not much different from the interests of boys who like to . . . read about Wild West desperados? . . . [M]aybe it isn't possible to stand next to murder piled on murder and not be touched by it" (279). These questions derive some of their power from their not being answered.

In contrast, Todd's search for "truth" and Dussander's return to "truth" force knowledge and are totally destructive. Both seekers believe that they are alone and are hence amoral: "And Todd, like everyone else he knew, was only tailoring his lifestyle to fit his own particular needs as he grew older. Really, he was no different than anybody. You had to make your own way in the world; if you were going to get along, you had to do it by yourself" (209). Knowing "the other," whether Jew or "boy" or the inner self, cannot be a moral act in the way Todd and Dussander define terms like "know" or "person." After all, Todd initially "knows" Dussander through comic-book Nazism. The kind of design the Nazi torturers had to construct for themselves of "the Jew" is the model for Todd's and Dussander's views of each other and of all people. Dussander and Todd commit a mutual epistemological rape: though they talk to each other, these speakers are most definitely not engaged in a dialogic community. Dussander will not even say Todd's name, perhaps because it means "death" in German.

Todd's pretext to his parents for visiting Mr. Denker is to read to the old man and help him write letters, and this lie characterizes many other lies. As history is subsumed into one voice, that of the Nazi, essentially a monological presence, the tension "Apt Pupil" mounts through dialogue is twisted and strained into a series of falsehoods that touches all the characters. For example, Todd's dialogues with his parents are all failures. They and their son share a flabby sort of fellowship; Todd even calls them by their first names. Their conversations, wearily perfunctory while maintaining the veneer of laid-backness, are full of cliches. For example, Todd's father masks his failure of communication with a manly, off-handed tone: " 'Well . . . okay. We'll try it your way, slugger. But I want to see a big improvement in your marks come January, you understand me? I'm thinking of your future. You may think junior high's too soon to start thinking about that, but it's not. Not by a long chalk.' As his mother liked to say *Waste not, want not,* so Dick Bowden liked to say *Not by a long chalk.*" Dick Bowden thinks, wrongly, that "he could read his son like a book. It had always been that way" (138). One of the reasons presented for Dick Bowden's failure to realize the evil in Todd is his failure to address it in himself:

He and his son had always been friends, and Dick wanted things to stay that way. They had no secrets from each other, none at all (except for the fact that Dick Bowden was sometimes unfaithful with his secretary, but that wasn't exactly the sort of thing you told your thirteen-year-old son, was it? . . . besides, that had absolutely no bearing on his home life, his *family* life). (137)

We also learn that meaningful dialogue, especially about the past, is rare between Todd's parents (182–183). And their misreading of Todd is complete: they attribute his silence on the subject of Mr. Denker to his modesty about his kindness in reading to the lonely old man (184).

Like Todd's parents, the school counselor Todd murders in the last scenes of the book, "Rubber" Ed French, thinks that he can communicate with his students. But despite his hip phraseology ("He had real *rapport* with his kids. He could *get right down to it* with them; he could *rap* with them and be silently sympathetic if they had to do some shouting and *kick out the jams*" [166]), he might as well *be* speaking in French. Dussander seems more a spiritual father to Todd than his own, and certainly more than an institutional father like Rubber Ed. This relationship is highlighted when Dussander plays Todd's grandfather for a visit to Rubber Ed. Such failures in dialogue permit and encourage the monology of evil.

When sane objections intrude into either of the two protagonists' minds, they are phrased in terms of dialogue. Todd, upon receiving another bad report card, hears, *"Maybe that's best,* an inner voice spoke up suddenly. *Maybe you even did it on purpose, because a part of you wants it to end. Needs for it to end. Before something bad happens."* But, as he decides, "[t]alking to yourself was bad shit — crazy people talked to themselves. He had picked up the habit over the last six weeks or so" (143). Dussander too talks aloud to himself: *"The boy . . . the cursed boy!* 'Be honest,' he said

aloud, and the sound of his own voice in the quiet room made him jump a
little. He was not in the habit of talking to himself, and it was the first
time he had ever done so" (146). But such sane inner voices are drowned
out by the evil monology each protagonist's obsessions inflict upon the
other. "Apt Pupil" cannot promise any more than the destruction of Todd
and Dussander, along with the sketchy community it presents between
the Israeli and American officers of law and victims of "laws," but it does
bring about inner dialogue within the reader because of its many unanswered questions.

In contrast to the abortive attempts to create dialogue in "Apt Pupil," in
It successful dialogue significantly extends important ideas of King's earlier fiction. In the dualistic personality of Pennywise the Clown, the most
frequent manifestation of It in the novel, and in the shared polyphonic
narrative of the protagonists are orchestrated the horror as well as the
moral of this extraordinary dialogic novel. *It*'s dialogics allow us better to
appreciate the moral opposition between the monologic monster, who
stands for self-love, and the "Loser" friends, who enact communality. Dialogics also makes *It* highly self-conscious about *being* a novel, with "It" as
the centerpiece of interpretation for characters and readers.

The clown in *It* is a grotesque figure of psychic transformation functioning with a dual purpose, similar to the ways such figures function in
Hawthorne's and Faulkner's work. As It serves as the town's soul, a historical collective self of the sins of the town fathers, It also represents the
dark personal unconscious the young developing psyches of the novel
must confront in order to live, while on a meta-level It points to the jar-
ring psychological function of the novel itself. Pennywise could be called
a grotesque image of the artist, particularly in Its insistence on upsetting
usual ways of "seeing" or "knowing."

The shape-changing It in its Pennywise figuration is a classic grotesque,
for in Pennywise the required grotesque elements of comedy and horror
are startlingly intermingled. Here the grotesque function connects picture and frame, much as do the grotesque medieval gargoyles and pew
carvings in cathedrals and churches or seventeenth-century "grotesque"
book decorations, both derived from the Roman and Italian tradition of
"grottesca" paintings. The grotesque as a bridge between states of being is
an important tradition in Western and non-Western art and literature,
and the clown or trickster figure is its human form. In this sense
Hawthorne's and Faulkner's "marble fauns" and other grotesques are related to It.

Mikhail Bakhtin defines the clown figure in literature as a "carnivaliz-
ing," or psychologically subverting force that manipulates language in order to reveal a failure to acknowledge otherness. Bakhtin finds that the
clown, rogue, and fool are the oldest characters of the European novel.
Like the novel in general, the clown "carnivalizes" society by overturning

its hierarchies: he is "a rogue who dons the mask of a fool in order to mo-
tivate distortions and shufflings of language and labels, . . . [he] is the one
who has the right to speak in otherwise unacceptable languages and the
right to maliciously distort language that *are* acceptable." The clown is the
"Ugly King" of the Mexican Fiesta, for example. He is the inversion and
exhibition at the same time, for such a clown appears in fictions that emphasize a looseness of structure by dialogically promoting lack of resolution, what Bakhtin calls a "prose cyclicity" that directs attention to the
meta-process of reading itself. The dialogic nature of the clown, as well
as the novel in which he (or she) is allowed to speak, questions our conventional modes of knowing and offers alternatives that force us into
confrontation with "other" truths (Bakhtin, *Dialogic Imagination,* 405).

In *It* the clown is accompanied by a host of carnival imagery, and
carnivalization takes place in the public square. The Barrens may seem to
be a private place, but its name is ironic – this weedy bog is anything but
barren. It is the public, social ground on which the protagonists become
friends and build their clubhouse and sense of community. Most scenes,
however, except for the conclusion in the public sewer, take place in
more obviously public places: the library, the streets, a baseball lot, a department store, a movie theater, or a town park. Our first real glimpse of
Pennywise occurs during Derry's Canal Days Festival when Adrian Mellon is beaten and killed. The book is full of confetti, calliope music, balloons, toys, and clown makeup and costume. Important moments,
Bakhtin would remind us, occur during public "carnivals": the official
openings of town facilities, a Fourth of July parade, a nightclub, the movies, the dedication of a statue, even the massacre of gangsters by townspeople.

But Derry's carnivals do not accomplish the communal aims of carnival
Bakhtin describes, as It, Derry suffers from a perversion of communality,
and the town's carnivals are accordingly contaminated by evil. Tony Magistrale characterizes the heroes of *It* as moving from the innocence of
childhood toward the corruption of adulthood, with the monster as "the
collective representation of the town's adult crimes and darkest impulses." Because the social outcasts in *It* are children, it seems that the
real enemy is the clown as Derry's parents and other adults. As Pennywise inhabits the town sewers, Magistrale suggests, so It represents a collection of moral waste (Magistrale, 110–11). Furthermore, it is important
in *It* that the focus is on the prejudices of the town It so convincingly mirrors. In Pennywise, the social evil in this novel is both carnivalized and
profoundly in need of carnivalization; that is, the clown's presence fills
the void left by the absent consciences of the adults of Derry.

On the personal level, in commenting on the role of the carnivalized
unconscious in the lives of its characters – their inner "other" – *It* allows a
healing dialogue with forces that come from "outside" self-knowledge and

knowledge of others. Characters are asked to admit that darkness is addressable and knowable. Elsewhere in King's work, characters such as Dick Hallorann of *The Shining,* who also figures in the history of Derry, *recognize* evil, that is, *address* it, and are thus able to fight it; characters such as Jack Torrance die in their independent pride. It's strange dual location in outer space (or rather, *outside* outer space in the "Deadlights") and in the sewers of Derry indicates Its psychological nature. It comes from within the deep recesses of the human mind, and is perceived, paradoxically, by the conscious mind as "other" or "outside." While It demands to be faced, none of the adults in the Losers' town is up to facing It; indeed, they cannot even see It. In contrast, by engaging in personally revealing dialogues amongst themselves—by *sharing* their dark personal fears—the Losers manage in the end to defeat "inner" and "outer" creatures of horror. This focus on the sharing of the inner self with other inner selves is healing personally and socially, for we sense Derry will be a better town after It. Such communal engagement with dark truths is a function of the novel as art. As Bill Denbrough remarks, "writers take the right word at the right time, as a simple gift of that outer space (*otherspace*) where the good words come from sometimes" (King, *It,* 697).

As to narrative form, the grotesque nature of Pennywise as the unconscious archetype accompanies a set of multiple perspectives in the novel that engage each other as the Losers must each find some part of the puzzle to share with the others. The characters' narratives are attempts to explain, to *tell* about, the darkness of It in order to survive. It thus comes as no surprise that the two most credible voices in this community are those of the two writer characters, Mike Hanlon and Bill Denbrough: Mike calls them all together while Bill acts as their leader. These writers mimic their creator. Both for them and for King, the "It" is the central event to which all refers. By telling about It they approach It, then by engaging in a dialogue with It they find that allowing oneself, character or reader, to confront the unconscious and "the other" and allay its fearsome aspects, whatever that may entail, demands a new personal and social psychology altogether.

Many readers wonder why King's endings don't seem as good as the rest of his texts; his books seem ruined by "showing the monster." But the endings are psychologically quite fitting. Like the things we manage to confront in real life, the It of the conclusion, reduced to a giant female spider, a Shelob of the Stars, doesn't seem quite as frightening once "it" is brought to light. This transformation is the natural result of addressing the unknown. Furthermore, the spider's reductiveness as this Saturday afternoon monster form represents no lack of imagination on King's part, but rather ironically *references* that horror cliche to indicate Its growing weakness. As knowers, the Losers, like King, pass on the lore of the tribe, and communal knowledge involves such metafictive play. With its constant turning and exploration of surfaces that conceal depths, *It*'s movement is always towards dialogue in community, while its title "character's" movement is always toward solitude. The defeated Its name is perfect: the third-person neutral pronoun is a nonperson, and as such a *nonaddressable* entity. The defeat of It at the end lies not just in killing It, but in killing her "community," her unhatched eggs, those creatures who would potentially end her isolation.

The entire form of the novel opposes Its monology. King likes borders that invite inspection of the relation between book and audience. In *It* he makes liberal use of inserts between chapters, in particular the ongoing interpolated first-person "Derry Interludes." Mike's "Derry Interludes" structurally enact dialogicity and promote community. The Interludes trace his personal development (addressing mainly his father and the town's racial discrimination) and his mission to bring the others back to Derry and themselves. But they are also an attempt at a history of the town, specifically of Its appearances. Mike's dual role as personal and social historian, his comprehension of the past and of the personalities of his friends, allows him to recognize the cyclic patterns associated with Its returns. In the First Interlude he wonders whether "it has started again"; he can only wait, "[a]nd fill up the waiting with words in the notebook and long moments of looking into the mirror to see the stranger the boy became. . . . I'm the only one who hears the voice of the Turtle, the only one who remembers, because I'm the only one who stayed in Derry." He further notes his mission of "re-creating" in his mind so he can show the others the "identical patterns their lives have taken." In order "to bring them back, to show them that pattern" (141–142), Mike must help prepare the adult Losers for the return to childhood—he even has Silver's gear stowed away. In the Second Interlude, Mike writes: "One [story] leads to the next, to the next, and to the next; maybe they go in the direction you wanted to go, but maybe they don't. Maybe in the end it's the voice that tells the stories more than the stories themselves that matters" (431).

Instead of a single narrative voice, there are thus two major ones, the overall narrator's and Mike's, and dozens of other ones. And instead of one hero there are many, just as there are two sexualities present and two distinct periods in the heroes' lives, childhood and adulthood, 1958 and 1985. Accordingly, the narrative style involves repetition with elaboration, cutting back and forth between characters and times and places, flashbacks, interior monologues, subtitles, and many interpolated texts. These texts self-consciously reinforce qualities of the novel's overall sense of narrativity—the "telling" function of the story. Borders also provide thematic context. King's epigraphs juxtapose lines from William Carlos Williams' *Paterson* with Joe South's "Don't It Make You Wanna Go Home?" and Bruce Springsteen's "Born in the USA." Though upon first glance the epigraphs seem drawn from widely diverse sources, they all have one very important theme in common: they are all songs and poems about *community*.

Nearly all scenes with the Losers are dialogues; the novel's brief early reliance on narrative exposition is replaced by heavy use of dialogue. Interior monologue is replaced with a shared "interior dialogue" with other characters. This transcends even chapter breaks, as chapter jumps occur quite deliberately in the midst of dialogues, and it becomes especially important in the concluding scenes. Repeated confessions, telling and retelling of events, remembering and sharing – all telling is important to the group. The dramatic revelatory scene in the Chinese restaurant forms a model for many scenes to come, as the Losers begin to remember, to speak, and to address the past and its evil influence on their present lives. All important decisions to act are henceforth made in dialogue.

The novel's reliance on capital letters, italics, ellipses, and line breaks to indicate voice is accompanied by a stress on phonetics, on the spoken and heard voice: "Hi yo Silver, AWAYYY!" Certainly the most constant emphasis on an individual's voice is on Richie Tozier, "the man with a thousand voices." His voiced wit saves the Losers more than once, as when in the house at 29 Nieboldt Street, a sudden dose of Mr. Nell, the Irish Cop, not only stops It but causes It intense pain: "Let him go, boyo, or I'll crack your thick head! I swear to Jaysus!" (362). The narrator tells us: "When referring to verbal zingers and loud farts, Richie's terminology was the same: he called it Getting Off a Good One, and he Got Off Good Ones of both types frequently" (287), but though he could "drive you bugshit . . . it was still nice to have him around" (289). Richie's grotesque exaggeration is a humorous obverse of Its own play with voices.

Opposed to dialogic voices in the novel is Its voice: profane, intimate, cruel, mimicking, cajoling, sneering. Its voice haunts each of the characters in a different way; as It appears to them in the form of their own worst fears, so Its voice comes to them through their own personal "inner ear." This devilish voice is amazingly varied, yet of course it is always the same, as consistent in its humiliating cruelty as in its self-protection and self-enclosure. It quotes the Bible, rock songs, and nursery rhymes. It makes bad puns, toys with cliches, twists the children's favorite words into weapons. In conversation It uses words designed to trigger fear, as when It calls Mike "the nigger" and uses this label to tease Henry Bowers.

What proves to be the antidote to such an overpowering voice? The answer, like all solutions to riddles, is simpler than anyone at first imagines. It is happiness expressed through simple laughter – *shared* laughter. This feature of the novel seems to emphasize the idea of the need for children to have contact through group dialogue; that is, the idea that to learn how to speak children must first hear language spoken. These children become themselves through language. Richie's momentary success against

Pennywise as Mr. Nell is an early and important clue. In large part simply *being* children, with children's beliefs and games and sense of wholeness, is the avenue to escaping Pennywise. When making the silver
bullets, for example, Ben and Bill feel that despite the fact that no one is
sure a silver bullet will stop a monster, "they had the weight of what
seemed like a thousand horror movies on their side" (807). Recalling the
orange fluffs on the giant bird's tongue, Richie compares Pennywise to a
comic book villain, "Lex Luthor or the Joker or someone like that" who
also "always leaves a trademark." Bill thinks that it is "kid's stuff" Pennywise thrives on, and fears (682). When Eddie thinks, "I'm scared. . . . That
was at the bottom of it. Just being scared. That was everything. But in the
end I think we turned that around somehow. We used it. But how?" (276),
he is recalling and imagining how the Losers can triumph.

Such grotesque laughter, the ambivalent laughter of the carnival, acknowledges horror even as it rises above it. It knows of this possibility,
and fears it. Disguised as Vic, It visits Henry in the insane asylum and
says, "They can't hurt Me if they only half-believe . . . But there have
been some distressing signs" (590). The Losers must "believe" enough in
evil to confront it, but they must also "unbelieve" in its monological control over them. If the Losers were to laugh at It instead of succumbing to
Its terrors, It would not only be threatened but destroyed.

Bev thinks of how girls always talked of "doing It," and insist they never
will. She wonders at their terrified laughter in talking about "It": "You
laugh because what's fearful and unknown is also what's funny, you
laugh the way a small child will sometimes laugh and cry at the same
time when a capering circus clown approaches, knowing it is supposed to
be funny . . . but it is also unknown, full of the unknown eternal power"
(1039–1040). The Losers' experience with Pennywise is something they
cannot tell their adult "protectors" for fear of being laughed at, punished,
or even thought insane, but they can band together and fight It on their
own childlike terms. Their shared community of joy proves the only real
weapon against It.

One of Pennywise's most alarming maneuvers is appearing in George's
photo album:

"NO!" Stan Uris screamed. His eyes bulged above bruised-looking crescents of
skin — *shockflesh*, Bill thought randomly, and it was a word he would use in a
novel twelve years later, with no idea where it had come from, simply taking it,
as writers take the right word at the right time, as a simple gift from that outer
space
   (*otherspace*)
where the good words come from sometimes. (697)

This scene is important not only because it demonstrates the boys' fear of
Its being able to make old pictures move or bleed or contain Pennywise's

face, but because of how it contrasts Stan's total rejection of what he "sees" with Bill's writerly *address* of the situation. Bill makes words out of it and uses it instead of being used by it. Ocularity per se, of course, is not negative; but what one *makes* of "it," observed reality, or one says about it is important. Stan is the only one who does not make it to the triumphant reunion, for he commits suicide out of not being able to face Pennywise and tell the others his fears. He keeps his fears bottled up inside, never feeling able to talk about them. Even as a child he was the most self-contained of the Losers, the least inclined to dialogue. As an adult, for him the "everything" he silently faces only leads to nothingness. In contrast, Bev's dialogues with Bill allow her to tell the hidden, painful things that she thought she would never reveal: "Tom looks small compared to [what the Losers face in Derry]. I can see him better now. I loathe myself for the years I spent with him. . . . You don't know . . . the things he made me do, and oh, I was happy enough to do them, you know because he worried about me. I'd cry . . . but sometimes there's too much shame. You know?" (890). As occurs so often, here honest conversation leads to healing.

Becoming a hero for stuttering Bill in particular involves finding a voice. His brother's death opens the novel, and Bill journeys inward and outward to confront that fact in his battle against Pennywise. It seems fitting that a phrase designed to help stutterers overcome their handicap in communicating to others, "He thrusts his fists against the posts and still insists he sees the ghosts," more than once helps Bill, especially when he hurls it at Pennywise in the final riddle game. All the "Losers" have some skill or quality to contribute, and for Bill that means contributing his words.

Perhaps Bill's most important contribution to the Losers' victory over It is his scholarly investigation. Looking for information in the library under the heading, "werewolf," Bill discovers the term, "glamour," which is identified as a Gaelic word for a particular kind of monster. He finds that the Plains Indians called it a "manitou," the Himalayans a "tallus" or "taelus," the Central Europeans an "eyelak," and the French "le loup-garou." These terms describe a shape-changing monster that often transforms itself into that which the observer most fears, a form that King used before It under the names "Wendigo" and "manitou" in *Pet Sematary*. Bill explains to the others what he has read about the attempts to defeat a glamour, specifically the Himalayan Ritual of Chüd, an ancient riddle game in which the human opponent and the glamour wrap their tongues around each other's tongue and then bite down to "staple" them together. Eye to eye they tell jokes and riddles through telepathy. If the human opponent, the chosen holy man, laughs first, the taelus could then eat him; if the glamour laughs first, it has to go away for a hundred years. The opposition of vision—the "glamour" of appearance—and the voice of the riddle game is nowhere more powerfully presented in *It* than here. Despite the horrible visuality of the spider, through the dialogic Ritual of Chüd the Losers conquer Pennywise once and for all. The Ritual is for the most part between Bill and It, but as a dialogic participant Bill gets significant help from the other Losers along with advice from the Turtle.

"Something new had happened. For the first time in forever, something new. Before the universe there had been only two things. One was Itself and the other was the Turtle," It unhappily realizes. The riddle game of 1958, which does not succeed, and the game of 1985, which does, are dialogically alternated in the novel's concluding chapters. During the second Ritual, It finally realizes the Losers' strength, and through a heretofore unprecedented interior monologue, we learn much more about who It is and how she is threatened by the adult Losers' willingness to enter into dialogue a second time. As It recalls, the "stupid old thing" of a Turtle vomited up the universe and then retired to its shell. It thinks that the Turtle may be dead. The Earth attracted It with its rich food, its *"depth of imagination . . . that was almost new, almost of concern. . . . Its teeth rent flesh gone stiff with exotic terrors and voluptuous fears."* With the Losers It makes a great "self-discovery," that *"It did not want new things, ever. It wanted only to eat and sleep and dream and eat again."* But *"a last new thing had come to It, this not an emotion but a cold speculation: suppose It had not been alone, as It had always believed? Suppose there was Another? And suppose further that these children were agents of that Other? Suppose . . . suppose . . . It began to tremble"* (966). As the Losers take turns engaging with It in the riddle game, the shape-changer seemingly loses the ability to change shapes, and appears in the final scenes only as the spider. Ben "understood somehow that It was imprisoned in this final shape, the shape of the Spider, by their common unsought and unfathered vision. It was against this It that they would live or die" (1004).

The final scenes of cosmic dialogue are thrilling and strange, carrying the story from the city sewers into the "outerspace" or "otherspace" of the joined minds of the ancient monster and the twentieth-century children and adults, as the mind of the child is brought back into dialogue with the mind of the adult. As It throws Its opponents through the cold of space toward the edge of creation itself, the borderland of the Deadlights, perhaps the oddest part is the conversations Bill has with the vastness of the Turtle, floating in the outer reaches of space. The child Bill hears the old and kind voice of the Turtle, drowning out the yammering and buzzing voice of It:

The Turtle spoke in Bill's head, and Bill understood somehow that there was yet Another, and that that Final Other dwelt in a void beyond this one. This Final Other was, perhaps, the creator of the Turtle, which only watched, and It which only ate. This Other was a force beyond the universe, a power beyond all other power, the author of all there was. (1009)

Bill suddenly realizes that It means to thrust him beyond the edge of existence into the "macroverse" where "It really lived," where "he would see It naked, a thing of unshaped destroying light" (1009). Bill begs the Turtle for help, and the Turtle replies,

there is only Chüd. And your friends. . . . son, you've got to thrust your fists against the posts and still insist you see the ghosts . . . that's all I can tell you. Once you get into cosmological shit like this, you got to throw away the instruction manual. (1009–1010)

The Turtle's words counsel Bill and the others to get in touch with the inner child, to believe, act, and survive as a child.

The phrase, "the voice of the Turtle," recurs in most of the characters' minds at different points throughout the novel, usually at climactic moments. Until the final scenes, though, the phrase is mysterious. The source, a sung dialogue between a maiden and a king in *Song of Solomon,* is never given in the novel:

My beloved spake, and said unto me, Rise up, my love, my fair one, and come away.

For lo, the winter is past,the rain is over and gone;

The flowers of the field appear on the earth; the time of the singing of birds is come, and the voice of the turtle is heard throughout our land. . . .

Oh my dove, that art in the clefts of the rock, in the secret places of the stairs, let me see thy countenance, let me hear thy voice; for sweet is thy voice, and thy countenance is comely. . . .

Until the day break, and the shadows flee away, turn, my beloved. (Song of Sol. 2:7–17, King James Version)

The voice of the turtledove announces peace, love, and resolution. The Biblical passage references many aspects of *It:* the "secret places of the stairs" in which this battle occurs, the shadows "fleeing" daybreak, and most importantly the coming together of the "beloved" partners in dialogue.

As he moves further and further out toward the Deadlights, Bill starts to lose contact with Its "human" voice and realizes that It wants "to break their mental communication," just as his parents cut him off with their "refrigerator coldness." Bill bellows his saving rhyme, recalling his childhood friends and all the things they struggled to believe in, that policemen are your friends, the Tooth Fairy, Captain Midnight, Santa Claus, "baby stuff, that your mother and father will love you again, that courage is possible and words will come smoothly every time; no more losers, . . . believe in yourself, believe in the heat of that desire" (1011–1013). He laughs suddenly, realizing too that he still believes in all these things; as It screams in pain It releases Bill to his beliefs and to his friends. Interestingly, in a reversal of the ancient Ritual of Chüd, these players are saved by laughing first instead of being laughed at. Perhaps this cataclysmic change helps explain why the Turtle (and later It) can die. It and Its eggs are destroyed, and the friends make their way out of the sewers into the light of a post-Deluge world.

In the "Epilogue – Bill Denbrough Beats the Devil (II)," Bill muses as he leaves Derry: "Children I love you. I love you so much. . . . *Be true, be brave, stand. All the rest is darkness*" (1087). The novel's themes are summed up by the others, too: " 'Nothing lasts forever,' Richie repeated. . . . 'Except maybe for love,' Ben said. 'And desire,' Beverly said. 'How about friends?' Bill asked, and smiled" (1063). "To pass beyond communication," we learn in *It,* is "to pass beyond salvation" (1055). Stephen King teaches us once again that language is important, a person's words are of note, and novels are important means for understanding all our lives. As King himself has put it, "[f]iction is the truth inside the lie, and in the tale of horror as in any tale, the same rule applies as when Aristophanes told his horror tale of the frogs: morality is telling the truth as your heart knows it" (King, *Danse Macabre,* 403–404).

REFERENCES

Bakhtin, Mikhail. *The Dialogic Imagination: Four Essays.* Edited and translated by Michael Holquist and Caryl Emerson. University of Texas Slavic Series, No. 1. Austin: University of Texas Press, 1981.

———. *Problems of Dostoevsky's Poetics.* Translated by Caryl Emerson, Theory and History of Literature Series, Vol. 8. Minneapolis: University of Minnesota Press, 1984.

King, Stephen, "Apt Pupil." In *Different Seasons.* New York: Viking, 1982; New American Library, 1983.

———. *Danse Macabre.* New York: Everest House, 1981; Berkley, 1983.

———. *It.* New York: Viking Penguin, 1986; New American Library, 1987.

Magistrale, Tony. *Landscape of Fear: Stephen King's American Gothic.* Bowling Green, Ohio: Bowling Green State University Popular Press, 1988.

14

Stephen King Reading William Faulkner: Memory, Desire, and Time in the Making of *It*

MARY JANE DICKERSON

It should come as no surprise to readers of Stephen King's fiction to learn from Tony Magistrale's 1986 interview with Burton Hatlen that King's undergraduate interest in William Faulkner led him to spend one year reading Faulkner's stories and novels (114). Magistrale, in his study *Landscape of Fear,* has briefly discussed how *It* reflects traces of both *The Sound and the Fury* and *Absalom, Absalom!* in its stylistic and thematic concerns. From King's acknowledged reading of Faulkner and from Magistrale's suggestive remarks, I believe a more detailed exploration of Faulknerian traces in *It*'s artistry reveals a subtly internalized literary influence at work.

In Faulkner's handling of how the past insinuates itself into the present and how the landscape reflects the corruption of human potential for love and renewal, Stephen King would recognize what another American writer had achieved who shared something of the same vision and who also tended to draw on popular forms to fashion serious fiction. Also, the evil that emerges from the social and cultural fabric of American society fascinates both writers and links what William Faulkner accomplishes in *Absalom, Absalom!* to what Stephen King attempts in the making of *It*. In his own ambitious novel, the younger writer explores his version of the nightmare of history through a multilayered textual production that represents the inner workings of the history of Derry, Maine, and exemplifies what Stephen King learned from reading William Faulkner. This study focuses upon these inner workings of Derry's history as they reveal the unconscious layering of memory and desire affected as they are by space and time.

"AGO AS IN ONCE UPON A TIME"

Through the interactions of memory, sexuality and the creative imagination, the interplay of multiple voices and texts, and the intersections of "was" and "is" that traverse the individual and communal stories in *It,* Stephen King transforms the psychological terrain of the American Gothic through *It*'s own departures from that generic tradition. These particular features of *It* give us ways to examine just how subtle and significant Faulkner's influence may be on King's ongoing fictional explorations of an American regional society. From the loss of childhood innocence and the many betrayals of family and community begun in *The Sound and the Fury* and brought to bear on the larger scope of *Absalom, Absalom!,* Faulkner's artistry is suggestive for what King tries to do in his own remaking of late twentieth-century American Gothic fiction in writing *It.* Both writers probe the past for a necessary understanding of the present even if the knowledge gained can only be partial and no insurance against a future untainted by the past's failures at love and compassion.

Just as Faulkner recognized *The Sound and the Fury* as a turning point in his artistic development that eventually made *Absalom, Absalom!* possible, "With The Sound and the Fury [sic] I learned to read and quit reading" (75), Stephen King almost echoes Faulkner in his own admission to Douglas Winter that "The book [*It*] is a summation of everything I have learned and done in my whole life to this point" (184). For each writer, too, belief in art's interrelationships with life is central to his fiction. For example, Faulkner's implications about writing as satisfying the human desire to be a part of recorded history in *Absalom* set up resonances with King's later reflections on writing in *It.* In *Absalom,* Miss Rosa Coldfield says to Quentin Compson: "maybe some day you will remember this and write about it" (6). In *It,* Bill Denbrough promises himself that, "I will write about all of this one day" (1090). Faulkner and King believe the writer has an obligation to record what has taken place, revealing the inhumane forces that continue to dominate American culture. Therefore, writing and memory for both writers become mutually reinforcing acts: storytelling itself makes further story-telling possible—for the characters inside the novels as well as for the writers outside the novels. And memory's greatest treasures are always rooted in childhood, its joys and pain identified in the long ago of once upon a time.

But it is architect Ben Hanscom's description of an ambitious building project near the beginning of the novel that stimulates us to read *It* as King's most innovative fiction to date and the one whose structural and thematic concerns show the subtle extent of embedded Faulknerian influences:

*When it's done people are going to say it looks like a giant-kid left his toy blocks all over
a flight of stairs, . . . Some will, anyway, and they'll be at least half-right. But I think it's
going to work. It's the biggest thing I've ever tried and putting it up is going to be scary
as hell, but I think it's going to work.* (70)

Ben's words about the structure he has designed and plans to build also
serve to describe the process of textual production that engages all the
main characters through both communal and individual acts of memory,
even though *It*'s conclusion does not measure up to its overall conception
and execution. Childhood's imaginative structures will not be abandoned
by the creative adult, whether the creation be a building or a fiction. For
both Faulkner and King, the intricacies of memory activate desire to create narrative from fragments of the past tying childhood to adulthood, tying earlier acts of inhumanity to the unfolding horrors of the present. In
Absalom and in *It*, the passage from innocence to knowledge as it is tra-
versed through the successful use of language renders the past in ways
that illuminate the present and give life to the future.

In one of the central scenes of *It*, the smoke-hole vision, fiction making
exposes its origins in memory and desire located within the context of
childhood's power to transcend ordinary place and time. The vision takes
place as the Losers enter what Mike names the "ago" to Richie, a prehis-
toric point of origin for the coming of It and the locus for story-telling itself:

Richie nodded. Ago, as in once upon a time, long long ago. . . . *We're in the ago,
a million years back, maybe, or ten million, or eighty million, but here we are and
something's going to happen . . .* There was a steady low vibration – he could feel it
more than hear it, . . . buzzing the tiny bones that conducted the sound. It grew
steadily. It had no tone; it simply *was:*
(the word in the beginning was the word the world the). (722)

In this brief foray into prelinguistic "ago" of "once upon a time," the
Losers discover that It came before It could be named. Thus, story-
telling, in its multiplicity of voices intersecting the real and the imaginary
in the past and the present works to give name to evil and to pit the naming of things against the chaos of the inchoate.

While listening to his father describing the town's collusion in caring
for Miss Rosa Coldfield, Quentin Compson undergoes a similar recognition of the child's prelinguistic knowledge of human desires ending in
tragedy:

*But you were not listening, because you knew it all already, had learned, absorbed it
already without the medium of speech somehow from having been born and living beside it, with it, as children will and do; so that what your father was saying did not tell*

you anything so much as it struck, word by word, the resonant strings of remembering,
who had been here before, seen these graves more than once in the rambling expedi-
tions of boyhood. (Faulkner, *Sound*, 266)

Quentin goes on to remember how he and playmates would frighten
themselves with imagined ghosts at the Sutpen graves and the "rotting
shell" of Sutpen's Hundred, long before he ever actually knew anything
about the lives of the Sutpens and the Coldfields or his own family's involvement. Such a revelation of what *has* happened, in turn, becomes the
fulfillment of the human desire to live and to create. The polyphonous
qualities of both *Absalom, Absalom!* and *It,* with their myriad voicings, fill
in the void and satisfy longing that existed before there was language.

In these story-telling ventures, a single voice would not be enough to
penetrate such an immensity of space and time. Language used crea-
tively to name emotional needs and desires makes possible the human
story as an ongoing cultural narrative with many narrators speaking from
multiple perspectives. Such use of language enables the system of story-
telling to proliferate among the various storytellers in both oral and written traditions represented in *It.* And, likewise, story-telling supports the
ongoing cultural development of fictional and historical narrative: from
the Native Americans (the origins of the smoke-hole vision and the voice
of the turtle – vital sources of knowledge for the Losers) and old-timers'
recollections of Derry's past to magazine writer Adrian Mellon, Mike
Hanlon's carefully researched "Derry Interludes," and Bill Denbrough's
anticipation of another novel at *It*'s conclusion. Surely a large segment of
what King had learned while reading Faulkner has gone into the writing
of *It,* from *It*'s excavation of the meaning of place in the lives of that region's inhabitants to the resonant presence of memory in their confronta-
tions with desire and mutability. And, not least, King learned something
of what it means to write within and against traditional narrative forms –
to both acknowledge mastery and challenge boundaries.

VOICES OF THE FATHERS

Stephen King may be telling a bit of what has gone into writing his own
fiction within the knowledge of a literary heritage when he gives us Bill
Denbrough's memory of a painful creative writing class. It's interesting
that Faulkner and Shakespeare, artists whose resistance to generic
boundaries radically altered their art, are those whose names enter the
exchange, the figures who, rather than the teacher, send young Denbrough off to write stories true to his own beliefs:

"Why does a story have to be socio-anything? Politics . . . culture . . . history . . .
aren't these natural ingredients in any story, if it's well told?"

No one replies. . . .

Finally the instructor says softly, . . . "Do you believe William Faulkner was just telling *stories?* Do you believe Shakespeare was just interested in making a *buck?* . . ."

"I think that's pretty close to the truth," Bill says after a long moment in which he honestly considers the question, and in their eyes he reads a kind of damnation.

"I suggest," the instructor says, . . . "that you have a *great deal to learn.*" (120)

In this exchange between teacher and pupil, the pupil learns from his real teachers and literary fathers, Faulkner and Shakespeare. The need to tell stories completes what it means to be part of one's world as well as to earn a living. It's as if King knows about Faulkner's own sense of rejection and failure that shaped the context out of which he wrote *The Sound and the Fury,* expressed here in an early version of an introduction to the novel:

This hope [of having *Flags in the Dust/Sartoris* published] must have died at last, because one day it seemed as if a door had clapped silently and forever to between me and all publishers' addresses and booklists and I said to myself, Now I can write. Now I can just write. Whereupon I, who had three brothers and no sisters and was destined to lose my first daughter in infancy, began to write about a little girl . . . the entire story, . . . seemed to explode on the paper before me. (72)

Following his classroom experience, Bill writes a story that marks his total commitment to writing, described in terms not unlike Faulkner's memory of what writing *The Sound and the Fury* meant to his art:

. . . he [Bill] has written a story called "The Dark," a tale about a small boy who discovers a monster in the cellar of his house. . . . He feels a kind of holy exaltation as he goes about the business of writing this story; he even feels that he is not so much *telling* the story as he is allowing the story to *flow through* him . . . his head seems to *bulge* with the story; it is a little scary, the way it needs to get out. . . .

If someone had suggested to him that he was really writing about his brother, George, he would have been surprised. (120–121)

Similar to Faulkner, Bill Denbrough's act of writing (perhaps King's as well) answers deep-seated needs and completes the process of being and staying alive. ("The Dark" also sells for two hundred dollars, payable on publication.) In each instance, the writing act occurs in response to a significant human loss, to replace what death has taken away: "His [Bill's] folks had given it [an old Underwood office model typewriter] to him for Christmas two years ago and Bill sometimes wrote stories on it. He did this a bit more frequently since George's death. The pretending seemed to ease his mind" (319). Also, families in *It* are either crippled or nonexistent, causing the Losers to create their own circle of love and caring; in *The Sound and the Fury* and *Absalom,* the Compson and Sutpen inability to love and nourish their children mirrors communal loss of love and human bond. For King and Faulkner, narrative takes on a life of its own and becomes larger than the writer himself—essentially acting to hold at bay the world's capacity for death and destruction.

Of all families in *It,* the Hanlons possess the necessary capacity for love even as their heritage places them in a marginal position in the community; therefore, Mike, though leading a lonely existence within the community, is able to become its chronicler from the strength of his father's example and love. Even as the family disintegrates around them, Quentin and his father are able to relate briefly through their mutual fascination with what *was,* as Quentin remembers it when he and Shreve are creating their version of the Sutpen tragedy:

Yes. Maybe we are both Father. Maybe nothing ever happens once and is finished . . .
but like ripples maybe on water after the pebble sinks, the ripples moving on, spread-
ing, the pool attached by a narrow umbilical water-cord to the next pool . . . Yes, we
are both Father. Or maybe Father and I are both Shreve, maybe it took Father and me
both to make Shreve or Shreve and me both to make Father or maybe Thomas Sutpen
to make all of us. (326–327)

The subtleties of these common concerns determine a literary influence that inscribes itself deeply within the pages of *It* much as described by Mike Hanlon, the librarian-archivist-documenter, as he contemplates how stories work and what the relationships between writers and their material mean:

One [story] leads to the next, to the next, and to the next; maybe they go in the direction you wanted to go, but maybe they don't. Maybe in the end it's the voice that tells the stories more than the stories themselves that matters.
    It's his voice that I remember, certainly: my father's voice, low and slow. . . . That voice, which is for me somehow the voice of all voices, the voice of all the years, the ultimate voice of this place—one that's in none of the Ives interviews nor in any of the poor histories of this place—nor on any of my own tapes.
    My father's voice . . .
I think I've finally found my way to my father's final story. (431–432)

It's as if the writer—Mike Hanlon in this instance—must listen for the voice of both his literal father *and* one who looms even larger than his father in order to enter the flow of cultural narrative. And with the inscription of the father within the text—and I am suggesting Faulkner as the figurative presence in this passage for this novel (for King, another text, such as *The Shining*, might contain the inscribed presence of a "mother" like Shirley Jackson) – the issue of literary influence is further complicated.

It's also significant that Mike's father's voice is the one telling him the particular story of Derry's past evil in connection with the 1930 fire of the Black Spot, the black soldiers' nightspot. As with Quentin and his father, sons must take into account their fathers' memories and perspectives. By naming the father's black soldier-friends who were among those killed, Stephen King both resurrects Faulkner's own fictional presence and transforms Yoknapatawpha names into black Americans who become victims of racism as virulent in Derry, Maine as in Jefferson, Mississippi: "Henry Whitsun . . . Stork Anson . . . Alan Snopes . . . Everett McCaslin . . . Horton Sartoris . . . all my friends" (425). Except for the McCaslin name with its allusion to the black and white McCaslins, those such as Anson, Snopes and Sartoris are references to white Faulkner characters. By incorporating a black narrator with the power to reveal the history of Derry's racist practices, *It* fulfills what Shreve anticipates at the end of *Absalom:* "in a few thousand years, I who regard you will also have sprung from the loins of African kings" (471). Language and the entrance into the cultural narrative that its power brings belong to Mike Hanlon, enabling him to voice and to record the evidence of racist horror in the northernmost reaches of late twentieth-century America.

With *It*, Stephen King "learned to read" his Faulkner as well as his Williams and Dickens. Close readings of all King texts consistently reveal that this is an American writer always conscious of the literary fathers and mothers over his shoulder as he writes. While he only *names* Faulkner indirectly and in extremely subtle shadings, Faulkner's may be the voice that Stephen King hears and listens to most intently while he tackles the shifting historical and narrative complexities of *It*. Their literary relationship suggests King's awareness of inserting his story into the culture's narrative tradition even as he transforms specific elements from the American Gothic tradition.

THE NIGHTMARE OF HISTORY

With *It*, Stephen King has shifted from Dick Hallorann, the black character as stand-in for dead writer Jack Torrance in *The Shining*, to Mike Hanlon, a black character who performs the major act of writing that sets in motion and drives the novel's narrative. The shift has been from the writer's stand-in to the writer *who writes* in ways that directly affect and shape the unfolding nightmare of history. Mike Hanlon's "Interludes" form the core text within the larger text of *It;* they are the informing text much as Mr. Compson's and Charles Bon's real letters and other imagined letters frame the text of *Absalom, Absalom!*, or as the ledgers provide the historical source material underlying Ike McCaslin's discovery of his patrimony in "The Bear." Having a (fictionalized) documentary text within a fiction sets up a creative tension between the world of the text and a world outside the text and suggests some credibility for events and characters whose distinction lies in their sheer incredibility.

What makes *It*'s brief allusion to an inclusive range of Faulkner characters especially provocative is that Mike Hanlon is the vehicle recording and, in the process, revising Derry's history to bring the full story of its racism into the chronicle. It's as if Stephen King insists that the story of the black American permeates the history of the American northeast as much as it does the history of the south. Racism is part of the cultural narrative, this nightmare of history. Therefore, the voice of the black writer has to be central in the making of *It*. Here, and throughout the story-telling's wheel-like spokes, King has placed the connective "Derry Interludes," the results of Mike's accumulated and painstakingly researched history of Derry, in order to understand the evil lurking within the town. Here, the African-American tells his own story and participates in a role that engages the other members of the Losers' Club in the communal act of memory to challenge It. By such oblique references to Faulkner, King both resurrects and consigns to death those Faulknerian echoes; as if he is adding the black writer's voice to the process of the recovery of the past — a Mike Hanlon to join Quentin Compson and Shreve McCannon in that cold Harvard dormitory room. The black man joins the Canadian and the alienated southerner as privileged outsiders, and, with Quentin, Mike becomes both scapegoat and savior. Perhaps King took careful note of Faulkner's choice of the northeast as story-telling site for disclosing central parts of *The Sound and the Fury* and *Absalom, Absalom!*.

Much in the handling of *It*'s narration strengthens the subtle relationship between Faulkner and King. Consider, for example, how Mike describes what he is doing as he researches and writes Derry's story: "He sat down and flipped through the pages he had written, thinking what a strange, crippled affidavit it was: part history, part scandal, part diary, part confessional" (878). Here Mike describes what the fiction writer as well as the historian draws from to make his or her fiction; fiction itself is comprised of both inside and outside the writer's personal experience. Again there is a telling resonance from Faulkner's passages in *Absalom, Absalom!* that speak to the nature of writing itself as well as to what is going on in the novel.

First, Mr. Compson muses on the gap between language's ability to bridge the present and the past and, from what we possess, to construct ourselves:

We have a few old mouth-to-mouth tales; we exhume from old trunks and boxes and drawers letters without salutation or signature, in which men and women who once lived and breathed are now merely initials or nicknames out of some now incomprehensible affection which sounds to us like Sanskrit or Chocktaw; we see dimly people, the people in whose living blood and seed we ourselves lay dormant and waiting. (124)

Second, the act of composing from these resources, as Quentin and Shreve continue their joint creation of the past in their "happy marriage of speaking and hearing" (395), comes close to what happens to the Losers when, as adults, Mike brings them together again to recover what they once knew. They must undergo such remembering in order to create from that communal act the power to say no to death:

. . . both thinking as one, the voice which happened to be speaking the thought only the thinking became audible, vocal; the two of them creating between them, out of the rag-tag and bob-ends of old tales and talking, people who perhaps had never existed at all anywhere, who, shadows, were shadows not of flesh and blood which had lived and died but shadows in turn of what were (to one of them at least, to Shreve, shades too) quiet as the visible murmur of their vaporising breath. (378–379)

The subtle play here on words such as "shade" and "shadow" suggests the desire rooted in writing to make substantial that which is shadowy. One of the horrors of Pennywise the Clown is that he casts no shadow, making it all but impossible to trace his existence and to discover and name his true shape. This representation of horror underlines the novel's central and pervasive horror – the name "It" refers to the third-person pronoun, a thing without its own identity. One way to represent the unconscious as Freud uses the word "means 'it' in German – *das Es*" (Meltzer, 147). King's choice of "It" as title sets such speculation in motion. If language in part represents the attempt to name the unknowable, the elusive other, then piecing together the fragments that language yields, even translated from an almost indecipherable French Canadian, is what Mike Hanlon must do if he is to give the Losers the opportunity to pursue and to name It.

For Quentin and for Shreve in Faulkner's *Absalom,* it was important to get the facts as straight as possible, but even with as many facts as they could piece together from the "rag-tag and bob-ends of the old tales and talking," too much defied full understanding. What they became primarily involved in, then, is the attempt to understand beyond what facts and evidence reveal about family and community relationships and what these past events reveal about lives in the present – the psychological implications of human motivations and acts. In both Jefferson and Derry, the writer's task in naming the unnameable becomes formidable because of history's complications, the difficulty of ascertaining truths, and the essential fallibility and mystery of human beings.

This interrelated nature of the conscious and the unconscious, the

known and the unknown, the self and the other that drive narrative desire in *Absalom, Absalom!* also center on It in the novel of the same name.
Following their communal act of remembering to add to what Mike has
recorded through the intervening years, the Losers must descend into the
underworld – the sewer system of Derry, Maine – to chart the unknown
on their way toward It.

THE WEB OF TIME

The Losers' descent as adults into Derry's labyrinthine sewer system, as
well as their childhood descent into "ago" through the smoke-filled underground club house, acts as a symbolic site for King's most significant handling of time in *It*. Time – the intersection of *is* and *was* – is closely related
to these sites of the unconscious in *It*. Time takes on psychological dimensions that add considerably to what King attempts to name in his
American Gothic.

Yet before examining the psychological dimensions of the temporal as
part of the reading and writing experiences of *It*, it's necessary to look at
ways King constructs the more straightforward temporal dimensions of
narrative. Already, we've mentioned Tony Magistrale's discussion of similarities between Faulkner's narrative innovation in *The Sound and the
Fury, Absalom, Absalom!* and *It*. The most obvious way Stephen King in-
tersects *is* and *was* lies in his overall design in which the five parts of the
novel reflect intermingled slices of the 1985 present, the 1984 immediate
past, and the 1957 and 1958 parts of the Losers' childhood – a design that
expands on the time slices in *The Sound and the Fury* (four parts: April
Seventh, 1928; June Second, 1910; April Sixth, 1928; April Eighth, 1928).
Similar to Faulkner, King uses time to title interchapters and major parts
perhaps not as consistently as Faulkner, but the effect of calling attention
to temporal representations as crucial in the fictions remains central, especially since time for both writers does not refer to a linear concept or
process of time. Any named time, whether it be the 1910 date of Damud-
dy's funeral in *The Sound and the Fury* or the 1957 flood in Derry, Maine,
bears the weight of time past that always intrudes on and influences the
present.

It opens with the 1957 flood as a marker for the more recent events and
ends with a summer day in June, 1985, in the aftermath of a cataclysmic
storm that saw the destruction of It and her babies and the destruction of
Derry itself. In this way, King encompasses the twenty-eight year span of
the actual time of the Losers' involvement and embeds their time within
the more remote nineteenth- and earlier twentieth-century times recorded through Mike's Interludes set between each part. And all of these
instances within historical recorded notions of time are set against the
time before time, the "long long ago" that Richie names but that can never
be recorded, even by Mike.

The marked times are clearly delineated during opening sections but as memory and desire take hold and become more actively engaged, time becomes less distinct, and occasionally merges within chapters late in the novel as the numbered parts of chapters themselves begin to proliferate. This movement resembles the way memory itself begins to operate under stimuli of talking and writing, echoing what Faulkner does with memory's effect on time through the many voices who contribute their versions to the story of Thomas Sutpen in *Absalom*. What such a web-like and spliced pattern also discloses about King's conception of time in *It* is that what happens remains attached to a larger historical narrative, shaped by "the force of memory and desire . . . and love" (1046), just as It represents the unleashed horrors of the social unconscious in a society that increasingly isolates and fragments human intercourse. These web-like time patterns provide a key to understanding as they intersect with the many underground sites that dominate the novel to produce King's version of how *was* and *is* turn into the nightmare of history. Time therefore assumes a psychological dimension as well as demarking an elusive reality.

Mike Hanlon appears to recognize a heightened visibility in the intersections of time and space as he learns to see things under his father's tutelage:

But Mike enjoyed most of the places in Derry his father sent or took him to, and by the time Mike was ten Will had succeeded in conveying his own interest in the layers of Derry's history to his son. Sometimes, as when he had been trailing his fingers over the slightly pebbled surface of the stand in which the Memorial Park birdbath was set, or when he had squatted down to look more closely at the trolley tracks which grooved Mont Street in the Old Cape, he would be struck by a profound sense of time . . . time as something real, as something that had unseen weight, the way sunlight was supposed to have weight (some of the kids in school had laughed when Mrs. Greenguss told them that, but Mike had been too stunned by the concept to laugh; his first thought had been, *Light has* weight? *Oh my Lord, that's* terrible!) . . . time as something that would eventually bury him. (262)

Mike's "terrible" realization anticipates the horror of the "deadlights" that occur in these underground habitations of It – a manifestation of It as a deathlike weight of combined time and light that buries by bringing down the darkness on those who challenge its inevitability. In this passage, time and space, as created by light, interact and intersect to take on a palpable quality for Mike. As the novel progresses, the weight of time intensifies as the adult Losers descend into Derry's underground to seek out It: the chapters themselves are marked by a slowed down time such as "In the Tunnels/4:59 A.M.," and "Derry/5:00 A.M."

Images associated with time, especially variations on "was" and "is," also become closely intermixed with space through sexual imagery in *It* in

ways that evoke Faulkner's own tortured reflections on the sexual implicit in "was" and "is." The copula connects the knower with the known,
self with other, the initiate with the initiation, and the child with the
adult. The process of making connections involves both birth and death.
Again, Mike Hanlon speculates on these things as he sets about the
process of excavating those "layers of Derry's history" that his father's
careful tutelage prepared him for: "To know what a place *is*, I really do
believe one has to know what it *was*" (144).

In the interview with Albert Carson, which Mike later sees as the beginning of his formal research, Carson's words anticipate the beginning
of the Losers' own childhood research into the nature of Derry's evil, entering the house on Neibolt Street through its basement window:

A town's history is like a rambling old mansion filled with rooms and cubbyholes
and laundry-chutes and garrets and all sorts of eccentric little hiding places . . .
not to mention an occasional secret passage or two. If you go exploring Mansion
Derry, you'll find all sorts of things. Yes. You may be sorry later, but you'll find
them, and once a thing is found it can't be unfound, can it? Some of the rooms are
locked, but there are keys . . . there are keys. (145)

The crumbling Sutpen mansion, from its incredible origins to its fiery
end, also held the keys that unlocked the secrets of the Sutpen and the
South's saga of a society dependent on dominance and power over others
for its survival.

One of the keys that enables the Losers' Club members to escape the
Derry tunnels in 1958 is bound up in the love they continue to have for
one another that again saves them in 1985. The final significant memory
to emerge from the communal remembering as the Losers regroup as
adults is Bev's of having made love to all of them, anticipating their own
"happy marriage of speaking and hearing": what Bill Denbrough recognizes when he tells her it's "y-y-your way to get us out!" (892). That sexual
initiation triggered the necessary psychic and physical energy for them to
keep the circle of love intact long enough to find their way home. In her
breakthrough memory of this communal sexual experience, Beverly
transforms the final "was" into "is" so that they can once again "break
through into the lifelight together" (1040) and move toward "the sound of
running water" (1041).

A WHEEL

The constant presence of water as source of life and as a destructive
agent (with its attendant smells of growth and decay) suggests that Beverly's role in *It* provides a contrast to the tragic figure of Faulkner's Caddie Compson whose sexuality finally signals suicide by drowning for her

brother Quentin. In *The Sound and the Fury,* Quentin's dissolution into a state of being "was" is resistant to the present reality "is." He cannot shape reality in his own desire to become his sister's lover, nor is he capable of acknowledging her own active sexuality: "I was I was not who was not was not who" (195). And, in *Absalom,* the coupling that transforms the "was-not" so briefly into "is" can only be imagined as incestuous, even by Shreve as he and Quentin are engaged in their "happy marriage of speaking and hearing . . . in order to overpass to love where there might be paradox and inconsistency but nothing fault or false" (395):

And who to say if it wasn't maybe the possibility of incest, because who (without a sister: I dont know about the others) has been in love and not discovered the vain evanescence of the fleshly encounter; who has not had to realise that when the brief all is done you must retreat from both love and pleasure . . . the dreamy immeasurable coupling which floats oblivious above the trammelling and harried instant, the: *was-not: is: was:* . . . but maybe if there were sin too maybe you would not be permitted to escape, uncouple, return. (404)

In contrast to the shadowy presences of Caddie and Judith behind the above passage, Beverly Marsh readily assumes something of sister, mother, and lover to answer her own and her friends' various needs in order to keep intact "that meagre and fragile thread" (Faulkner, *Absalom,* 313) of language, of communication. Through Quentin's role in this creative "marriage of speaking and hearing" – the communication that keeps alive the intersection of memory and desire, he participates in the cultural narrative that keeps death at bay through the power of memory and imagination: "saying No to Quentin's Mississippi shade who in life had acted and reacted to the minimum of logic and morality, who dying had escaped it completely, who dead remained not only indifferent but impervious to it, somehow a thousand times more potent and alive" (350).

Following this insight into the power of language to breathe life and meaning into a speechless past, Faulkner almost anticipates the imagery of King's own Ritual of Chüd invoking language's power to slay death by stapling the past to the present through its multitongued probing of the past: "since Quentin did not even stop. He did not even falter, taking Shreve up in stride without comma or colon or paragraph" (350). When Ben revisits the Derry Library in 1985 and hears a librarian reading the fairy story of Billy Goat Gruff, he experiences a powerful sense of *deja-vu: "How can it be the same story? . . . Is something really stapling the past and present together here, or am I only imagining it?"* (514–515). It's as if "story" refers both to the scene of children listening to the tale of Billy Goat Gruff *and* to the larger story of the monster "It" and the unfolding narrative in which Ben and the Losers are the storytellers and the principal characters.

And the story is as well Derry's history being told from within the cultural narrative of the fairy tale embedded within the ongoing life of present-day Derry. Later in the text but earlier in time, Bill Denbrough places the imagery of "stapling the past and present together" firmly within the Ritual of Chüd as he explains it to the young Losers:

If you were a Himalayan holy-man, you tracked the *taleus* ["an evil magic being that could read your mind and then assume the shape of the thing you were most afraid of"]. The *taleus* stuck its tongue out. You stuck *yours* out. You and it overlapped tongues and then you both bit in all the way so you were sort of stapled together, eye to eye. (642)

Once the stapling took place, the holy-man and the *taleus* began to take turns telling jokes and riddles. The first one to laugh was either killed (the human) or banished for a hundred years (the *taleus*). Once again, similar to his more deliberate creation of *Misery* as a Scheherazadean narrative, King has written a variation on telling stories to prolong life.

At times Stephen King's narrative strategy both echoes and revises what it means to read Faulkner. When Quentin and Shreve finish reconstructing and imagining the Sutpen story and, in the telling add substance and meaning to their own lives (especially Quentin's), the story that has already been written in *The Sound and the Fury* looms beyond the final pages of *Absalom*: the loss of Caddie, Quentin's death, Mr. Compson's death by alcohol, and the final dissolution of the family. But, in *It* the Losers, through the combined forces of their memories and their creativity, manage to staple the past to the present and to slay the monster of many shapes: "it was their combined force, augmented by the force of that Other; it was the force of memory and desire; above all else, it was the force of love and unforgotten childhood like one big wheel" (1046). But, their moment of transcending individual limitations cannot last. As soon as the deed is done, the surviving Losers begin to forget each other and what has happened. All that will remain is the evidence of Mike Hanlon's diary and the book that Bill Denbrough says he will write someday. Memory itself is transient, to be captured only partially in written texts that enter the narrative flow of recorded history.

In "Derry: The First Interlude," Mike Hanlon anticipates *It*'s place in Stephen King's vision of American Gothic as a serious segment of the cultural narrative that constructs and probes the nightmare of history: "The gothic conventions are all wrong. My hair has not turned white. I do not sleepwalk. I have not begun to make cryptic comments or to carry a planchette around in my sportcoat pocket" (141). Douglas Winter's mention of Faulkner's story "Ad Astra" is pertinent here for the particular ways *It* reveals the extent of Faulkner as a major influence on King's deepening grasp of Gothic possibility in *It:*

And the darkness, the night, the eternal negation of the grave, give us access to truths we might not otherwise obtain. In "Ad Astram [*sic*]," William Faulkner wrote a fitting credo for horror fiction: "A man sees further looking out of the dark upon the light than a man does in the light and looking out upon the light." (154)

From the perspective of the marginalized Other, these are the words spoken by the Indian subadar to his fellow Caucasian World War I soldiers. The Indian also points out that "In my country I was prince. But all men are brothers" (408). The story itself, like *Absalom* and *It,* centers on a brief period of time in which there is a bond of brotherhood forged against the threat of death and destruction.

As children who suffer various degrees of alienation from both adults and other children in Derry, the Losers' Club members also speak from the loneliness of their various marginalized positions in Derry's world. The evil represented by the many shapes of "It" concerns matters of power, sex, class, and race that act in complex and interrelated ways to isolate and separate human beings from one another. As Mike has acknowledged, "The Gothic conventions are all wrong." It is therefore fitting that African-American Mike Hanlon be the character in *It* who examines historical evidence and who reassembles the Losers to set the narrative wheel back in motion. Also, King's major accomplishment in *It* is to portray contemporary figures who come together briefly to act together in ways that keep alive the hope for communities of love and compassion against the forces of unnamed darkness.

Stephen King's innovations with the handling of time and the recurring significance of the past on events in the present, the intertwined impact of the forces of memory and sexuality on creative acts, and the human needs for love and community in an increasingly barren landscape are what link the younger writer with his famous precursor, a worthy literary father. In earlier King novels, the literary influence of Poe and others was a much more obvious element to pinpoint; in *It*, Faulknerian influences are much more deeply embedded in ways that go far to move King's work beyond popularized expectations of Gothic forms and closer to the concerns of serious post-modern fiction. Similar to what Faulkner describes as a key vantage point for observation, King is "looking out of the dark upon the light" where he has long worked to transform his chosen genre into a literature worthy of serious attention. Without harming those "natural ingredients" of story-telling in *It*, King confronts present-day horrors of intolerance, ignorance, and inequity in a society lurching toward the twenty-first century.

REFERENCES

Faulkner, William. *Absalom, Absalom!* New York: Random House, 1936; Vintage ed., corrected text, 1987.

———. "Ad Astra." In *Collected Stories of William Faulkner.* New York: Random House, 1950.

———. *The Sound and the Fury.* New York: Jonathan Cape & Harrison, 1929; Random House, corrected ed., 1984; Vintage, 1987.

King, Stephen. *It.* New York: Viking Penguin, 1986.

Kinney, Arthur F., ed., "An Introduction to *The Sound and the Fury.*" In *Critical Essays on William Faulkner: The Compson Family,* pp. 75–77. Boston: G. K. Hall, 1982. (Reprinted from *Southern Review* 8 (October 1972): 708–710.)

Magistrale, Tony. *Landscape of Fear: Stephen King's American Gothic.* Bowling Green, Ohio: Bowling Green State University Popular Press, 1988.

Meltzer, Françoise. "Unconscious." In *Critical Terms for Literary Study,* edited by Frank Lentricchia and Thomas McLaughlin. Chicago: University of Chicago Press, 1990.

Meriwether, James B., ed. "An Introduction to *The Sound and the Fury.*" In *Critical Essays on William Faulkner: The Compson Family,* pp. 70–74. Boston: G. K. Hall, 1982. (Reprinted from *A Faulkner Miscellany,* edited by James B. Meriwether, pp. 156–161. Jackson, Miss.: University of Mississippi Press, 1974.)

Winter, Douglas E. *Stephen King: The Art of Darkness.* New York: New American Library, 1986.

15

"The Face of Mr. Flip": Homophobia in the Horror of Stephen King

DOUGLAS KEESEY

All fear is more or less social. If there is such a thing as the transhistorically and crossculturally monstrous, it can still only be manifested in socially specific monsters. One idea of horror fiction sees it as a politically conservative force, identifying threats to the social order as monstrous and celebrating the story of their successful elimination. Stephen King has said that "Monstrosity fascinates us because it appeals to the conservative Republican in a three-piece suit who resides within all of us. We love and need the concept of monstrosity because it is a reaffirmation of the order we all crave as human beings . . . the creator of horror fiction is above all else an agent of the form" (*DM*, 50, 58). Recently, Noel Carroll has used King's remarks to form the basis of a *Philosophy of Horror:*

What King may have in mind here . . . is that the horror narrative appears to proceed by introducing something abnormal—a monster—into the normal world for the express purpose of expunging it. That is, the horror story is always a contest between the normal and the abnormal such that the normal is reinstated and, therefore, affirmed. The horror story can be conceptualized as a symbolic defense of a culture's standards of normality; the genre employs the abnormal, only for the purpose of showing it vanquished by the forces of the normal. The abnormal is allowed center stage solely as a foil to the cultural order, which will ultimately be vindicated by the end of the fiction. [Carroll, 199]

Carroll's temptingly lucid theory seems like a fair extrapolation of King's comments, until we notice that Carroll has solemnized King's playful irony. Is "the conservative Republican in a three-piece suit" really the major part of us? How "normal" is that part? Is such "normality" really "always" reinstated and reaffirmed at the end? And finally, is "the conservative Republican" in us really the only part to which monstrosity appeals?

More recent comments by Stephen King would indicate that his philosophy of horror is rather more complex: "one thing that reviewers and scholars have missed so far is that I have tried to have some fun in these novels and that I've tried to poke some fun along the way. I guess that if people have missed one glaring point it is that fantasy and horror can be wonderful tools of satire" (Magistrale, *Stephen King,* ms. 28). Perhaps the "conservative Republican in a three-piece suit who resides within all of us" is as much object as subject of satire; maybe the deadly serious business of culturally conservative horror is being made fun of as one of the monsters! King himself believes that critical interest in his fiction is due largely to the fact that his "work underlines again and again that I am not merely dealing with the surreal and the fantastic, but more important, using the surreal and the fantastic to examine the motivations of people and the society and institutions they create" (Magistrale, *Stephen King,* ms. 23). It would seem that any full study of the relationship between King's novels and society's norms would have to be ready to find examination as well as affirmation, satire as well as reinstatement. The monstrous may appeal to both the conservative and the radical within us, alternately and sometimes simultaneously.

One of the socially specific fears most often represented in King's horror is homophobia. Variously defined as a fear of homosexuality, homoerotic excitement, effeminacy, passivity, or weakness in other men or in oneself, "homophobia" is clearly so overdetermined as to be practically an umbrella term covering any threat to male gender identity. Interestingly, when King reaches for an example of effective horror, he comes up with a scene that plays on homophobia. Calling Anne Rivers Siddons' *The House Next Door* "the best" horror novel he's read lately, King describes a scene where "There's this one guy who's very proud of his masculinity, and the house makes him sort of sexually 'hot' for this other guy, and everybody's at this party, and these two people are making love! And the guy later – POW! – blows his brains out. . . . it's nasty; it's a nasty book. A NASTY BOOK!!!" (Van Hise, 20). King goes on to explain how the terror of this fiction draws its power from the social:

The essence of the horror in this scene . . . lies in the fact that social codes have not merely been breached; they have been exploded in our shocked faces. . . . much of the walloping effect of *The House Next Door* comes from its author's nice grasp of social boundaries. Any writer of the horror tale has a clear – perhaps even a morbidly overdeveloped – conception of where the country of the socially (or morally, or psychologically) acceptable ends and the great white space of Taboo begins. Siddons is better at marking the edges of the socially acceptable from the socially nightmarish than most.(*DM*, 264)

One might say that in this novel, which King considers the epitome of horror, heterosexual society is frightened to death by the spectacle of homosexuality: when "They find Buddy Harralson and Lucas Abbott embracing, naked," Buddy's father-in-law "expire[s] of a stroke," Buddy's wife "screams on . . . and on . . . and on," and Buddy himself commits suicide (*DM*, 264). Does Siddons' novel show the elimination of (homosexual) abnormality and the reinstatement and reaffirmation of the (heterosexual) norm? Perhaps; homosexuality is expunged, but so is much of society along with it! It seems just as likely that the novel shows the self-destructive consequences of homophobia, that this horror fiction may be read as a satire on heterosexist society, with its "morbidly overdeveloped" conception of what is and is not socially acceptable. Which is more horrible, a heterosexual husband's gay attraction or his and others' homophobic response? Is it the homosexuality or the homophobia that leads to death?

In a scene prominently placed near the beginning of *It*, a group of young men beat up two homosexuals and throw one into a canal. Asked why he wrote this scene of homophobic destruction, King responded by saying that he based his horror fiction on social fact: during Bangor's 150th anniversary celebration, a gay man did die after being thrown into the Kenduskeag Stream. "If the chapter strikes you as homophobic," King said, "please remember that this is a case of 'We don't make the news, we just report it!' " (SK, 5). Here King refuses to let his attitude toward homosexuality be confused with that of his homophobic characters; it is not he but the society he writes about with reportorial accuracy that fears gays. King makes a similar distinction in countering the charge that his "fictional violence," even if modeled on actual events, may yet serve as a model for further violence in "real life." After recalling a "homosexual-murder case" that may have been influenced by a scene from *The Shining*, King admits to some concern, but argues that "these people would all be dead even if I'd never written a word. The murderers would still have murdered. So I think we should resist the tendency *to kill the messenger for the message*" (Beahm, 42; italics added). King's comments imply that, if society is disturbed by the homophobic violence in his fiction, it should recognize and criticize its own homophobia rather than blaming the writer for it. In such accusations, the writer becomes the scapegoat for homophobic attitudes that society can continue to hold unconsciously as long as scapegoats make self-recognition unnecessary.

But how does *It* read without King's spirited extratextual defense? Does the novel come across as a satire on homophobic society or as a demonization of homosexuality and a consequent reaffirmation of heterosexuality as the norm? Michael R. Collings describes the "treatment of homosexuality" in *It* as "more openly vicious" than in any of King's previous fiction. Collings believes that King as author shares his characters' homophobia: "Not only do the characters react negatively and strongly to the suggestion of homosexuality, but the narrative links (i.e., the narrator's voice itself) continue that harsh, stereotypic attitude. The gay man killed never rises above the slickest of stereotypes, nor do reactions to his death ever overcome the hurdle of his sexual orientation" (Collings, 23). While it's true that the relationship between gay Don and Adrian is presented largely in terms of butch/femme stereotypes, it should be noted that King seems to have more on his mind than the perpetuation of heterosexist cliches. King makes Adrian effeminate in order to show up the homophobes' attitudes and actions as all the more deplorable. Garton, Unwin, and Dubay are exposed as cowards when they pick on the less "masculine" Adrian because they think he will be less able to defend himself. Garton's hatred for Adrian is represented not as a natural fear of the unnatural (the effeminate man), but as a childish inability to resolve his own gender insecurities. When Adrian makes a flirtatious remark, Garton believes that "His masculinity had borne an insult which he felt must be avenged. *Nobody* suggested he sucked the root. *Nobody*" (*It*, 22). A nearby policeman realizes that Garton's defensiveness ("He called me a queer!") is rooted in the fear that he might really be gay (*It*, 23). Bashing gays and dressing tough, Garton is desperately trying to find a proper male role model with which to identify but is ever fearful that he is acting "queer": "Like his two friends, he was dressed in unconscious imitation of Bruce Springsteen, although if asked he would probably call Springsteen a wimp or a fagola and would instead profess admiration for such 'bitchin' heavy-metal groups as Def Leppard, Twisted Sister, or Judas Priest" – groups which are themselves gender benders, an irony King may have intended (*It*, 20). Garton is like the local citizens who won't enter a gay bar "for fear all the muscles would go out of their wrists, or something"; he wields a switchblade to assure himself of phallic prowess and "punche[s] Adrian in the groin" to fix the latter as feminine in relation to his own masculinity (*It*, 26, 32).[1]

King extends his satire on homophobia from three boys to the town as a whole, closing off society's option of using them as scapegoats for its own homophobic beliefs. King writes of the "town's tightly homophobic attitude, an attitude as clearly expressed by the town's preachers as by the graffiti in Bassey Park," thus equating the words of the town's most respected members with the crudest anti-gay threats scrawled by the likes of a Garton (*It*, 28). No one in town helps Don or Adrian as they're being beaten; this negligence amounts to a tacit condoning of the act. Finally, in his most uncompromisingly satiric touch, King describes the gay bashing and killing as an unwritten part of the town's anniversary celebration, "one final event which everyone had somehow known about but which no one had quite dared to put down on the Daily Program of Events. . . . Ritual sacrifice of Adrian Mellon officially ends Canal Days" (*It*, 21). Here what Noel Carroll described as characteristics of horror fiction – the expulsion of the abnormal in order to reconfirm the norm – is revealed by King to be a *real life ritual* exposed in all its horror by fiction. Gay Adrian is eliminated so that the townspeople can feel more at home with their gender and sexuality. After all, what really rankles Garton is that he is unable to win the town's celebratory hat ("I Love Derry!") that Adrian had successfully won at a carnival game: how can a gay man express and "win" a town's love while he is shut out? (*It*, 30). Never mind that, as the one Derry resident who really knows them realizes, "these men, fags or not, seemed to have learned a secret of getting along with each other which their heterosexual counterparts did not know" (*It*, 26). The most important thing to the townspeople is to ensure their own sense of belonging (to the town, to their sex), even if they become in the process the very alien sex perverts they fear.[2]

It should now be clear that, unlike Collings, I do not see *It*'s implied author or narrator as homophobic; on the contrary, homophobia would seem to be the target of the book's satire. It's true that the policemen from whose perspective much of this chapter is written have no special liking for gays ("About the bum-punchers I'm neutral" [*It*, 23]), but, in addition to King's extratextual defense of his novel's real-life accuracy ("I took notes on the police interrogation . . . a lot of the conversation in the chapter is reputedly what was said" [SK, 5]), there is also the fact that even the police and the D.A. in the novel feel that gay bashing is wrong: "Averino did not like gays, but this did not mean he believed they should be tortured and murdered"; " 'The guy was a fruit, but he wasn't hurting anyone,' Boutillier said" (*It*, 24, 38). In a bizarre thought that both expresses and struggles to transcend homophobia, the police imagine the gay bashers' retribution as occurring in the form of what they most fear and desire: "I'm going to put them in the slam, my friend, and if I hear they got their puckery little assholes cored down there at Thomaston, I'm gonna send them cards saying I hope whoever did it had AIDS" (*It*, 38).

The gay bashing, the police interrogation, even this imagined retribution: all of these form what might be called the "realistic" background to what is essentially a surrealistic or fantastic novel. When the veritable monster, the supernatural horror is introduced, what does It represent? Does It challenge or defend social norms? Is It the threat of homosexuality, the danger of homophobia, or some indefinite combination of both? We might begin by noting that It finishes the job begun by the gay bashers: It kills Adrian. This continuity may suggest that It is largely the supernatural embodiment of human evil: It is the boys' and the town's own homophobia monstrously out of control. This supposition receives some confirmation in the fact that It seems to have been the author of the particularly inhuman anti-gay graffiti in Bassey Park (*It*, 28–29). It is also associated with "thousands" of "I Love Derry" balloons, which remind one of the hat for which Garton jealously beat Adrian. Don says that " 'It was Derry . . . It was this town,' " suggesting that in his mind It is the monstrous embodiment of the town's homophobia (*It*, 36). With "great big teeth," It takes a bite out of Adrian's armpit, " 'Like it wanted to eat him, man. Like it wanted to eat his heart' " (*It*, 35). Does It carry out in a horribly literal sense the metaphorical threat made by Garton to Adrian earlier on in the chapter? Garton: "I ought to make you *eat* that hat, you fucking ass-bandit!" Adrian: "If you want something to eat, hon, I can find something *much* tastier than my hat" (*It*, 22). Does Its penetrating teethwork give It the sense of potency and sexual satisfaction Garton craves? Noting that "there was a big chunk of meat gone from [Adrian's] right armpit," an officer speculates that "One of the [gay bashers] really liked to bite. Probably even got himself a pretty good bone-on while he was doing it. I'm betting Garton, although we'll never prove it" (*It*, 38). Is It the town's unacknowledged homophobia, the responsibility they all share for Adrian's death, a culpability they deny by scapegoating Garton and the other two boys as the only ones deserving conviction?

Well, if It is the town's homophobia wreaking havoc on Derry's gays, then why does It manifest Itself in the form of a clown whose uncertain sex mirrors that of Its victim? It "looked like a cross between Bozo and Clarabell, who talked by honking his (or was it her? – George was never really sure of the gender) horn," much as Don and Adrian are first seen as a "couple of girls," their gender difficult to determine (*It*, 13, 21). Is It homophobic other or homosexual double? The D.A. thinks that It might be "Kinko the Klown or a guy in an Uncle Sam suit on stilts or Hubert the Happy Homo" (*It*, 37). Later on in the novel, the police speculate that It may be a "sexfiend," a "fiend for boys" (*It*, 180). And, as if in response to young boys' fears ("It's one of the queers the big kids are always talking about"), It appears as a hobo, frightening the boy Eddie with the proposition, "Come back here, kid! I'll blow you for free" (*It*, 260, 309) – an invitation disturbingly reminiscent of Adrian's words to Garton.[3] The other guys tell Eddie that the hobo has syphilis, "a disease you get from fucking . . . another g-g-guy if they're kwuh-kwuh-queer. . . . Some guys with the Syph, their noses fall right off. Then their cocks" (*It*, 309–310). Eddie thus comes to associate homosexual contact with castration and death. Not surprisingly, when another boy meets the hobo-clown, he hears It say, "Want to play some more, Richie? How about if I point at your pecker and give you prostate cancer?" (*It*, 590).

If It was formerly the town's monstrous homophobe, the embodiment of gays' worst fears, now It would appear to be the monstrous homosexual, heterosexual society's worst nightmare. Has King moved from gay rights' activism and social satire to heterosexism and cultural conservatism? Certainly, *It* can be read that way. In one subplot, a boy is edged toward insanity by the sexual advances of another boy. Led in a circle jerk and then masturbated by Patrick ("You liked it! You got a boner!"), Henry balks at fellatio – but it is too late. He is finally overcome by doubts about his own sexuality: "On the day when he had allowed Patrick Hockstetter to caress him, that bridge [over some mental abyss] had narrowed to a tightrope" (*It*, 823, 914). Henry goes crazy, trying to eliminate his own fear of effeminacy by projecting it onto others and cutting it out ("Okay, fag," Henry calls Eddie, planning to knife him) and attempting to prove his manly strength by thrusting his knife into women (*"Kill her"*) (*It*, 967, 914). The circle jerk and masturbation scenes are both viewed through the horrified eyes of Beverly, female and representative of the natural (social) order. She thinks of the circle jerk as something "so strange, so ludicrous and yet at the same time so deadly-primitive that she found herself, in spite of the giggling fit, groping for the core of herself with some desperation" (*It*, 816) – as if trying to get a hold on normal (hetero)sexuality? The thought of her boyfriend's penis makes her "flush" and "almost sick to her stomach," but this is the natural modesty and maidenly excitement expected in a young girl when she dreams of what (hetero)sexuality will be like; in contrast, Beverly's response to the circle jerkers' *"things"* and to Patrick's masturbation of Henry's *"thing"* is "terror," seemingly the proper attitude toward (homo)sexual perversion (*It*, 815). Not coincidentally, Beverly figures prominently in the book's main plot: she is the girl who saves Eddie, Richie, and other boys from Henry's fate; by making love to all of them, she guides them successfully through their gender insecurities and into a safely normal (hetero)sexuality (*"I made love to all of you?"* / "That was y-y-your way to get us o-out" [*It*, 931]).

Thus, in one reading of *It*, homosexuality (effeminacy, perversion) is the monster, the gender-indefinite hobo-clown that can only be destroyed by heterosexual experience – "this essential human link between the world and the infinite, the only place where the bloodstream touches eternity" (*It*, 1082–1083). Michael R. Collings finds a "certain justification" (logical reasoning or moral rightness?) in what he considers to be King's homophobic "attitude in the novel": "By its nature, homosexuality opposed heterosexuality, the linking of man and woman in the deepest emotional bonds. And that intense bonding lies at the center of *It*" (Collings, 23). Does same-sex attraction "naturally" "oppose" heterosexual bonding? Are homosexuals by their very nature a threat to the security of heterosexual couples, their sexual orientation and their gender identity?

Let us see if *It* can be read in another way, one that does not ratify society's homophobia. The answer to the question of whether It represents the threat of homosexuality or the danger of homophobia can be found late in the novel, where we learn that It *depends*. It takes the form of whatever Its victim at the time most fears: "all of [Its] glamours were only

mirrors, of course, throwing back at the terrified viewer the worst thing
in his or her own mind" (*It*, 1015). So gay Don sees it as the town's homophobia, while insecurely heterosexual Eddie and Richie fear it as a
gay advance threatening their masculinity. It, it turns out, is afraid of any
Otherness, "that maddening, galling fear . . . that sense of Another. It
hated the fear, would have turned on it and eaten it if It could have . . .
but the fear danced mockingly out of reach, and it could only kill the fear
by killing them" (*It*, 1015). It tries to project Its fear of Otherness onto specific others because others can be eliminated, but the trick doesn't work:
the Otherness It fears is within Itself, an inner insecurity, that cannot be
allayed through the murder of outsiders.

In this too, It mirrors Its victims, whose own insecurity leads them to
see Otherness as monstrous. Richie's vision of a threatening gay hobo –
"How about if I point at your pecker and give you prostate cancer?" –
seems to say more about his own sexual anxieties than about predatory
homosexuality; from an adult perspective, the threat is ridiculous, the
product of adolescent nightmare (*It*, 590). Patrick may be something
other than a gay fiend who gets a sexual charge out of molesting another
boy; instead, he might be seen as a psychologically disturbed youth unable to feel much of anything. After all, he does not even get an erection
from masturbating Henry; Patrick is so insecure that only the feeling of
being in complete control, as when he kills, gives him a "hard-on" (*It*,
831). And Patrick does not drive Henry insane so much as Henry's fear
that "he had allowed" Patrick to caress him; Henry is driven crazy by his
own fear of the Otherness within, his inability to live with his own homosexual impulses (*It*, 914). Finally, Beverly's terrified reaction to the circle
jerk may be more complex than a heterosexual girl's natural repulsion for
perverted, quasi-homosexual behavior. Beverly's strongest fear is not that
the world will be tainted by the boys' homosexuality, but that their *homophobia* will lead them to rape or kill her if they discover her watching.
The circle jerkers feel guilty about their act, knowing what (homophobic)
society thinks of males masturbating together; if a girl were to see them,
they might have to prove their heterosexuality by raping her, or kill her to
ensure her silence about what she has seen.[4] If It represents a fear of the
Otherness within and the monstrous desire to kill that fear by killing
others, then It may well be the embodiment of homophobic society: men
who would kill each other (and women who see too much) in a desperate
attempt to deny the effeminacy within.

Just as It mirrors Its victims, so *It* will to some extent mirror *It*'s readers: as I have shown, homophobes can certainly find monstrous confirmation of their worst fears and a ratification of their heterosexist world
view, while those more sympathetic to gays can find social satire, homophobia demonized and exorcized. My own sense, as I have tried to
demonstrate, is that readers who look closely won't miss the social sati-

rist behind the three-piece suit, the radical inside the conservative republican. As a child, King himself suffered under the rules of a homophobic
society and felt compelled to conform to its macho prescriptions: "I had
to play football, because I was big. If you didn't play football and you
were big, it meant you were a fucking faggot, right? That's what it's like
when you come from a small town" (Winter, 18). Many of King's fictions
address the problem of how one can be something other than a football
player – say, a writer – and still retain respect for oneself as a man.

The Stephen King stand-in or author surrogate in 'Salem's Lot is Ben
Mears who, because he is a writer, is suspected of being a "sissy boy" or a
"faggot": the people "distrusted the creative male with an instinctive
small-town dislike" (SL, 191, 106). Ben has come to write a book about the
town's evil Marsten House which frightened him as a child; readers of It
will recall that gay Adrian, also an author, "had come to Derry to write a
piece about the Canal" into which he is eventually dumped (It, 27). Ben's
first book included a "homosexual rape scene in the prison section,"
which the town reads as "Boys getting together with boys" (SL, 21). Ben's
arrival coincides with that of Straker and Barlow, two men who "may be
queer for each other"; at the same time, young boys start disappearing,
and the town can't make up its mind which one of the three – Straker,
Barlow, or Ben – is the "sex pervert" that did it (SL, 142, 139).

How can a writer defend the manliness of his vocation in a homophobic, anti-intellectual society? First, he can do so with what he writes.
Ben's first novel sounds a lot like an early Stephen King novella, "Rita
Hayworth and Shawshank Redemption." In this fiction, Andy is raped by
the prison's "sisters" or "killer queens," but, instead of letting himself "just
get taken," he decide[s] to fight" (DS, 21, 23). Through his financial genius,
Andy gains power over the men who raped him; rather than allow himself to be beaten or "turned" gay, Andy breaks out of prison through a
"hole" he has dug behind a girlie poster, thus escaping to freedom and heterosexuality (DS, 21, 80). The narrator and author of Andy's story is a fellow prisoner and rape victim who learns from Andy's example. Andy
may have been forced to "bend over" by the rapists and the guards who
searched his anal cavity upon his entrance to prison, but he fought back,
defeating his enemies using the money he secreted in a part of his anus
that remained inviolate (DS, 19). Similarly, the narrator smuggles his
story out "the same way," thus triumphing as a writer and as a man over a
violently intrusive world (DS, 95). In a tale that obviously contains certain homophobic elements, King does take pains to portray the prison
rapists as able to find joy only in violence, as more antisexual than homosexual, as, in fact, homophobes, preying on "the young, the weak, and the
inexperienced" in order not to feel so effeminate themselves (DS, 21).
And the relationship between the narrator and Andy is described as involving mutual concern and the exchange of "pretty" rocks, as if to claim

sympathy and beauty as manly occupations in spite of what homophobes might say (*DS*, 29).

If Ben's first novel is like "Rita Hayworth and Shawshank Redemption," it might almost have been written to counter suspicions like those entertained by the homophobic townsfolk of *'Salem's Lot* concerning a writer's manliness. Not only what he writes, but also his purpose in writing seem part of his masculine defense. Ben plans to write about the Marsten House as a way of "Confronting my own terrors and evils"; with the writing he hopes will come "control of the situation, and that would make all the difference" (*SL*, 113). Numerous passages in King's work make it clear that he sees the writing of fiction as a means of gaining control over his fears, of shaping amorphous anxiety into manageable form. In "The Body," fledgling author Gordie remembers "the first time I had ever really used the places I knew and the things I felt in a piece of fiction, and there was a kind of dreadful exhilaration in seeing things that had troubled me for years come out in a new form, *a form over which I had imposed control*" (*DS*, 336). And many years later, in a recent interview, King himself still describes the advantage of writing in similar terms: "Fiction is in my hand, and that means I can control it" (Magistrale, *Stephen King*, ms. 13).

In *'Salem's Lot*, Ben plans to wield his writer's pen as proof that he is man enough to overcome the town's suspicions about his effeminacy and his own doubts concerning possible inner weakness. Like It, the vampire Barlow plays on his victims' worst fears – Ben's terror that he is nothing but a bookish wimp; that, as a writer and as a man, he is impotent:

Look and see me, puny man. Look upon Barlow, who has passed the centuries as you have passed hours before a fireplace with a book. Look and see the great creature of the night whom you would slay with your miserable little stick. Look upon me, scribbler. I have written in human lives, and blood has been my ink. Look upon me and despair! (*SL*, 411)

But Ben succeeds in taking pen and stake in hand and vanquishes the vampire; by giving his fears fictional form, he is able to overcome them. In the beginning Ben's imaginative capacity as a writer may have contributed to his fear of effeminacy, but in the end it helps him prove his masculinity.[5]

Perhaps King is hinting that those, like writers of horror fiction, who can win the war against sexual fears in their imaginations are stronger than the unimaginative who end up fighting and killing real others in a desperate attempt to destroy the Otherness within. In "Graveyard Shift," Hall, unable to handle being ridiculed by a foreman who continually denigrates his manhood by calling him "college boy," turns his phallic hose on the man and causes him to be eaten by rats (*NS*, 50). In the end, however, Hall's macho display gets him nowhere; his hose isn't strong enough to stop the rats (his own insecurities) from eating him up too. In "I Am the Doorway," an astronaut, returned from a failed mission to the planet of love, finds himself giving a beach boy the eye ("He was tanned almost black by the sun, and all he was ever clad in was a frayed pair of denim cutoffs"), but the eyes turn out to be peering from the astronaut's hand, as if aliens had entered his body and were looking through him (*NS*, 67). What the alien eyes see is not a beautiful boy, but something horribly other, hateful, and "they" kill the boy: "I didn't kill him, either—I told you that. They did. I am the doorway" (*NS*, 63). And when the astronaut looks into his own face through the eyes, he sees a "monster" which must be destroyed (*NS*, 70). One can read this tale as the story of a man whose inability either to accept or deny his homoerotic impulses leads to murder and suicide, or one can take it as a more abstract parable about a man's failure to live with Otherness outside or within himself.

King's longer works develop these same themes in revealing depth. *The Stand* gives us Kit Bradenton, whose homoerotic dream of "the most beautiful boy in the world, tall and tanned and straight, . . . wearing lemon-yellow bikini briefs" is horribly interrupted when the boy's face turns out to be that "of a Goya devil and from each blank eyesocket there peers the reptilian face of an adder" (*St*, 268–269). Kit's fear is that the 1960s are over and the country has since turned conservative and homophobic, that some macho man (like the Walkin Dude) will come and stab him for his homosexuality, and that Kit himself is now too old and decrepit to attract anyone but a monster: "The boy in the yellow briefs had been long ago, and in Boulder Kit Bradenton had been little more than a boy himself. *My God, am I dying?*" (*St*, 269). In *The Shining*, Jack Torrance finds himself looking at another boy:

Tall and shaggily blond, George had been an almost insolently beautiful boy. In his tight faded jeans and Stovington sweatshirt with the sleeves carelessly pushed up to the elbows to disclose his tanned forearms, he had reminded Jack of a young Robert Redford, and he doubted that George had much trouble scoring— no more than that young football-playing devil Jack Torrance had ten years earlier. (*Sh*, 110–111)

Like Claggart in Melville's *Billy Budd*, Jack, though he refuses to admit it to himself, is jealous of George's good looks, athletic and sexual prowess, and unselfconscious masculine identity. Like Claggart, Jack allows his own gender insecurity to lead him to defame another: using George's stutter as an excuse (as if that made the boy less of a man), Jack drops him from the debating team (for his impotence as a debater). When George attempts to reassert his manhood by taking a knife to Jack's tires, Jack cannot bear the affront to his masculine authority and viciously strikes out at the boy. Jack is, not coincidentally, a *failed* writer.[6]

Again and again, the defeated characters in King's fiction are revealed to be men who cannot imagine a constructive resolution to the battle of the sexes raging within them. Sometimes King seems almost callous about their fate, as if he were afraid that their effeminacy might threaten him or as though he were imaginatively killing off his own fear of weakness. In *The Tommyknockers,* a mama's boy named John Leandro manages to break his mother's injunction against eating fast-food cheeseburgers (*"Microbes,* his mother's voice spoke up in his mind. *Food in places like that can make a person very, very sick"*), but eventually he succumbs to his fear of her disapproval and is killed by contact with a Coke machine (*TK,* 438). King considers the passage detailing Leandro's death "a scene that I like as well as anything I've ever done"; his attitude toward the victim: "One of the main characters is a real wimp. I was glad to see him go" (Underwood, 83).

But King can also be extraordinarily sympathetic toward the "wimps" of this world, as if he himself were feelingly engaged in their struggle and did not take their loss lightly. This is the Stephen King whose art rises above kneejerk homophobia and the demonization of Otherness. In a scene from *'Salem's Lot,* which may be viewed as paradigmatic of the (self-)confrontations in King's fiction, Father Callahan comes face to face with the vampire Barlow, a face which, though "strong and intelligent and handsome," also "seemed almost effeminate"; Callahan thinks: "Where had he seen a face like that before? And it came to him, in this moment of the most extreme terror he had ever known. It was the face of Mr. Flip, his own personal bogeyman, the thing that hid in the closet during the days and came out after his mother closed the bedroom door (*SL,* 352). "Flip": flip out, flip side, flippant; Mr. Flip, now suddenly "out of the closet" and "staring . . . with his clown-white face and glowing eyes and red, sensual lips," is Callahan's own fear of his other side, the side that mocks his attempts at manly action, the exterior embodiment of an inner effeminacy that threatens to drive him insane (*SL,* 352). And, like many another brave but insufficiently hardy souls in King's fiction, Callahan has faith in his identity (religious, adult, male)—but not faith enough: "The cross [held by Father Callahan] flared with preternatural, dazzling brilliance, and it was at that moment that Callahan might have banished [the vampire, his own fears] if he had dared to press forward" (*SL,* 353). From the moment Callahan gives up fighting to resolve his insecurities, from the moment he lets his childhood fear of weakness get the better of him, he is lost. Again and again, and most insistently near the end of *'Salem's Lot,* the male reader is implored to recognize that the "transvestite," the "strangely masculine face bleeding with rouge and paints," is "his own face" (*SL,* 417–418). Only by facing up to one's fear of effeminacy, only by acknowledging the monstrousness of homophobia, can one learn to live with others and with the Otherness in oneself.

NOTES

1. Garton is just one in a long line of macho, homophobic, and sexually inse-cure characters in King's fiction. Other examples include the 1950s-imitation tough-guy Billy Nolan in *Carrie* ("he was going to have her until every other time she'd been had was like two pumps with a fag's little finger" [*Ca,* 164]) and that "miniature streetpunk from hell," The Kid in *The Stand,* who rapes Trashcan with his ".45" (*St,* 608).

2. Derry's "ritual sacrifice" of gay Adrian, all but outlined in the sermons of the "town's preachers," reminds one of the homophobic scapegoating called for by the boy evangelist in "Children of the Corn": "No room for the defiler of the corn. No room for the hommasexshul" (*NS,* 263).

3. Compare King's novella, "Apt Pupil," in which a wino proposes to the boy Todd, "For a buck I'd do you a blow job, you never had better. You'd come your brains out, kid" (*DS,* 198). Todd later has a wet dream in which he stabs the wino, thus getting a sexual charge out of violently proving his masculinity. Todd's gen-der anxiety is exacerbated by his relationship with the former Nazi Dussander, a bad father who encourages Todd to take pleasure in inflicting pain. In another wet dream, Todd tortures a Jewish girl with a combination dildo/cattle prod sup-plied by Dussander; under the Nazi's tutelage, Todd attempts to straighten out his confused sexual orientation through rape. The fact is, as Tony Magistrale points out, "Dussander is symbolically raping Todd"—fucking with the boy's mind in a desperate attempt to restore the sense of potency he lost with age and the Third Reich (Magistrale, *Landscape,* 87). In a later scene, Dussander actually masquer-ades as the "old faggot" he fears he is, propositioning a wino and then, as if trying to project and eliminate his own effeminacy, kills the bum (*DS,* 209).

4. The fear that male bonding will be seen as gay attraction—what Eve Ko-sofsky Sedgwick has termed "male homosocial panic"—is pervasive in King's fic-tion. See Dennis's concern about embracing Arnie in *Christine* (*Ch,* 58) and Gordie's and Chris's embarrassment at their warmth for each other in "The Body" (*DS,* 430). Bookish, nerdy, diminutive, or overweight young males troubled by the fear that they may be—or be perceived as—gay include Charlie in *Rage (BB,* 106); Harold in *The Stand* (*St,* 971, 978); Randy in "The Raft" (*SC,* 279); the narra-tor in "Nona" (*SC,* 377); and (the only one in this list who overcomes his ho-mophobia) Garraty in *The Long Walk* (*BB,* 179, 288).

5. Given the theme of this essay, perhaps something should be said about the critical controversy surrounding the relationship between Ben Mears and the boy Mark Petrie in *'Salem's Lot.* King has made his position clear: "People say to me . . . that what I wrote there was a classical sub rosa homosexual relationship. I say bullshit, it's father-son" (Underwood, 122). King's response may seem less ho-mophobic if one remembers that in the novel Ben is under suspicion of being a gay *fiend,* a child molester: *this* may be the charge that King is really repudiating. One should also remember that King has written often on the theme of the bad father who takes advantage of his son (Jack and Danny Torrance in *The Shining,* for example); King may want to make certain that readers view Ben as he was intended to be seen—as a good (surrogate) father to Mark.

Probably the most detailed and determined reading of the Ben-Mark relation-ship as containing homosexual undercurrents is Joseph Reino's. It seems that, where King claims to have meant only paternal love, Reino sees (also or instead?) homoerotic attraction. The trouble with Reino's interpretation is that it is based almost entirely on verbal ambiguity: King's "fairy-light" is read "subsurfacely" as a reference to the "fairy-feelings" between Ben and Mark; King's "the moment seemed to undergo a queer stretching" becomes an "ithyphallic innuendo," a reference to gay erection (Reino, 27, 29). These readings seem strained to me, despite the fact that I elsewhere find Reino to be a subtle and perceptive critic of King.

6. Beating George does not help Jack feel like any more of a man, because fears of effeminacy cannot be dispelled through attack on another. This, however, is a lesson Jack never learns, for his jealous assault on George is unconsciously repeated on his son Danny when Jack begins to suspect that the hotel prefers the boy's masculinity to his own. Jack's greatest fear is that his relation to the hotel is like that of the man in the dog suit trying to fellate his impotent master: submissive and yet unrewarded (*Sh*, 334). The point of the servile dogman as representative of Jack's fear of unmanliness is lost in Stanley Kubrick's film version of the novel, where the dogman becomes a pigman and the connection with Jack is not made. A bewildered Pauline Kael commented, upon seeing the film, that "Kubrick has an odd sense of morality: it's meant to be a hideous debauch when [Wendy] sees the two figures in the bedroom – one of them, wearing a pig costume, looks up at her while he or she is still bent over the genitals of a man in evening clothes on the bed" (Kael, 4).

In addition to using the dog to symbolize man's fear of effeminacy (the cowardly cur subject to another man's phallic rule), King also employs the dog as a figure for the sexually insecure man who overcompensates by acting like a hypersexed animal, even if this leads him to raping men. Consider the rapist Frank Dodd whose vicious spirit inhabits the rabid dog Cujo and assaults George Bannerman: "Hello, Frank. It's you, isn't it? Was hell too hot for you? . . . What's he done to me down there? Oh my God, what's he done?" (*Cu*, 285).

REFERENCES

Works by Stephen King

[*BB*]   *The Bachman Books.* New York: New American Library, 1985.

[*Ca*]   *Carrie.* New York: New American Library, 1975.

[*Ch*]   *Christine.* New York: Viking, 1983.

[*Cu*]   *Cujo.* New York: Viking, 1981.

[*DM*]   *Danse Macabre.* New York: Everest House, 1981.

[*DS*]   *Different Seasons.* New York: Viking, 1982.

[*It*]   *It.* New York: Viking, 1986.

[*NS*]   *Night Shift.* New York: Doubleday, 1978.

[*SL*]   *'Salem's Lot.* New York: New American Library, 1976.

[*Sh*]   *The Shining.* New York: New American Library, 1978.

[SC]   *Skeleton Crew.* New York: New American Library, 1985.

[St]   *The Stand: The Complete and Uncut Edition.* New York: Doubleday, 1990.

[SK]   "Stephen King Comments on *It.*" *Castle Rock* (July, 1986): 1, 5.

[TK]   *The Tommyknockers.* New York: Putnam, 1987.

Criticism

Beahm, George. *The Stephen King Companion.* Kansas City: Andrews & McMeel, 1989.

Carroll, Noel. *The Philosophy of Horror or Paradoxes of the Heart.* New York: Routledge, 1990.

Collings, Michael, R. *The Stephen King Phenomenon.* Mercer Island, Wash.: Starmont House, 1987.

Kael, Pauline. *Taking It All In.* New York: Holt, Rinehart & Winston, 1984.

Magistrale, Tony. *Landscape of Fear: Stephen King's American Gothic.* Bowling Green, Ohio: Bowling Green State University Popular Press, 1988.

———. *Stephen King: The Second Decade,* Danse Macabre *to* The Dark Half. New York: Macmillan, forthcoming, 1992.

Reino, Joseph. *Stephen King: The First Decade,* Carrie *to* Pet Sematary. Boston: Twayne, 1988.

Sedgwick, Eve Kosofsky. *Between Men: English Literature and Male Homosocial Desire.* New York: Columbia University Press, 1985.

Underwood, Tim and Chuck Miller, eds. *Bare Bones: Conversations on Terror with Stephen King.* New York: McGraw-Hill, 1988.

Van Hise, James. *Stephen King and Clive Barker.* Las Vegas: Pioneer, 1990.

Winter, Douglas E. "Talking Terror: Interview with Stephen King." *Twilight Zone Magazine* 5 (February, 1986).

16

Reading, Writing and Interpreting: Stephen King's *Misery*

LAURI BERKENKAMP

I began reading *Misery* lying in a hammock one sunny summer afternoon. Hours later I came inside, bleary-eyed from reading. I had read the entire novel in one sitting; I didn't plan on it, but I couldn't put it down. I had followed Annie Wilkes into that mysterious realm that Paul Sheldon in the novel calls "the gotta" (*Misery,* 242): the need to know how things will turn out. "The gotta" is what makes readers of novels fall under the power of the writer, and what makes writers fall under the sway of their own ideas. *Misery* is a novel that not only creates "the gotta," but also is *about* "the gotta," the relationship between reading and writing and the reciprocal effects each process has on the other.

Much reader-response criticism explores this complex relationship, and concentrates on the role of the reader in making sense of a text. Some reader-response critics, most notably Wolfgang Iser, posit that readers of texts and writers of texts share power in experiencing a literary work: the writer of a text provides the reader with building blocks, or "correlatives" (Iser, 100), of meaning with the words he writes, to which the reader brings her own preconceptions and expectations. Through a recreative process the reader makes meaning by combining what she finds in the text with what she brings to it, in some ways "rewriting" the text for herself as she reads. Thus, for these critics, the reader and the writer are involved in a reciprocal participatory relationship, where the reader's contribution to the text is as important to its meaning as are the literal words on the page.[1]

Stephen King addresses the shifting, cyclical reader-writer relationship in *Misery*. In the novel, King examines the interactive roles of reader and writer through the characters Paul Sheldon and Annie Wilkes. Paul and Annie are introduced at the start of the work as writer of novels and reader of novels, respectively, but in the course of the book the two characters' perceptions of each other and of their roles as writer and reader blur, at times even becoming indistinguishable.

Many kinds of reading and writing go on in this novel, and on many levels. Each character learns to "read" the other: learns to interpret signals, actions, and signs the other makes to understand and predict what he or she will do next. In the act of reading, Paul and Annie gain greater insight into each other, how the other character thinks, feels, and acts. Through the course of *Misery* the power dynamics shift each time a change occurs in one character's level of insight, so that finally both Annie and Paul become creators as well as interpreters of each other as texts.

Paul Sheldon is a character who begins the novel viewing himself wholly as A Writer: "he had spent most of his adult life thinking the word writer was the most important definition of himself" (*Misery*, 29). Paul sees this role of writer – his role – as inherently powerful, and in many respects, he considers this power entirely one-sided: he creates the worlds in which his readers become so wholly involved, he dictates what "truths" they will experience through his words.

Paul consequently has very little respect for his readers, because he considers the work for which he is known, his *Misery* novels, his personal prostitution. By continuously writing about Misery Chastain, Paul has given in to what King calls the "great siren's song to keep giving [the readers] whatever it is they want" (Magistrale, ms. 29). Paul writes his *Misery* novels to make a buck, and he resents every word.

Paul refers to Annie throughout the text as a Bourka Bee-Goddess, but he also sees himself as such a being in his role of writer: a removed and omnipotent figure dispensing knowledge to be absorbed by his grateful followers. This self-perception, however, is shattered when Annie forces him to burn *Fast Cars*. At first Paul is outraged that this reader of his *Misery* novels who "wouldn't know good if it bit (her) nose off" would have "the nerve to *criticize* the best thing he had ever written" (28). However, it soon becomes clear that Annie has the nerve to do more than merely criticize his new novel, and it is at this point that Paul comes to some hard realizations about the power inherent in his role as writer. When Annie Wilkes, reader, makes *him* burn what *he* has created, Paul recognizes that what he's considered his omnipotence has been challenged and usurped. More importantly, perhaps, Paul sees that this power is challenged *by his reader*. Annie forces Paul into a position where he must realize that the writer is not the only authority over a text; for perhaps the first time Paul recognizes that the relationship between himself and Annie, between writer and reader, is undergoing some rather drastic revisions.

Paul burns *Fast Cars* because Annie Wilkes tells him to; she administers the ultimate bad review. And as Paul burns what he "knew about the . . . TRUTH!" (45), in this scene, he comes to a moment of traumatic realization: no longer a Bourka Bee-Goddess, he is, rather, a crippled junkie in a great deal of trouble. And yet the act of burning this manuscript, of being forced to destroy a part of himself by his "number one fan" offers Paul a means of saving himself in more ways than one. By burning the novel Paul obtains not only the medicine he needs to help him survive physically, but also gains a psychological reason for surviving. He vows he will kill Annie Wilkes for what she made him do, but to do this requires Paul to become a reader, himself: he learns to interpret Annie as a kind of text, to decipher her moods and behave in a way that will present her with the least opportunity for inflicting punishment. Paul's ability to read Annie is initiated by his desire for revenge for having his power and source of control (as both a writer and a physical being) challenged and so manipulated, but it is precisely *by reading*—by learning how to read Annie accurately and successfully—that Paul manages not only to kill Annie and save his own life, but also to create his most successful novel.

Paul becomes a skilled reader quickly: he has to in order to stay alive. He learns how to interpret the physical cues Annie provides him to make judgments and expectations about what she will do, and how she will react to what he does. Paul learns to recognize what I call "markers" in Annie's psychological text: patterns of behavior that offer him a means for evaluating Annie's actions while likewise providing him with predictable patterns she is likely to follow. Early in the novel when Annie becomes "unplugged" for the first time, Paul looks at her face and sees "the black nothing of a crevasse" (12). He processes this information and is "alerted" by it to conclude that "everything she said was a little strange, a little offbeat" (12). Paul learns to recognize these "blips," and to recognize that changes in Annie's routines signal changes in her "cycles" of behavior. Paul eventually can read Annie like the weather; when he notices she is not behaving in her usual manner, he thinks, "Here's a special weather bulletin for residents of Sheldon County—a tornado watch is in effect until 5:00 p.m. tonight. I repeat, a tornado watch" (118).

As Paul learns to read the clues Annie provides him, he combines this reading with his skills as a writer. Annie offers Paul small bits of information about her past, information that is not complete or clear. Paul takes these small pieces of information, these "correlatives" of Annie's text, and based on the judgments he has made about her by reading her physical cues and her actions, Paul "writes" the parts of Annie's history she doesn't provide him. As he says, "he had a little extra information on which to judge just how *much* of her gear wasn't stowed right, didn't he?" (29); consequently, Paul writes a version of Annie even as he reads a version of Annie, to come up with a complete view of the woman who holds him captive.

Paul reads Annie's scrapbook, entitled "Memory Lane"; but the memories he "reads" in it are those he creates as a result of his reading and writing Annie. Paul writes a complete history of Annie's crimes based on the bits of information the scrapbook provides him and what he knows about Annie already; in fact, "in an act of self preservation, part of his imagination had, over the last few weeks, actually *become* Annie" (188), and consequently Paul is able to create an uncannily accurate portrait of Annie's past. Further, Paul's writing of Annie helps him as a reader, as well; as he "becomes" Annie through his writing of her history, Paul becomes more and more adept at anticipating what Annie will do next, and thus can prepare his own reactions accordingly. Paul's growing ability to foresee and predict what will happen—"writing" what will happen—is based on his growing ability to "read" what *is* happening. This combination of skills, ultimately, is the key to Paul's empowerment when he and Annie confront each other in the battle over the final copy of *Misery's Return.*

Paul learns through his reading—and his writing—of Annie that readers assert control over the texts they read in as powerful, but different, a way as their writers. In the act of reading, the text becomes the reader's, in fact becomes a part of the reader, who places himself within the confines of the narrative and perhaps (as Georges Poulet suggests)[2] melds with the author to participate in the world of fiction. Paul eventually discovers the reciprocity inherent in creating meaning from a text, creating individual truths based on interpretation. As King says, "It's like digging something out of the ground . . . It might look to me as if I dug a steam engine up out of the earth, but to someone else that steam engine could look like a car" (Magistrale, ms. 13). Paul recognizes the different views of reader and writer by becoming a reader, and because he is able to switch roles, to see from the outside in, he comes to a new understanding of the relationship between readers and writers and the power and responsibility of each.

Paul proves himself to be both an adept reader and adept writer of Annie Wilkes; however, he is not a perfect reader, and he misreads Annie on two occasions with disastrous results. Paul again underestimates the power of Annie Wilkes as a reader, and this underestimation has dire consequences. In a grotesque parallel to the psychic mutilation Paul undergoes when he is forced to burn *Fast Cars,* Paul is mutilated again by Annie when he fails to interpet and respond accurately to her as a text. Paul recognizes this the second time he misreads Annie. He says of his thumb amputation: "I bitched about the typewriter . . . Not a lot; I only bitched about it once. But once was enough, wasn't it?" (249). Paul recognizes his mistakes, and these recognitions make him a stronger reader of Annie in the future. Finally, in fact, Paul becomes so accomplished at reading Annie—he "learns from her," as he tells her when he kills her—that he is able to predict accurately what she'll do at the completion of

Misery's Return. Paul gambles everything on this interpretation of Annie, and it's a gamble he wins because he's learned how to read Annie as a text – and to manipulate and exploit the power inherent in his newfound reading ability.

In contrast to Paul, who views himself at the start of *Misery* solely as a Writer, Annie Wilkes begins *Misery* as a Reader. But Annie isn't just any reader; rather, she is the epitome of the "Constant Reader" (63), a fan so loyal to Paul's *Misery* novels that she "read each of his eight novels at least twice, and had read her *very* favorites, the *Misery* novels, four, five, maybe six times" (9). While Annie identifies herself as Paul's "number one fan," and sees herself as a loyal reader of *Misery* novels, she actually does many different kinds of reading in King's novel: for example, she not only reads, but casts judgment on *Fast Cars*, based on her expectations of what "good" writing is. It is quite ironic that Annie's perception of "good" writing is based on what Paul sees as his personal prostitution. This irony isn't lost on Paul, who begins the novel mocking Annie's fanatical fanship; rather, he comes to realize quite quickly that this "Constant Reader" "reads" far more than Misery Chastain's exploits. Throughout *Misery* Annie reveals to Paul that, "Constant Reader did not mean Constant Sap" (107).

Annie is a much more adept reader, at many different kinds of "reading," than Paul gives her credit for at the beginning of the novel. In fact, it is her ability to read – to interpret and respond to situations presented to her – that helps teach Paul to become an active reader, as well. Not only does Annie read and judge the novels Paul writes, but she "reads" Paul himself in a way that he emulates and imitates throughout the novel. She tells him when she is "hobbling" him that "my eyes were opened. I saw how much of your color had come back . . . And your arms were getting stronger again, as well . . . That was when I started to realize I could have a problem with you even if no one from the outside suspected a thing" (216). Annie recognizes signs Paul gives her based on what she knows about him and what she experiences with him, to make interpretations about what she thinks he will do. Paul recognizes and learns from Annie how to detect signs and signals in her behavior; he then "reads" her in much the same way she has been reading him.

While Paul comes to a new understanding through the course of the novel that readers of novels have a direct effect on the power and control of the writer of the books they read, Annie shows throughout the novel that she has an almost innate sense of what kinds of power a careful reader can have; she illustrates this understanding often throughout the novel. Annie knows that "Keeping up appearances is very, very important" (68), and thus painstakingly maintains the appearance of a "normal" household so the neighbors don't "yap" (68). Annie reads how she is expected to act, what she must do to appear "normal," and recognizes the consequences of deviating from the norm. She shows an uncanny ability to read her situation and respond accordingly. Annie knows when she must leave for her "Laughing Place" (175), for example, and she goes there before she gets out of control.

Annie's understanding of her role as a reader, and what privileges and responsibilities are inherent in that role, help her to make the transition from reader to "writer." She is very much in control of Paul and in control of Paul's "text." She "writes" his survival, not only by controlling his medication and recovery, but also by forcing him to burn *Fast Cars,* and by shaping the narrative direction of *Misery's Return.*

Annie writes the scenarios in her house, while Paul becomes the submissive, if reluctant reader of Annie's moods. Like Paul, Annie takes what she reads about Paul and is able to "write" possible scenarios for how he will respond or behave; she places hairs around her house because she is sure Paul will manage to escape from his room, and in fact leaves out her scrapbook because she "knew" Paul would read it (208, 209). Thus, she, too, "writes" a script for Paul while she simultaneously reads one. And while Paul "writes" Annie's story when he discovers Annie's "Memory Lane" scrapbook, he also discovers that Annie is writing his story at the same time, as well. Paul finds his own newspaper clipping at the end of the scrapbook, and finds he is part of Annie's written "memories," as well. In fact, Paul eventually acknowledges Annie's abilities as both a reader and a writer: "he was almost afraid she would read his thoughts on his face, like the bare premise of a story too gruesome to write" (57). Paul recognizes Annie's power as a reader and writer here, and realizes that his storyline, at least to some extent, is in Annie's hands.

Annie's control as a writer of Paul's situation carries through both his reading and his writing. She forces him to write for her yet another *Misery* sequel, a coercive act that ultimately becomes the impetus for his finest novel. She also gives him the ideas for key elements in the work, offering him the suggestion about the bee stings, which Paul acknowledges to be what "had shaped the book and given it its urgency" (164).

Because Annie is in control of Paul's life, she makes Paul play "Can you" every day. In fact, Annie proves herself to be an accomplished "Can you" player in her own right and joins Paul in his "game." She reveals to Paul that the story she told him about how she found him was false: that she made up—"wrote"—the story about going into Sidewinder, because she didn't "know him well then" (175). Similarly, Annie "writes" what will happen when the state troopers come looking for the young officer she has killed: "When they come I'll stand right out there in the driveway and say yes, there was a state trooper that came by here . . . I'll say he showed me your picture. I'll say I hadn't seen you" (277). Here she writes what may happen much like Paul has been writing what may happen throughout the novel. In fact, Annie and Paul trade roles in playing "Can you" throughout the novel, each writing possible scenarios that ominously foreshadow what actually does occur.

By the end of the novel, Annie appears to be able to "write" what Paul will do as well as Paul can write what she will do. She puts him down in the basement because "If I gave you a flashlight, you might try to signal with it. If I gave you a candle, you might try to burn the house down with it. You see how well I know you?" (280). However, just as Paul is neither a perfect writer nor a perfect reader, Annie, too, both misreads and miswrites what occurs in the novel. Just as Paul's misreading of Annie's moods brings about disastrous consequences for him, Annie's misreading and miswriting of Paul's capabilities prove to be her downfall. And in the novel's climactic scene, the focus of Annie's misreading of Paul revolves around the written word.

Paul's *Misery* novels mean as much to Annie as *Fast Cars* did to him, and just as Paul finds it inconceivable that Annie would make him burn his book because she didn't like the language in it, she cannot comprehend that Paul would be willing to burn the truths she finds in *Misery.* Annie misreads Paul not because she has misjudged him as a character, but because she has misjudged him as a fellow reader. Annie cannot accept any truths that differ from her own, and her refusal, or, perhaps, inability to recognize that her truth differs from Paul's is the crux of her misreading of him. This misreading finally shifts the balance of power back to Paul, and eventually results in Annie's death.

Paul has shown throughout the novel that he is capable of both creating and accepting other truths, those present in a novel such as *Fast Cars,* for example, or the grotesque truth of his macabre imprisonment. Truth is transitory for Paul, where different truths apply to different novels, different situations, and he is accordingly able to create truths that are relevant to both his "serious work" and his *Misery* novels. But as Annie shows again and again, her truth is the only truth she'll accept: she reads only what confirms what she already believes, and interprets what she wants to interpret. Annie "reads" the world not to expand her self-knowledge, but to affirm the narrowness of her own psychotic view of reality. Only one interpretation exists for Annie: her own. Ultimately, Annie's inability to recognize and accept other truths, her inability to be a flexible or open reader, causes her to lose the final game of "Can you" to Paul.

The relationship between these two readers and writers throughout the novel is thus both antagonistic and eerily complementary. While Paul reads Annie as a necessary means of survival, and Annie reads Paul to maintain control over him (and thus over herself), the reading processes of these two characters become as reciprocal as they are adversarial. Each reader has power over the other: Annie has power over Paul's medicine and their physical survival, but Paul has power over the book, which is also a kind of drug upon which Annie has become dependent. Annie feels herself very much a part of the new *Misery* novel, just as Paul felt *Fast Cars* was a part of himself. Similarly, each character has a part of him or herself destroyed in the barbecue pot, because both novels represent texts that are reflective of the authors' personal vision. *Misery's Return* is nothing less than a collaborative writing exercise.

Annie and Paul prove to be quite equal adversaries and collaborators in this novel: so equal, in fact, that there seems to be a good deal of each character in the other – a bit of Annie in every writer, and a bit of Paul in every reader. Each writer must write in part with an audience in mind, even if that audience is the writer himself. And each reader, as many theorists of reader-response criticism have argued, brings herself to each text and invests a certain degree of meaning that is unique to her alone.

Where does the reader of King's novel fit in here? As a reader of *Misery*, I started out liking neither character, but ended up respecting both. Like Annie and Paul, I am given the opportunity in this novel to be an active reader, to make connections and conclusions based on what the text provides me and the assumptions I bring to it. And like Annie and Paul, I must do a great deal of "writing" – making connections *through* the text which are not necessarily *in* the text – to understand this work fully.

King offers me extensive allusions throughout *Misery* not only to other works, such as Fowles' *The Collector*, which *Misery* eerily parallels, but also to other novels he has written. He incorporates places such as The Overlook Hotel from *The Shining* into the novel as a "real life" event, for example. As an active reader of *Misery*, I have to "read" these allusions into the novel to determine their significance.

I also must make sense of what is almost an affronting relationship with the two characters through the visual typescript of the novel being composed within *Misery*. I am brought into the action of *Misery* and thrust into a relationship between reading and writing (and thus between Paul and Annie) in an immediate way through King's technique of altering the type in *Misery's Return*, and of presenting in a visual way the difficulties Paul has *writing* his new novel. When I read Paul's manuscript of *Misery's Return* within the confines of King's novel, and see the "handwriting" of characters within that novel also creating a novel, the boundaries between reality and fiction, life and art, even fiction and metafiction, collapse. I, too, become a part of the novel Paul and Annie create, and become a character in King's novel as I mentally fill in missing letters for Paul just as Annie physically inserts "n's" into his manuscript. By the end of Paul's novel only he, Annie, and I know what the sentences he has created say; only the three of us have the extra information necessary to make meaning from the unfinished words on the typewritten pages. I become a collaborator in *Misery's Return* much like Annie Wilkes, and I become an active reader – and misreader – like Paul Sheldon.

King has placed me, his reader, in a position to write for myself a version of his novel. As he says, "I sometimes think that with a really good tale or novel, the theme is there before you recognize it, before you create it. Before you write it down, the story exists, but it takes the actual writing to recognize it" (Magistrale, ms. 13). King provides me the chance to write for myself the story of Annie and Paul, by offering me information both through and about the characters and what will happen to them, and giving me the opportunity to recognize the story through (and sometimes in spite of) the information I'm given.

In many ways, then, I "wrote" my own version of *Misery,* and created my own "gotta" by being an active reader of Paul and Annie's story. By enabling me to be a creative reader, by empowering me through reading to write for myself an interpretation of his novel, King has performed the ultimate balancing act: he has created a work in which all roles are blurred, self-defining, and essentially unrealized, and this makes all readers of *Misery* writers of *Misery,* as well.

NOTES

1. For more on Iser's reading process, see Wolfgang Iser, *The Implied Reader: Patterns of Communication in Prose Fiction from Bunyan to Beckett* (Baltimore: Johns-Hopkins University Press, 1974). For an extensive bibliography of reader-response criticism, see Jane Tompkins, ed., *Reader-Response Criticism: From Formalism to Post-Structuralism* (Baltimore: Johns-Hopkins University Press, 1980).

2. See Georges Poulet, "Criticism and the Experience of Interiority," in *Reader-Response Criticism: From Formalism to Post-Structuralism.*

REFERENCES

Iser, Wolfgang. "Narrative Strategies as a Means of Communication." In *Interpretation of Narrative,* edited by Mario J. Valdes and Owen J. Miller, pp. 100–117. University of Toronto Press, 1978.

King, Stephen. *Misery.* New York: New American Library, 1988.

Magistrale, Tony. *Stephen King, The Second Decade: From Danse Macabre to The Dark Half.* New York: Macmillan, forthcoming, 1992.

A Stephen King Bibliography

PRIMARY TEXTS

Novels

Carrie. Garden City, New York: Doubleday, 1974; New American Library, 1975.

Christine. West Kingston, R.I.: Donald M. Grant, 1983; New York: Viking, 1983; New American Library, 1984.

Cujo. New York: The Mysterious Press, 1981; Viking, 1981; New American Library, 1982.

Cycle of the Werewolf. Westland, Mich.: Land of Enchantment, 1983; New York: New American Library, 1984.

The Dark Half. New York: Viking, 1989; New American Library, 1990.

The Dark Tower: The Gunslinger. West Kingston, R.I.: Donald M. Grant, 1984; New York: New American Library, 1988.

The Dark Tower II: The Drawing of the Three. New York: New American Library, 1987.

The Dark Tower III: The Waste Lands. New York: New American Library, 1991.

The Dead Zone. New York: Viking, 1979; New American Library, 1980.

The Eyes of the Dragon. New York: Viking, 1987; New American Library, 1987.

Firestarter. Huntington Woods, Mich.: Phantasia Press, 1980; New York: Viking, 1980; New American Library, 1981.

It. New York: Viking, 1986; New American Library, 1987.

The Long Walk [Richard Bachman, pseud.]. New York: New American Library, 1979.

Misery. New York: Viking, 1987; New American Library, 1987.

Needful Things. New York: Viking, 1991.

Pet Sematary. Garden City, New York: Doubleday, 1983; New York: New American Library, 1984.

Rage. [Richard Bachman, pseud.]. New York: New American Library, 1977.

Roadwork. [Richard Bachman, pseud.]. New York: New American Library, 1981.

The Running Man. [Richard Bachman, pseud.]. New York: New American Library, 1982.

'Salem's Lot. Garden City, N.Y.: Doubleday, 1975; New York: New American Library, 1978.

The Shining. New York: Doubleday, 1977; New American Library, 1978.

The Stand. Garden City, N.Y.: Doubleday, 1978; New York: New American Library, 1979; 2nd ed. rev. and unexpurgated, New York: Doubleday, 1990.

The Talisman [with Peter Straub]. West Kingston, R.I.: Donald M. Grant, 1984; New York: Viking and Putnam, 1984; Berkley, 1985.

Thinner. [Richard Bachman, pseud.]. New York: New American Library, 1984.

The Tommyknockers. New York: G. P. Putnam, 1987; New American Library, 1988.

Collections

The Bachman Books: Four Early Novels. New York: New American Library, 1985.

Creepshow. New York: New American Library, 1982.

Different Seasons. New York: Viking, 1982; New American Library, 1983.

Four Past Midnight. New York: Viking, 1990.

Night Shift. Garden City, N.Y.: Doubleday, 1978; New York: New American Library, 1983.

Skeleton Crew. New York: Putnam, 1985; New American Library, 1986.

Nonfiction

Danse Macabre. New York: Everest House, 1981; Berkley, 1982.

Nightmares in the Sky: Gargoyles and Grotesques. New York: Viking, 1988.

Interviews

"Interview: Stephen King." *Gallery* (January, 1986).

"Stephen King." *Interview* (February, 1986).

"Stephen King." In *The Faces of Fear: Encounters with the Creators of Modern Horror,* edited by Douglas Winter. New York: Berkley, 1985.

"Stephen King." *WB* [Waldenbooks] (November/December 1989).

"Talking Terror with Stephen King." *Twilight Zone Magazine* (February 1986).

Bare Bones: Conversations on Terror with Stephen King. Underwood, Tim, and Chuck Miller, eds.: New York: McGraw-Hill, 1988.

FULL-LENGTH BOOK STUDIES OF KING'S WORK

Beahm, George, ed. *The Stephen King Companion.* Kansas City, Mo.: Andrews and McMeel, 1989.

Blue, Tyson. *The Unseen King.* Mercer Island, Wash.: Starmont House, 1989.

Browne, Ray, and Gary Hoppenstand, eds. *The Gothic World of Stephen King: Landscape of Nightmares.* Bowling Green, Ohio: Bowling Green State University Popular Press, 1987.

Collings, Michael R. *The Films of Stephen King.* Mercer Island, Wash.: Starmont House, 1986.

———. *Infinite Explorations: Art and Artifice in Stephen King's* It, Misery, *and* The Tommyknockers. Mercer Island, Wash.: Starmont House, forthcoming.

———. *The Many Facets of Stephen King.* Mercer Island, Wash.: Starmont House, 1985.

———. *The Stephen King Concordance.* Mercer Island, Wash.: Starmont House, 1985.

———. *Stephen King as Richard Bachman.* Mercer Island, Wash.: Starmont House, 1985.

———. *The Stephen King Phenomenon.* Mercer Island, Wash.: Starmont House, 1986.

Collings, Michael R., and David A. Engebretson. *The Shorter Works of Stephen King.* Mercer Island, Wash.: Starmont House, 1985.

Connor, Jeff. *Stephen King Goes to Hollywood.* New York: New American Library, 1987.

Docherty, Brian, ed. *American Horror Fiction: From Brockden Brown to Stephen King.* New York: St. Martin's, 1990.

Herron, Don, ed. *Reign of Fear: Fiction and Film of Stephen King.* Los Angeles: Underwood-Miller, 1988.

Horsting, Jessie. *Stephen King at the Movies.* New York: Starlog Press & New American Library, 1986.

Magistrale, Tony. *Landscape of Fear: Stephen King's American Gothic.* Bowling Green, Ohio: Bowling Green State University Popular Press, 1988.

———. *The Moral Voyages of Stephen King.* Mercer Island, Wash.: Starmont House, 1989.

———, ed. *The Shining Reader.* Mercer Island, Wash.: Starmont House, 1991.

———. *Stephen King, The Second Decade:* Danse Macabre *to* The Dark Half. New York: Macmillan, forthcoming, 1992.

Murphy, Tim. *The Darkest Night: A Student's Guide to Stephen King.* Mercer Island, Wash.: Starmont House, forthcoming.

Reino, Joseph. *Stephen King, The First Decade: From* Carrie *to* Pet Sematary. Boston: G. K. Hall, 1988.

Schweitzer, Darrell, ed. *Discovering Stephen King.* Mercer Island, Wash.: Starmont House, 1985.

Spignesi, Stephen J. *The Shape Under the Sheet: The Complete Stephen King Encyclopedia.* Bangor, Maine: Philthrum Press, 1991.

Underwood, Tim, and Chuck Miller, eds. *Fear Itself: The Horror Fiction of Stephen King.* San Francisco, Calif: Underwood-Miller, 1982; New York: New American Library/Plume, 1984.

———. *Kingdom of Fear: The World of Stephen King.* New York: New American Library, 1986.

Van Hise, James. *Enterprise Incidents Presents Stephen King.* Tampa, Fla.: New Media, 1984.

Winter, Douglas E. *The Reader's Guide to Stephen King.* Mercer Island, Wash.: Starmont House, 1982.

————. *The Stephen King Bibliography.* West Kingston, R.I.: Donald M. Grant, forthcoming.

————. *Stephen King: The Art of Darkness.* New York: New American Library, 1984, rev. ed. 1986.

Zagorski, Edward J. *Teacher's Manual: The Novels of Stephen King* [pamphlet]. New York: New American Library, 1981.

CRITICAL ARTICLES

Adams, Michael. *"Danse Macabre."* In *Magill's Literary Annual 1982,* Vol. I, edited by Frank N. Magill. Englewood Cliffs, N.J.: Salem Press, 1982.

Alexander, Alex E. "Stephen King's *Carrie* — A Universal Fairy Tale." *Journal of Popular Culture* (Fall 1969).

Allen, Mel. "The Man Who Writes Nightmares." *Yankee Magazine* (March, 1979).

Ashley, Mike. "Stephen King." In *Who's Who in Horror and Fantasy Fiction.* New York: Taplinger, 1977.

Babington, Bruce. "Twice a Victim: Carrie Meets the BFI [British Film Institute]." *Screen* 23 (September/October, 1982).

Bleiler, Richard. "Stephen King." In *Supernatural Writers: Fantasy and Horror,* edited by Richard Bleiler and Everett Franklin. New York: Scribners, 1985.

Bradley, Marion Zimmer. "Fandom: Its Value to the Professional." In *Inside Outer Space,* edited by Sharton Jarvis. New York: Ungar, 1985.

Breque, Jean-Daniel. "Stephen King: L'horreur moderne." *Revue litteraire mensuelle* 707 (March, 1988).

Bromell, Henry. "The Dimming of Stanley Kubrick." *Atlantic* (August, 1980).

Brown, Royal S. "Dressed to Kill: Myth and Fantasy in the Horror Suspense Genre." *Film/Psychology Review* 4 (Summer/Fall 1980).

Bunnell, Charlene. "The Gothic: A Literary Genre's Transition to Film." In *Planks of Reason: Essays on the Horror Film,* edited by Garry Keith. Metuchen, N.J.: Scarecrow, 1984.

Caldwell, Larry W., and Samuel J. Umland. " 'Come and Play with Us': The Play Metaphor in Kubrick's *The Shining."* *Literature/Film Quarterly* 14 (1986).

Cheever, Leonard. "Apocalypse and the Popular Imagination: Stephen King's *The Stand."* *Artes liberales* 8 (Fall 1981).

Cook, David A. "American Horror: *The Shining."* *Literature/Film Quarterly* 12 (1984).

Egan, James. "Antidetection: Gothic and Detective Conventions in the Fiction of Stephen King." *Clues* 5 (Spring/Summer 1984).

————. "Apocalypticism in the Fiction of Stephen King." *Extrapolation* 25 (Fall 1984).

————. "A Single Powerful Spectacle: Stephen King's Gothic Melodrama." *Extrapolation* 27 (Spring 1986).

————. "Technohorror: The Dystopian Vision of Stephen King." *Extrapolation* 29 (Fall 1988).

Ehlers, Leigh A. *"Carrie:* Book and Film." *Literature/Film Quarterly* 9 (Spring 1981). Reprint in *Ideas of Order in Literature and Film,* edited by Peter Ruppert. Tallahassee, Fla.: University of Florida Press, 1980.

Ferguson, Mary. *"The Stand."* In *Survey of Modern Fantasy Literature,* edited by
    Frank N. Magill. Englewood Cliffs, N.J.: Salem Press, 1983.
————. " 'Strawberry Spring': Stephen King's Gothic Universe." *Footsteps V* (April
    1985).
Fiedler, Leslie. "Fantasy as Commodity, Pornography, Camp and Myth." *Fantasy
    Review* (June, 1984).
Gallagher, Bernard J. "Breaking Up Isn't Hard to Do: Stephen King, Christopher
    Lasch, and Psychic Fragmentation." *Journal of American Culture* 10 (Winter
    1987).
Gareffa, Peter M. "Stephen King." *Contemporary Authors,* New Revision Series, I.
Geduld, Harry M. "Mazes and Murders." *The Humanist* (September/October,
    1980).
Gibbs, Kenneth. "Stephen King and the Tradition of American Gothic." *Gothic* 1
    (1986).
Graham, Allison. " 'The Fallen Wonder of the World': Brian De Palma's Horror
    Films." In *American Horrors: Essays on the Modern American Horror Film,*
    edited by Gregory A. Waller. Chicago: Illinois University Press, 1987.
Grant, Charles L., David Morrell, Alan Ryan, and Douglas E. Winter. "Different
    Writers on *Different Seasons.*" *Fantasy Newsletter* (February 1983); in *Shadow-
    ings,* edited by Douglas E. Winter. Mercer Island, Wash.: Starmont House,
    1983.
Greenspun, Roger. *"Carrie,* and Sally and Leatherface Among the Film Buffs."
    Film Comment 13 (January/February, 1977).
Handling, Piers, ed. *The Shape of Rage: The Films of David Cronenberg.* Toronto:
    Toronto General Publishing, 1983.
Hatlen, Burton. "The Destruction and Re-Creation of the Human Community in
    Stephen King's *The Stand.*" *Footsteps V* (April, 1982).
————. "The Mad Dog and Maine." In *Shadowings,* edited by Douglas E. Winter.
    Mercer Island, Wash.: Starmont House, 1983.
————. " *'Salem's Lot* Critiques American Civilization." *The Maine Campus* (Decem-
    ber 1975).
————. "Steve King's Third Novel Shines On." *The Maine Campus* (April, 1977).
Heldreth, Leonard G. "Rising Like Old Corpses: Stephen King and the Horrors of
    Time-Past." *Journal of the Fantastic in the Arts* 2 (Spring 1989).
Hicks, James E. "Stephen King's Creation of Horror in *'Salem's Lot:* A Prolego-
    menon Towards a New Hermeneutic of the Gothic Novel." In *Consumable
    Goods: Papers from the North East Popular Culture Association Meeting, 1986,*
    edited by David K. Vaughan. Orono, Maine: University of Maine National
    Poetry Foundation, 1987.
Hoile, Christopher. "The Uncanny and the Fairy Tale in Kubrick's *The Shining.*"
    Literature/Film Quarterly 2 (1984).
Indick, Ben P. "Stephen King as an Epic Writer." In *Discovering Modern Horror Fic-
    tion, I,* edited by Darrell Schweitzer. Mercer Island, Wash.: Starmont
    House, 1985.
Jameson, Richard T. "Kubrick's *Shining.*" *Film Comment* (July/August, 1980).
Kauffman, Stanley. "The Dulling." *New Republic* 14 (June, 1980).
Keeler, Greg. *"The Shining:* Ted Kramer Has a Nightmare." *Journal of Popular Film
    and Television* (Winter 1981).

Kendrick, Walter. "Stephen King Gets Eminent." *Village Voice* 29 (April, 1981).

Kennedy, Harlan. "Kubrick Goes Gothic." *American Film* (June, 1980).

Kilbourne, Dan. *"Christine."* In *Magill's Cinema Annual 1984,* edited by Frank N. Magill. Englewood Cliffs, N.J.: Salem Press, 1984.

Kimberling, Ronald C. *Kenneth Burke's Dramatism and Popular Arts.* Bowling Green, Ohio: Bowling Green State University Popular Press, 1982.

King, Tabitha. "Living with the Bogey Man." In *Murderess, Ink,* edited by Dilys Winn. New York: Bell, 1979.

Klavan, Andrew. "The Pleasure of the Subtext: Stephen King's Id-Life Crisis." *Village Voice* 3 (March, 1987).

Lidston, Robert. *"Dracula* and *'Salem's Lot:* Why the Monsters Won't Die." *West Virginia University Philological Papers* 28 (1982).

Lorenz, Janet. *"Carrie."* In *Magill's Survey of Cinema,* Vol. I, edited by Frank N. Magill. Englewood Cliffs, N.J.: Salem Press, 1981.

Luciano, Dale. *"Danse Macabre:* Stephen King Surveys the Field of Horror." *The Comics Journal* 72 (May, 1982).

———. "E. C. Horror Stories Mistranslated into Film." *The Comics Journal* 79 (January, 1983).

Macklin, F. Anthony. "Understanding Kubrick: *The Shining." Journal of Popular Television and Film* (Summer 1981).

Magill, Frank N., ed. *Survey of Modern Fantasy Literature.* Englewood Cliffs, N.J.: Salem Press, 1983.

Magistrale, Tony. "Art Versus Madness in Stephen King's *Misery."* In *The Celebration of the Fantastic: Selected Papers from the Tenth Anniversary International Conference on the Fantastic in the Arts,* edited by Donald E. Morse, Marshall B. Tymn, and Csilla Bertha. Westport, Conn.: Greenwood, forthcoming.

———. " 'Barriers Not Meant to Be Broken': Where the Horror Springs in Stephen King." In *Consumable Goods: Papers from the North East Popular Culture Association Meeting, 1986,* edited by David K. Vaughan. Orono, Maine: University of Maine National Poetry Foundation, 1987.

———. "Crumbling Castles of Sand: The Social Landscape of Stephen King's Gothic Vision." *Journal of Popular Literature* 1 (Fall/Winter 1985).

———. "Free Will and Sexual Choice in *The Stand." Extrapolation,* forthcoming.

———. "Hawthorne's Woods Revisited: Stephen King's *Pet Sematary." Nathaniel Hawthorne Review* 14 (Spring 1988).

———. "Inherited Haunts: Stephen King's Terrible Children." *Extrapolation* 27 (Spring 1985).

———. "Native Sons: Regionalism in the Work of Nathaniel Hawthorne and Stephen King." *Journal of the Fantastic in the Arts* 2 (Spring 1989).

———. "Stephen King's Vietnam Allegory: An Interpretation of 'Children of the Corn.' " *Cuyahoga Review* (Spring/Summer 1984); *Footsteps V* (April, 1985).

Malpezzi, Frances M. and William M. Clements. *"The Shining."* In *Magill's Survey of Cinema,* Vol. V, edited by Frank N. Magill. Englewood Cliffs, N.J.: Salem Press, 1981.

Meyer, Richard E. "Stephen King." In *Beacham's Popular Fiction in America,* Vol. 2, edited by Walton Beacham. Washington, D.C.: Beacham, 1986.

Moore, Darrell. *The Best, Worst, and Most Unusual Horror Films.* Skokie, Ill.: Publications International, 1983.

Moritz, Charles. "Stephen King." *Contemporary Biography Yearbook 1981.* New York: H. H. Wilson, 1981.

———. *"Different Seasons."* In *Magill's Literary Annual 1983,* Vol. I, edited by Frank N. Magill. Englewood Cliffs, N.J.: Salem Press, 1980.

Morrison, Michael A. "Author Studies: Stephen King." In *Horror Literature: A Reader's Guide,* edited by Neil Barron. New York: Garland, 1990.

———. *Pet Sematary:* Opposing Views." *Fantasy Review* 64 (January, 1984).

Murphy, Patrick D. "The Realities of Unreal Worlds: King's *The Dead Zone,* Schmidt's *Kensho,* and Lem's *Solaris."* In *Spectrum of the Fantastic: Selected Essays from the Sixth International Conference on the Fantastic in the Arts,* edited by Donald Palumbo. Westport, Conn.: Greenwood, 1988.

Neilson, Keith. "Contemporary Horror Fiction, 1950–88." In *Horror Literature: A Reader's Guide,* edited by Neil Barron. New York: Garland, 1990.

———. *"The Dead Zone."* In *Magill's Literary Annual 1980,* Vol. I, edited by Frank N. Magill. Englewood Cliffs, N.J.: Salem Press, 1980.

———. *"Different Seasons."* In *Magill's Literary Annual 1983,* Vol. I, edited by Frank N. Magill. Englewood Cliffs, N.J.: Salem Press, 1983.

Nelson, Thomas A. "Remembrance of Things Forgotten: *The Shining."* In *Kubrick: Inside the Artist's Maze.* Bloomington, Ind.: Indiana University Press, 1982.

Norris, Darrell A. "Evolving Landscapes of Horror: Recent Themes in American Fiction." In *Consumable Goods: Papers from the North East Popular Culture Association Meeting, 1986,* edited by David K. Vaughan. Orono, Maine: University of Maine National Poetry Foundation, 1987.

Patrouch, Joseph F., Jr. "Stephen King in Context." In *Patterns of the Fantastic,* edited by Donald M. Hassler. Mercer Island, Wash.: Starmont House, 1983.

Pearce, Howard D. *"The Shining* as *Lichtung:* Kubrick's Film, Heidegger's Clearing." In *Forms of the Fantastic: Selected Essays from the Third International Conference on the Fantastic in Literature and Film.* Westport, Conn.: Greenwood, 1986.

Phippen, Sanford. "Stephen King's Appeal to Youth." *Maine Life* (December, 1980).

———. "The Student King." *Maine* 70 (Fall 1989).

Price, Robert M."Fundamentalists in the Fiction of Stephen King." *Studies in Weird Fiction* 5 (Spring 1989).

Radburn, Barry. "Stephen King and John Carpenter: Cruisin' with *Christine." Footsteps V* (April 1985).

Rudin, S. "The Urban Gothic, from Transylvania to the South Bronx." *Extrapolation* 25 (1984).

Schaefer, S. "The Director is King." *Film Comment* 22 (1986).

Schiff, Stuart David. "The Glorious Past, Erratic Present, and Questionable Future of the Specialty Presses." In *Inside Outer Space,* edited by Sharon Jarvis. New York: Ungar, 1985.

Schweitzer, Darrell. "Introduction." In *Discovering Modern Horror Fiction, I,* edited by Darrell Schweitzer. Mercer Island, Wash.: Starmont House, 1985.

Senf, Carol A. "Stephen King: A Modern Interpretation of the Frankenstein Myth." *Science Fiction: A Review of Speculative Literature* 8 (1986).

———. "Donna Trenton, Stephen King's Modern American Heroine." In *Heroines of Popular Culture,* edited by Pat Browne. Bowling Green, Ohio: Bowling Green State University Popular Press, 1987.

Snyder, Stephen. "Family Life and Leisure Culture in *The Shining." Film Criticism* 6 (Fall 1982).

"Stephen King." In *Contemporary Literary Criticism,* Vol. 12, edited by Dedria Bryfonski and Garard Senick. Detroit, Mich.: Gale Research, 1980.

"Stephen King." In *Current Biography Yearbook, 1981,* edited by Charles Moritz. New York: H. W. Wilson, 1981.

Stewart, Robert. "The Rest of King." *Starship: The Magazine About Science Fiction* 18 (Spring 1981).

Tuchman, Michael. "From Niagara-on-the-Lake, Ontario." *Film Comment* 19 (May-June, 1983).

Westerbeck, Collin. "The Waning of Stanley Kubrick." *Commonweal* 1 (August, 1980).

Wilson, William. "Riding the Crest of the Horror Craze." *Times Magazine* (May 11, 1980).

Winter, Douglas E. "The Art of Darkness." In *Shadowings,* edited by Douglas E. Winter. Mercer Island, Wash.: Starmont House, 1983.

———. "I Want My Cake! Thoughts on *Creepshow* and E. C. Comics." In *Shadowings,* edited by Douglas E. Winter. Mercer Island, Wash.: Starmont House, 1983.

Wood, Robin. "Cat and Dog: Lewis Teague's Stephen King Novels." *Action* 2 (Fall 1985).

———. "King Meets Cronenberg." *Canadian Forum* (January, 1984).

Index

About the Contributors

LAURI BERKENKAMP received an M.A. degree in English at the University of Vermont where she was also a graduate teaching fellow. She won the Frederick Tupper Award for the English department's outstanding graduate fellow in 1990. Currently, she is teaching writing and literature classes at Norwich University in Northfield, Vermont.

ARTHUR W. BIDDLE is an associate professor of English at the University of Vermont where he teaches courses in American literature and writing. His current research interest is the work of Thomas Merton, author and Trappist monk. Biddle is coeditor and coauthor of the recently published *Angles of Vision: Reading, Writing, and the Study of Literature.*

BERNADETTE LYNN BOSKY is the author of two other articles about Stephen King that appear in *Kingdom of Fear* and *Discovering Stephen King.* A longtime afficionado and scholar of fantastic literature, she has also published on other authors in the genre, particularly Charles Williams and Peter Straub, and on the development of academic criticism of the genre.

EDWIN F. CASEBEER is a professor of English at Indiana-Purdue University at Indianapolis. His publications focus on the areas of popular culture, fantasy, literary theory, and science fiction.

JOSEPH A. CITRO, born and raised in Vermont, does for the Green Mountain State what Stephen King does for Maine. His novels of horror and the supernatural include *Shadow Child, The Unseen,* and *Guardian Angels.*

RONALD T. CURRAN is an associate professor of English at the University of Pittsburgh. He is also a certified Jungian therapist with a practice in Pittsburgh, and has published work in a wide variety of academic journals, particularly those emphasizing the link between psychology and literature.

MARY JANE DICKERSON, an assistant professor of English at the University of Vermont, has written articles on William Faulkner and other modernists such as Jean Toomer and Sherwood Anderson. Her first study of Stephen King, "The Masked Author Strikes Again: Writing and Dying in *The Shining,"* was published in *The Shining Reader.* Currently, she is working on American autobiography as cultural dialogue.

GENE DOTY teaches in the English department at the University of Missouri, Rolla. He has published scholarship on Tolkien and various writers of supernatural horror fiction.

DOUGLAS KEESEY teaches English and American studies at California Polytechnic State University, San Luis Obispo. He has published essays on Thomas Pynchon, James Dickey, Henry James, and H. G. Wells.

TONY MAGISTRALE is the author of two books on Stephen King, *Landscape of Fear: Stephen King's American Gothic* and *The Moral Voyages of Stephen King,* and served as editor of *The Shining Reader.* He has just concluded writing *Stephen King, The Second Decade: From* Danse Macabre *to* The Dark Half. He is an associate professor of English at the University of Vermont where he teaches classes in American literature and directs the freshman composition program.

LEONARD MUSTAZZA is an associate professor of English at Pennsylvania State University. His Ph.D. is from SUNY at Stony Brook. He is the author of *Such Prompt Eloquence: Language as Agency and Character in Milton's Epics* and "The Red Death's Sway: Setting and Character in Poe's 'The Masque of the Red Death' and King's *The Shining"* in *The Shining Reader.*

MARY PHARR is an assistant professor of English at Florida Southern College. She has written extensively on Stephen King, horror film, women in fantasy films and literature, and comic-book heroes. She is the author of "A Dream of New Life: Stephen King's *Pet Sematary* as a Variant of *Frankenstein"* in *The Gothic World of Stephen King.*

JEANNE CAMPBELL REESMAN is an assistant professor of American literature at the University of Texas at San Antonio. She is the author of *American Designs: The Late Novels of James and Faulkner* and articles published in several academic journals. Her essay "Stephen King and the Tradition of American Naturalism" appears in *The Shining Reader.*

JAMES F. SMITH is a professor of English at Pennsylvania State University. He earned his Ph.D. in American studies at Pennsylvania State and is the author of *The Business of Risk: Commercial Gambling in Mainstream America* and "Kubrick's or King's—Whose *Shining* Is It?" in *The Shining Reader.*

MICHAEL N. STANTON is an associate professor of English at the University of Vermont. He has taught there since receiving his Ph.D. from the University of Rochester in 1971. His interests include Restoration literature, the Romantics, and Victorians, and the literature of science fiction and fantasy. He is the author of "Once, out of Nature: The Topiary" in *The Shining Reader.*

GREG WELLER received an M.A. degree from the University of Pittsburgh. He is the author of "The Redrum of Time: A Meditation on Francisco Goya's 'Saturn Devouring His Children' and Stephen King's *The Shining*" in *The Shining Reader.*